Praise From Higher Educati 

KP's and the chapter authors' expertise in transforming data into a driving force for decision-making and change shines brilliantly in "The Power of Strategic Accreditation." This insightful book redefines the accreditation process, turning it from a routine task into a dynamic and engaging journey. With a focus on teamwork and strategic innovation, the book provides an invaluable roadmap for institutions to harness accreditation as a powerful tool for future growth and success.

Aimee Sapp, PhD
President, Meredith College

Accreditation is often viewed by higher education administrators as a daunting task. However, the authors of this book illuminate how to leverage the accreditation process for institutional growth and transformation. This insightful guide is a must-read for all higher education leaders and stakeholders. I highly recommend it.

P. Daniel Chen, PhD
Director, Higher Education Program, George Mason University

The Power of Strategic Accreditation:Driving Institutional Impact is an excellent example of an integrated planning model or approach to accreditation.The book's key components provided by a distinguished and diverse group of authors address the comprehensive, collaborative, equity, and accountability measures and efforts necessary to view and move accreditation beyond mere compliance.It is a must-read for all higher education leaders, administrators, faculty, staff, and students involved in the accreditation process.

Waddell M. Herron, PhD
Associate Director, Analytic Studies Division
California State University, Office of the Chancellor – Emeritus

---

With far too little scholarship on accreditation, this book helps fill the gap in how-to guidance for both innovative and practical resources to best support institutions and professionals looking to combat a compliance mindset and instead instill good practice and student-centered decision-making. This book features insights, checklists, and nuggets of wisdom for people to engage in self-reflection and yield multiple beneficial byproducts applicable across the institution. With each chapter providing discussion questions and further resources to support the work, this book will prove to be an invaluable resource for institutions preparing for, going through, or looking to best support accreditation (and continuous improvement) efforts and beyond.

Dr. Joseph D. Levy
Associate Vice Provost of Accreditation and Quality Improvement
Excelsior University

The POWER of STRATEGIC ACCREDITATION:
Driving Institutional Impact

Edited by

Kristina 'KP' Powers, PhD

Foreword by: Amelia Parnell, PhD

First published 2024
by The Institute for Effectiveness in Higher Education
Menlo Park, CA 94025

Library of Congress Cataloging-in-Publication Data

A catalog record for this title has been requested.

ISBN: 979-8-950595-03-5

Dedication

To President Patrick J. Schloss, my mentor, colleague, and friend, this book is a tribute to your exceptional knowledge in book publishing, a pioneer in higher education leadership, and the enduring influence of your guidance during my early years in the field of higher education. Your mentorship and trust over the several decades have been integral to my ongoing professional success. I am forever grateful to you.

Table of Contents

Exhibits

Foreword

In 2018, in response to the question "What is student success?", I wrote a piece to encourage higher education professionals to expand the definition beyond the outcomes of retention, persistence, and graduation. I explained that while those goals should be the foundation of student success strategies, the broad nature of those objectives does not fully capture the nuance of various experiences that contribute to those milestones. So, I decided to define student success with a more specific and student-centered frame. In doing so, I posed the question "What should a successful student be able to do?" That question is one around which we can design and deliver high-quality learning experiences for students and measure the extent to which they acquire key skills, knowledge, and competencies.

That revised question is also one for which the answer will continue to evolve. For example, six years ago, I mentioned that one thing a successful student should be able to do is balance competing individual and community priorities. At the time, I was thinking of common scenarios in which the person might be in a collaborative working environment and have primary responsibility for a portion of a larger project. I envisioned college as a place where learners would regularly work in teams and accept both solo assignments and shared ones and develop the ability to manage both well. That was an acceptable assertion for that period. However, two years later, a global pandemic sparked my thinking again about that definition. I continued to delve into the question of what a successful student should be able to do and I determined that the list should be even more reflective of our changing world. In 2023, I wrote about it again and stated that a successful student should realize the scope and scale of various political, social, economic, health, and other systems. It was obvious that what happens in one industry can greatly affect another, and that college students should think about community as more than just the people in their direct proximity.

I recalled my exercise of trying to define student success after reviewing this new book, *The Power of Strategic Accreditation*. Just as the discussion of student success was ripe for a fresh perspective to nudge us to think more boldly, accreditation also needs a new narrative. In fact, I see a natural connection between these two things, as the first chapter of this book states that "the power of accreditation lies in its ability to advocate for student success." It is the perfect introduction, as one could assume that every higher education institution, regardless of its size, sector, location, or student population, has a cadre of professionals across all functions who desire to help students be successful.

Students obviously also have a desire to succeed, and often attend college with the hope that their experience will result in the education and opportunities that will position them to achieve their life and career goals. As a result, there is much pressure on professionals to meet students' expectations and to be accountable to many groups in doing so, including trustees and various other regulatory authorities. One such group is accrediting organizations.

Accreditation is one of the most important parts of an institution's operations. It is no secret that without it, a campus would have significant struggles, many of which could lead to declines in resources and student enrollment. It is common for accreditation discussions to focus on accountability, as senior leaders must provide thorough evidence that students are receiving a high-quality educational experience that adheres to the standards set by the accrediting organization. This typical depiction of the purpose and process of accreditation leaves much opportunity for new conversations that go beyond a focus on reporting. *The Power of Strategic Accreditation* takes advantage of that opportunity by providing one of the most interesting, forward-looking, and empowering discussions of accreditation to date.

This book is a resource for professionals who strive to explore the potential of accreditation as a lever for creating and sustaining new opportunities for their campus. Though the return on that pursuit can be significant, it is important to acknowledge that it can be difficult for professionals to appropriately balance three key actions: reviewing past results, continuing present activities, and planning for future objectives. This book weaves in and out of the continuum of past, present and future considerations by providing examples of things to remember from prior activities, illustrations of effective practices, and suggestions for planning next steps.

Four timely themes that are throughout this book are related to collaboration, data-informed decision making, knowledge sharing, and emerging opportunities. This is a great combination to frame accreditation as any institution that engages in the process will undoubtedly find better outcomes when groups of professionals align on the strategy, use data effectively, identify new opportunities, and learn along the way. The book is organized by six parts that focus on these themes to smoothly guide readers through the past, present, and future journey previously described. The sections are appropriately titled Breakthrough Blueprints, Igniting Information, Capacity Catalysts, Information Sparks, Post-Graduate Success Shaping, and The Aha Advantage.

The theme of collaboration is paramount for this publication because the depth and breadth of the accreditation process requires contributions from professionals across the institution. Collaboration for the purpose of measuring quality is essential, as indicators of success reflect myriad aspects of students' experiences. For example, as institutions continue to refine their campuswide learning outcomes, faculty and student affairs professionals often partner to help students collect examples of their learning from both classroom and out-of-classroom engagements. For accreditation purposes, emerging learning records such as ePortfolios, digital badges, and co-curricular transcripts offer the evidence of such learning and tangible examples for review teams to consider when assessing the quality of those experiences.

The second recurring theme, data-informed decision making, connects to nearly every aspect of strategic accreditation. Institutions will be evaluated on the extent to which investments in instruction, programs, and services are positively impacting students' progress toward graduation and other key outcomes. As a result, professionals have a recurring focus on determining which data and information are most relevant to showing the value and quality of various learning experiences. The previous example of faculty collaborating with student affairs to examine learning outcomes can be extended to include institutional research and effectiveness professionals. For example, Chapter 9 describes several ways in which institutional researchers can work with faculty to share results from student surveys about their learning experiences.

If it is true that experience is a good teacher, this publication is an ideal workbook from which one can learn, as it is filled with ongoing advice for professionals. The authors draw from decades of accreditation review experience and generously offer suggestions to help individuals navigate the process as smoothly as possible. Chapter 1 lists 10 lessons derived from institutions' experiences with accreditation and 10 risks of not strategically leveraging accreditation. Those two lists set the tone for readers to consider this publication as a resource designed to help them avoid common pitfalls, learn from the experiences of others, and develop a plan of action for managing their campus reviews. Chapters 6 and 15 add to the collection of guiding perspectives with a focus on mentoring and insights from accreditation commissions.

As mentioned earlier, this book presents a bold and refreshing discussion of accreditation by describing how institutions can consider it as a catalyst for change. The themes of collaboration, data-informed decision making, and knowledge sharing are an excellent connection to the fourth theme of emerging opportunities. From Chapter 13, which addresses career services to Chapter 17 which focuses on innovation, there is a constant narrative about how the accreditation process can help campuses discover new options for improving students' experiences. In essence, the book positions accreditation as a method to simultaneously create meaningful learning environments and gather the proof that the strategy for doing so is effective. This book is optimal for those who enjoy future-oriented discussions of higher education, as it can easily spur thoughts about countless possibilities to provide critical resources in new and considerate ways.

Chapter 1 states that another reason why accreditation can be powerful is because it "encourages colleges and universities to articulate their mission, vision, and educational objectives clearly". This highlights the importance of strategic communication, which is a key consideration for professionals who embark on leveraging accreditation for change. To maximize the power of accreditation as a tool for effectively advocating for student success, it is essential for the messaging of that goal to be widespread and consistent. The book makes an exceptionally compelling case for accreditation as an integral but underutilized resource for advocacy and systemic change. Therefore, senior leaders must create communication channels for professionals to share how their individual contributions connect to those of their colleagues and to broader campus objectives.

Perhaps the most important audience for such communication is students, as they seek alignment between their educational aspirations and the resources they receive to prepare and support them. Regardless of how our definitions of student success evolve over time, it is unquestionable that when learning opportunities are delivered collaboratively and measured with relevant data and information, students' needs will be addressed more thoughtfully and thoroughly. *The Power of Strategic Accreditation* confirms that accreditation can be both the mechanism that guides our present steps and the prompt to explore future opportunities to help students thrive. For any campus that unlocks such potential, it seems inevitable that recurring and longstanding success will follow.

Amelia Parnell, PhD

President, NASPA – Student Affairs Administrators in Higher Education

Preface

In today's fast-paced and ever-changing educational landscape, institutions are facing increasing demands for excellence, innovation, and improved outcomes. Accreditation is a widely recognized benchmark that institutions strive to achieve, but often, its potential benefits are not fully realized. *The Power of Strategic Accreditation: Driving Institutional Impact* aims to bridge this gap by providing educational leaders with a comprehensive resource on how to strategically leverage accreditation as a catalyst for institutional improvement and success.

The Power of Strategic Accreditation: Driving Institutional Impact highlights the missed opportunities that exist within the accreditation process and how to leverage them. Accreditation reviews provide a valuable chance for institutions to critically evaluate their operations, identify areas for improvement, and propel themselves towards excellence. However, many institutions view accreditation as a mere compliance exercise, missing the chance to truly transform and grow.

By reframing the perception of accreditation, this book empowers higher educational leaders, administrators, faculty, and staff to embrace a strategic approach to accreditation. Through engaging narratives, practical insights, and real-world examples, readers will gain a deep understanding of how strategic accreditation can become a driving force for positive change and institutional enhancement.

The book explores the key areas where institutions often miss the mark during accreditation reviews. It delves into how an accreditation process can be an opportunity to reflect on mission alignment, identify areas for growth, and implement evidence-based practices that drive institutional improvement. By focusing on these critical aspects, institutions can establish a culture of excellence and continuous improvement that goes beyond meeting minimum standards to exceed institutional expectations.

The Power of Strategic Accreditation: Driving Institutional Impact comprises six sections, each offering practical insights and tips on how to maximize the benefits of accreditation. The six sections are:

1. **Breakthrough Blueprints** - This section introduces readers to strategic planning and innovation, demonstrating how accreditation can be used to achieve institutional breakthroughs. Readers learn about the importance of aligning accreditation goals with the institution's strategic vision and establishing a culture of innovation, excellence, and continuous improvement.

2. **Igniting Innovation** - This section is dedicated to highlighting how accreditation can be a catalyst for innovation in higher education institutions. Readers will discover practical strategies that can be employed to foster a culture of innovation that is nurtured by accreditation. This section also feature real-world examples of institutions that have leveraged accreditation creatively to drive innovation.

3. **Capacity Catalysts** - This section emphasizes the importance of leadership in embracing the potential of accreditation in institutions. The section explores practical ways that institutional leaders can use accreditation to amplify their leadership and capacity-building skills. The section will also provide guidance on how to engage stakeholders meaningfully, establish partnerships, and leverage accreditation to build internal capacity.

4. **Information Sparks** - This section focuses on the importance of data-driven and information-driven decision-making during the accreditation process. Readers gain a deep understanding of how to collect, evaluate, and utilize data and information in accreditation reviews. The section offers practical tips on how institutions can use data and information to drive evidence-based improvements.

5. **Post-Graduate Success Shaping** - This section demonstrates how institutions can use accreditation to shape the success of their students beyond graduation. The section explores the role of institutions in preparing students for the job market, equipping them with valuable skills that they can use in their careers, and measuring their success once they leave the institution.

6. **The Aha Advantage** - This section concludes the book by reinforcing the importance of a strategic approach to accreditation. Readers gain important insights from the vantage point of key roles in the accreditation process as they share their perspectives so others can gain the "Aha" advantage, that is, the ability to see accreditation as a transformative tool that can drive institutional growth and excellence.

To provide readers with additional resources and opportunity for discussion and learning, each chapter includes discussion questions that can be used in graduate courses or by senior leaders in their planning (e.g., executives, boards of trustees, committees, etc.). Additionally, some chapters include a section that is called Discover and Propel, where chapter authors provide information and /or links to resources for further exploration at higher education organizations, social media, case studies, etc.,

In conclusion, *The Power of Strategic Accreditation: Driving*

Institutional Impact offers educational leaders a paradigm shift in their approach to accreditation. It encourages a strategic mindset that embraces the potential for growth, innovation, and enhanced performance that lies within the accreditation process. By adopting a strategic approach, institutions will not only meet accreditation standards but also position themselves for long-term success in an increasingly competitive educational landscape.

Acknowledgements

I would like to express my heartfelt appreciation to those who have made this book possible. First, I would like to acknowledge all of the chapter authors. I am grateful to them for their time and collective expertise, resulting in a resource of breadth and depth for current and future higher education leaders.

I deeply admire the editing expertise of Tracy Kendrick. Her attention to detail and passion for her profession were the patina that elevated the book. I was delighted when Tracy agreed to edit this book since her exceptional skills bring out its strengths.

This book visually comes to life with much thanks to two talented people. Diana Goldstein's utilized her design expertise for many of the exhibits throughout the book. She turned rough draft artwork into polished and aesthetically pleasing exhibits that amplified critical messages throughout the book.

Justin Oefelein created the front and back cover designs and formatted the manuscript for publication. His attention to detail in turning a 270-page Word document and 70 exhibits into a high-quality book in both print and Kindle formats contributed to the final product.

Finally, an honorable mention goes to the family and friends of all contributors to this book; with their support, we can complete the research about which we are so passionate. A special thanks to my husband (Tim) for his unwavering support in life and another book!

PART I

BREAKTHROUGH BLUEPRINTS

This section introduces readers to strategic planning and innovation, demonstrating how accreditation can be used to achieve institutional breakthroughs. Readers learn about the importance of aligning accreditation goals with the institution's strategic vision and establishing a culture of innovation, excellence, and continuous improvement through the lens of political strategy.

Chapter 1

Why Leaders Need to Leverage the Power of Accreditation

Kristina 'KP' Powers

This chapter focuses on inspiring institutional leaders to strategically leverage the power of accreditation and the gains created by doing so. Lessons from institutions that have received less than favorable accreditation outcomes (e.g., Notice of Concern, Warning) are shared so that other leaders can avoid similar pitfalls.)

Today's higher education institutional leaders face a myriad of demanding challenges, many unlike their predecessors. From enrollment pressures and financial constraints to evolving student needs and global competition, the demands on leaders are greater than ever before. In navigating these challenges, institutional leaders must embrace being nimble along with innovative strategies that not only meet accreditation standards but also position their institutions for long-term success.

Accreditation, a voluntary process that evaluates an institution's quality and effectiveness, plays a crucial role in the higher education ecosystem. It provides external validation that a college or university meets established standards of excellence and ensures that the institution is fulfilling its mission and serving its students effectively. Accreditation serves as a marker of quality and credibility, informing stakeholders about an institution's commitment to academic rigor and continuous improvement.

However, the power of accreditation extends far beyond compliance. Accreditation offers an opportunity for colleges and universities to go beyond the minimum requirements and strive for excellence. It serves as a catalyst for growth, innovation, and enhanced performance. By strategically leveraging accreditation, leaders can unlock the full potential of their institutions and pave the way for long-term success.

This chapter aims to inspire institutional leaders to tap into the power of accreditation strategically. By adopting a strategic approach to accreditation, leaders can harness its potential for growth, innovation, and enhanced performance. The first section of the chapter uses data to back up this assertion.

After (hopefully) convincing you that an accreditation strategy is needed, the chapter explores the power of accreditation. Accreditation can be a transformative process that enhances an institution's reputation, competitiveness, and ability to fulfill its mission.

All too often, institutions approach accreditation with a compliance mindset, ticking the boxes without fully capitalizing on the potential for improvement and innovation. This chapter discusses frequently missed opportunities that leaders can seize during accreditation reviews to maximize the benefits to their institutions.

Some institutions end the accreditation cycle with surprising negative results; I call this the "accreditation naughty list." This chapter presents lessons gleaned from institutions that have faced less than favorable accreditation outcomes. By examining these cases, leaders can gain insights into the mistakes and missteps that led to these negative results and avoid similar pitfalls.

Risk mitigation is a constant concern for college and university leaders. Choosing not to leverage accreditation strategically can have significant consequences for institutions. By neglecting to capitalize on accreditation, institutions become vulnerable to complacency, reputational damage, and missed opportunities for growth and innovation. The chapter explores these risks to further emphasize why leaders must take a strategic approach to accreditation.

Institutional leaders have a unique opportunity to leverage the power of accreditation strategically. By shifting mindsets and embracing accreditation as a catalyst for growth and improvement, leaders can position their institutions for success in an increasingly competitive higher education landscape. This chapter provides data, insights, and lessons for those who want to truly harness the power of accreditation and discover its potential.

What Are Our Chances for Accreditation Reaffirmation Success?

This section kicks off the chapter by making the case, using data, that accreditation reviews need to be strategically managed. Leaders will not achieve the desired outcomes simply by doing good work. We all believe we are doing good work. Doing good work and showing that you are doing good work are two different things. Savvy leaders should thus be asking, "What are our chances for accreditation reaffirmation success?"

This is probably THE top question that presidents have asked me during my nearly 15 years of deep accreditation work, and it is a tricky one to answer. What does one mean by "success"? In this section, I share data that I've analyzed from the Council for Higher Education Accreditation (CHEA) pertaining to the likelihood of accreditation success and offer suggestions—based on data—for answering this tricky question.

But more importantly, the data results show why leaders must strategically leverage the power of accreditation to achieve the results that they desire. Positive accreditation outcomes don't just magically happen. Even those that are the fruits of several years of purposeful work have and do result in follow-up reports and visits. There are many, many, many possible outcomes from an accreditation visit. These range from "See you in 10 years" to "We need a focused report in less than a year" to "The institution is on formal warning/notice of concern."

What the president is really asking usually comes down to these two questions:

- Will we pass or fail? (Will we be reaffirmed accreditation?)

- What area/range of accreditation outcomes is our institution likely to be in?

The first question is at a high level: Will we pass or will we fail? The second question is more granular: Which level of passing or failure are we in?

Consider, for example, an exam in a course. The class test results can be reported as the percentage that passed and failed. However, we know that passing with a perfect score of 100% is not the same as passing with a D grade. As with other evaluation processes, the normal distribution curve applies. Few are in the "top" category, and few are in the "lowest" category. Few students get 100%, and very few land in the lowest categories (e.g., 10% or 20%).

The same is true for accreditation—and the data from CHEA prove it.

CHEA Data Analyzed—Pass/Fail

Let's first look at the topic of pass/fail in the context of accreditation actions. I used CHEA's Almanac of External Quality Review, which presents data about annual accreditation activities of institutional and programmatic accreditors recognized by CHEA and/or the U.S. Department of Education. In its most recent report, using data provided by the accrediting agencies, CHEA notes that accrediting bodies took nearly 5,000 actions on colleges, universities, programs, and freestanding institutions in 2019. Of these, more than three-quarters (76.2%) resulted in "passing," as shown in Exhibit 1.1.

It is important to note that some of the other actions may not be considered a "fail" but they definitely are not passing. For example, "withdrew accreditation" could be at the institution's choosing so that it can put forth a more robust application at a later date.

Exhibit 1.1: Accreditation Action Results for Four-Year Institutions

Accreditation Action	2016	2017	2018	2019
Grant Accreditation	20.1%	22.7%	19.3%	17.7%
Reaffirm Accreditation	55.7%	54.6%	53.3%	58.5%
Deny Accreditation	0.8%	0.6%	0.5%	0.4%
Withdrew Accreditation	7.4%	6.2%	5.0%	6.9%
Defer Accreditation	5.8%	5.4%	9.1%	6.6%
Notice/Warning	2.5%	4.7%	5.0%	3.7%
Show Cause	2.0%	2.0%	3.9%	2.1%
Probation	5.6%	3.7%	3.8%	4.1%
Appeals	0.0%	0.0%	0.0%	0.1%
Total number of actions	**5,276**	**5,378**	**5,530**	**4,973**

Source: KP Powers analysis of CHEA data (Figure 28), 2021.

Setting Expectations for Accreditation Outcomes

Delving further into the CHEA data, there are different degrees of "passing" just as there are with a course exam (e.g., passing with a B grade is not the same as passing with a D-). A deeper dive into the formal actions taken on previously accredited institutions and programs reveals that more than half (55%) of institutions have consistently received high marks with "accreditation continued" (without a follow-up report), as shown in Exhibit 1.2. This is the category that all institutions strive for.

Exhibit 1.2: Formal Actions Taken on Institutions, 2009 through 2017

Formal Action Taken	2009	2011	2013	2015	2017
Accreditation Continued Following Comprehensive Review	55.0%	55.9%	54.5%	54.3%	55.4%
Accreditation Continued Following Comprehensive Review with Required Follow-up	27.9%	26.5%	29.7%	26.2%	30.2%
Notice or Warning	2.4%	2.7%	3.5%	6.2%	4.1%
Probation	2.0%	2.2%	3.4%	4.3%	4.3%
Show Cause	10.5%	10.3%	6.0%	6.3%	2.9%
Accreditation Terminated or Removed	1.7%	1.6%	2.0%	2.1%	2.8%
Actions Under Appeal	0.4%	0.7%	1.0%	0.5%	0.3%
Formal Actions Total for Accredited Institutions	**5,251**	**5,866**	**6,635**	**6,053**	**6,097**

Source: KP Powers analysis of CHEA data (Figure 29), 2021.

Next is the section that institutions can use to set expectations for reaffirmation of accreditation.

If 55% of institutions received an outcome of "accreditation continued without a follow-up report," then that means that 45% of institutions received an action that will require more institutional work. Before getting too worried, let's dig in a bit further. Of the 45%:

- 30% received the outcome of "accreditation continued," but it came with a requirement for a follow-up report. Not ideal, but not terrible. Essentially, this means that the institution will have to submit to the accreditor very soon—but only on a select number of topics requiring additional attention.

- Less than 5% of institutions fall into each of the remaining categories (Notice or Warning, Probation, Show Cause, Accreditation Terminated or Removed, Actions Under Appeal), so really, really bad accreditation actions are unlikely. They do happen, though. These less-than-desirable accreditation outcomes are intended to help the institution focus on the issues identified by the review team and resolve them as soon as possible.

Answering the Tough Question About Accreditation Success

So how do I answer the tricky question "What are our chances for accreditation reaffirmation success?"

My response might sound something like this:

> *More than 75% of institutions "pass" their accreditation review. After all, the institution is focused on making improvements and doing good work. In terms of "accreditation work" coming to a close after the visiting team leaves, you should know that about half of institutions have no follow-up work to do before their next visit. This means that we should do all we can to put extra effort into this accreditation report and visit. The next likely outcome is that we will pass but have a follow-up report, which happens to about 30% of institutions.*

The draft answer above needs to be tempered with institutional circumstances such as issues raised during the last review, known deficiencies in the current report, and comments from the off-site review team. When applicable, it is important to discuss the more unfavorable outcomes (e.g., notice of concern or warning). However, those comments should be backed by other recent institutional examples (which require more research by searching accreditor, institutional, and news websites).

Coordinating Accreditation Tasks

To save yourself and your accreditation team unnecessary work, it's essential to leverage the power of accreditation strategically. Your effort needs to be as effective, accurate, and comprehensive as possible to avoid adverse action. To return to the course exam analogy used earlier in this chapter, it is well worth spending time on the class each week so that the exam is simply a demonstration of the work already done.

Most things with a high benefit require a fair amount of work. The accreditation reaffirmation process is no different; it's a lot of work. Getting through it takes a great deal of time and effort on the part of many people within the institution.

Lastly, it is easy to get caught up in the busyness of accreditation reports and visits. *Remember that your accreditor is rooting for your institutional success.* They truly want you and your institution to succeed. I find that most staff at accreditors say, "We are here to help the institution; reach out if you have questions." I know many people wonder, "Do they really mean it? Can I really call if I have a question without it being held against the institution?" I have found the offer to help to be genuine and quite advantageous to the institution.

Having served on review teams many times, I can attest that nobody wants to write a negative report—unless one is really warranted. *There are many people on the accreditation review team and at the accreditation office cheering for your institutional success.* So take the time to leverage the power of accreditation.

What is the Power of Accreditation?

Accreditation is often viewed as a necessary process for institutions to maintain their credibility and ensure regulatory compliance. However, its power extends far beyond these conventional expectations. Accreditation has the potential to drive institutional transformation, enhance educational quality, and foster continuous improvement.

One of the key powers of accreditation is its ability to enhance an institution's reputation. Accreditation serves as a mark of quality and credibility, providing assurance to students, parents, employers, and the community at large. When a college or university proudly displays its accredited status, it sends a powerful message that it meets or exceeds rigorous standards of excellence. This instills confidence in stakeholders and attracts prospective students who are seeking a high-quality education.

Moreover, accreditation is not just a one-time validation of an institution's quality; it serves as an ongoing process of evaluation and improvement. Accrediting bodies regularly assess colleges and universities, ensuring that they continue to meet the established standards. This accountability promotes a culture of continuous improvement and drives institutions to strive for excellence in all aspects of their operations. By leveraging the power of accreditation, institutions can embrace a mindset of perpetual growth and refinement.

Connecting to the Mission

Accreditation encourages colleges and universities to articulate their mission, vision, and educational objectives clearly. Through the accreditation process, they are prompted to assess and align their programs, policies, and practices with their stated goals. This alignment ensures that institutions are purposefully working towards their intended outcomes, providing direction and focus to their efforts. By leveraging accreditation, colleges and universities can create a structured framework for institutional effectiveness and achievement.

Catalyst for Innovation

Another powerful aspect of accreditation lies in its role as a catalyst for innovation. As institutions strive to meet accreditation standards, they are motivated to explore new ways of teaching, learning, and addressing the needs of their students. Accreditation pushes colleges and universities to challenge the status quo, encouraging them to embrace innovative approaches and technologies. When leaders and faculty view accreditation as an opportunity for transformation, it can spark creativity and lead to breakthroughs in teaching methods, curriculum design, and student support services.

Evidence-Based Decision-Making

Accreditation also empowers institutions to develop a culture of evidence-based decision-making. Through the accreditation process, they are required to collect, analyze, and utilize data and information to assess their performance and drive improvement. This culture of data-driven decision-making ensures that colleges and universities rely on facts and evidence, rather than assumptions or personal biases, to inform their strategies. By harnessing the power of accreditation, institutions can establish a foundation of rigorous assessment and utilize data to guide their planning, resource allocation, and evaluation efforts.

Collaboration

Moreover, accreditation provides a platform for collaboration and learning among institutions. Accrediting bodies often facilitate peer review processes that allow institutions to take lessons from one another's successes and challenges. Through cross-institutional dialogue, leaders and faculty can share best practices, collaborate on research, and exchange innovative ideas. This exchange of knowledge and expertise fosters a culture of learning and continuous improvement that extends beyond individual institutions.

Decision-Making and Strategic Planning

Accreditation also serves as a valuable tool for institutional decision-making and strategic planning. The accreditation standards and processes prompt institutions to critically assess their strengths, weaknesses, opportunities, and threats. This self-reflection allows them to identify areas for improvement and develop strategic initiatives that align with their long-term goals. By leveraging the power of accreditation, higher education leaders can ensure that their institutional plans and actions are guided by a clear vision and evidence-based analysis.

Roadmap for Improvement

Furthermore, accreditation provides institutions with a roadmap for improvement. The accreditation standards outline the essential elements and characteristics of high-quality educational programs and services. By closely aligning their practices with these standards, colleges and universities can ensure that their programs are relevant, rigorous, and responsive to the evolving needs of students and society. This alignment ensures that institutions remain on the path of continuous improvement and maintain a forward-looking approach.

Advocate for Student Success

Lastly, the power of accreditation also lies in its ability to advocate for student success. Accreditation requires colleges and universities to demonstrate their commitment to student learning outcomes, development, and success. By prioritizing student support services, academic rigor, and career readiness, institutions not only enhance their educational quality but also equip their students with the skills and knowledge needed for success in the workforce. Accreditation serves as a mechanism for institutions to prioritize student success, ensuring that they deliver a high-quality education that prepares graduates for the challenges and opportunities of the future.

Accreditation possesses immense power to drive institutional transformation and enhance educational quality. It serves as a mark of quality and credibility, instills confidence in stakeholders, and attracts students seeking a high-quality education. Accreditation empowers institutions to cultivate a culture of continuous improvement, embrace innovation, utilize data for decision-making, and engage in peer learning. It guides institutions in strategic planning, supports evidence-based decision-making, and advocates for student success. By harnessing the power of accreditation, institutions can position themselves as leaders in higher education and create meaningful and lasting impact.

Ten Ways Leaders Can Unlock the Power of Accreditation

Cultivating Trust and Confidence

Guiding Evidence-Based Decision-Making

Catalyzing Innovation and Continuous Improvement

Fostering Collaboration and Exchanging Best Practices

Enhancing Student Experience and Success

Cultivating Ethics and Professionalism

Ensuring Financial Stability and Sustainability

Attracting Top Talent and Bright Minds

Enabling Socio-Economic Impact

Elevating Reputation and Prestige

Ten Ways Leaders Can Unlock the Power of Accreditation

Accreditation wields the potential to be a transformative force in the hands of leaders at colleges and universities. By understanding and harnessing the power of strategic accreditation, institutions can drive remarkable impact and navigate the intricate maze of higher education. Exhibit 1.3 and the following section offer 10 ways leaders can unlock this power, highlighting the positive outcomes accreditation can bring to their institutions.

1. Cultivating Trust and Confidence: Accreditation acts as a steadfast pillar of confidence, reinforcing trust in the institution's educational quality and effectiveness. Leaders can tap into this confidence to build stronger relationships with stakeholders, securing support for their strategic initiatives and fostering a collaborative environment conducive to driving impactful change.

2. Guiding Evidence-Based Decision-Making: Strategic accreditation compels institutions to conduct comprehensive self-assessments, resulting in meaningful insights for leaders. Armed with this data, they can make informed, evidence-based decisions to ensure their institutions stay agile in a rapidly evolving educational landscape, driving long-term success and relevance.

3. Fostering Collaboration and Exchanging Best Practices: Accreditation offers leaders an opportunity to engage with peer institutions, fostering an environment of collaboration and the exchange of innovative ideas. By collaborating and sharing best practices, institutions can collectively elevate their impact and contribute to advancement in the broader higher education sector.

4. Catalyzing Innovation and Continuous Improvement: Accreditation provides a catalyst for innovation and continuous improvement within institutions. Leaders can leverage accreditation standards to inspire an environment of progressive thinking, encouraging faculty and staff to explore new strategies, technologies, and teaching methodologies. This fostering of innovation promotes constant growth and drives institutional impact.

5. Enhancing Student Experience and Success: Accreditation reinforces an institution's commitment to student success, emphasizing the provision of high-quality education and support services. Leaders can leverage accreditation to drive initiatives that enhance the student experience by improving curriculum, expanding co-curricular opportunities, and nurturing a supportive learning environment, ultimately leading to improved student outcomes.

6. Cultivating Ethics and Professionalism: Strategic accreditation upholds institutions to ethical and professional standards, establishing them as beacons of integrity and responsible leadership. Leaders can seize this opportunity to reinforce a culture of ethical behavior and ethical decision-making, fostering an environment where professionalism thrives and impactful research and innovation flourish.

7. Attracting Top Talent and Bright Minds: Accreditation acts as a powerful magnet for top-tier faculty and staff, as it serves as a testament to the institution's commitment to excellence. Leaders can leverage accreditation to attract the best and brightest minds, enhancing the institution's intellectual capital, research capabilities, and overall academic prestige.

8. Ensuring Financial Stability and Sustainability: Through strategic accreditation, leaders can demonstrate the

institution's robust financial management practices, ensuring long-term stability and sustainability. Accreditation provides assurance to donors, sponsors, and funding agencies, making the institution an attractive investment and fostering partnerships that drive impactful initiatives.

9. Enabling Socio-Economic Impact: Accredited institutions have the potential to drive significant socio-economic impact within their communities. By utilizing the institution's impact, leaders can forge partnerships with local businesses, governments, and community organizations, fostering economic development, community engagement, and positive change at a regional level.

10. Elevating Reputation and Prestige: Accreditation serves as a mark of distinction, elevating an institution's reputation among peers and prospective students. Leaders can leverage this accolade to showcase their institution's commitment to excellence, attracting top talent, partnerships, and investment opportunities that ultimately drive institutional impact.

Strategic accreditation is a catalyst for driving institutional impact, fostering growth, and elevating the reputation of colleges and universities. Leaders who embrace the potential of accreditation can leverage it to enhance their institution's prestige, attract top talent, cultivate collaboration, foster innovation, and make a lasting positive impact within their communities. By optimizing the power of strategic accreditation, leaders can steer their institutions towards greater success and influence within the higher education landscape.

Missed Opportunities in Accreditation Reviews

Although often perceived as a bureaucratic hurdle, accreditation holds substantial untapped potential for colleges and universities. There

Nine Strategic Accreditation Opportunities Not to Be Missed

Designing an Accreditation Showcase

Reimagining Self-Assessment

Leveraging Data Analytics

Expanding Collaborative Assessment

Building External Partnerships

Celebrating Innovation Success Stories

Amplifying Student Voices

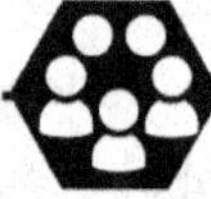

Accreditors as a Resource

Embracing the Continuous Improvement Mindset

are missed opportunities that lie hidden beneath the surface of the accreditation review process, waiting to be explored and harnessed by higher education leaders. In this section, I highlight nine such missed opportunities, urging leaders to embrace the hidden creativity and forward thinking inherent in accreditation and to utilize it as a catalyst to shape the future of their institutions (summarized in Exhibit 1.4).

Nine Strategic Accreditation Opportunities Not to Be Missed

1. Designing an Accreditation Showcase: Accreditation reviews don't have to be mere paperwork exercises. Leaders can flip the script and transform the review process into an opportunity to curate a captivating showcase. By presenting their institution's accomplishments, unique programs, and impactful initiatives, colleges and universities can capture the attention of accreditors and leave a lasting impression that bolsters reputation and elevates institutional impact.

2. Reimagining Self-Assessment: Instead of viewing self-assessment as a routine compliance exercise, leaders can infuse creativity and exploration into this process. Embracing alternative methods such as multimedia presentations, interactive visualizations, or storytelling techniques can transform self-assessment into a powerful tool for introspection and institutional growth.

3. Expanding Collaborative Assessment: Accreditation reviews provide a valuable chance for collaboration. Leaders can harness this opportunity by establishing partnerships with other institutions, pooling resources, and jointly addressing accreditation standards. This collaborative assessment not only lightens the load but also opens avenues for sharing innovative practices and fostering a spirit of collective growth.

4. Leveraging Data Analytics: Accreditation reviews generate a wealth of data that can drive evidence-based decision-making. Leaders can employ advanced data analytics tools to uncover patterns, identify areas for improvement, and make data-driven strategic decisions. This data-driven approach unlocks valuable insights that accelerate institutional progress and maximize impact.

5. Building External Partnerships: Many accreditors value the input of external stakeholders in the accreditation process. Leaders can seize this opportunity by cultivating partnerships with local businesses, government entities, and community organizations. Engaging external stakeholders not only enriches the review process but also builds stronger connections that extend beyond accreditation, fostering meaningful collaborations for societal impact.

6. Celebrating Innovation Success Stories: Accreditation reviews often focus on compliance, potentially overlooking stories of innovation and transformative initiatives. Leaders can highlight these success stories within the accreditation narrative, showcasing their institution's capacity for creative problem-solving, entrepreneurial spirit, and inventive approaches to current higher education challenges. By celebrating and sharing these narratives, institutions can promote a culture of innovation and inspire future breakthroughs.

7. Accreditors as a Resource: Accreditors are not just evaluators but can also serve as valuable catalysts for change. Accreditation liaison officers can engage accreditors in strategic conversations, seeking their expertise and guidance on transformative initiatives. By tapping into the collective wisdom of these professionals, institutions can accelerate growth, align with emerging trends, and drive impactful change.

8. Amplifying Student Voices: Accreditation reviews can be enriched by centering the student voice. Leaders can create avenues for students to share their experiences, perspectives, and ideas during the review process. By genuinely embracing student feedback, institutions can better align with student needs, enhance the educational experience, and foster a vibrant campus community.

9. Embracing the Continuous Improvement Mindset: Accreditation is not a static endpoint but rather a driver of continuous improvement and growth. Leaders can embed the ethos of continuous improvement into the institution's culture, encouraging faculty and staff to embrace innovation, challenge the status quo, and seek out opportunities for advancement. By fostering a mindset that goes beyond compliance, colleges and universities can unlock their true potential and achieve remarkable institutional impact.

The accreditation review process harbors untapped potential for creative and innovative approaches to institutional growth. Leaders who embrace these overlooked opportunities can revolutionize their institutions, shaping a future brimming with creativity, collaboration, and transformative impact. By adopting a positive and forward-thinking mindset, institutions can unleash the true power of accreditation and chart a course toward excellence, relevance, and lasting success.

Lessons From Institutions Who Were on the Accreditation "Naughty List"

Accreditation is a vitally important process that maintains academic standards and ensures quality in education. Unfortunately, some colleges and universities have found themselves on the naughty list

Lessons From Institutions Who Were on the Accreditation "Naughty List"

Lesson One:
Address Issues Proactively

Lesson Two:
Foster Internal Communication

Lesson Four:
Utilize Data for Improvement

Lesson Three:
Embrace Change

Lesson Five:
Implement Effective Project Management

Lesson Six:
Invest in Professional Development

Lesson Eight:
Foster a Culture of Ownership and Responsiblity

Lesson Seven:
Engage External Auditors Early

Lesson Nine:
Promote Transparency in Decision-Making

Lesson Ten:
Celebrate Achievements

due to neglecting the strategic potential of accreditation. This section shares lessons learned from these institutions, offering positive ways that leaders can avoid similar pitfalls and strengthen their own accreditation practices, and is summarized in Exhibit 1.5.

- Lesson One: Address Issues Proactively - Institutions on the naughty list often fail to address accreditation issues until it's too late. Leaders must proactively identify issues, implement corrective measures and communicate these solutions to relevant stakeholders. This will demonstrate the institution's commitment to quality and compliance with academic standards.

- Lesson Two: Foster Internal Communication - Communication problems can also land an institution in hot water. Departments and faculties may have different interpretations of requirements, leading to confusion or non-compliance. Leaders must promote proactive and effective communication within the institution, setting up channels to ensure everyone is working towards the same goals and understands the actions required for compliance.

- Lesson Three: Embrace Change - Complacency and resistance to change can also result in accreditation issues. Leaders must foster a culture of innovation, recognizing that staying competitive means adapting and evolving. This includes embracing new technologies, strengthening connections with stakeholders, and continually measuring and communicating progress.

- Lesson Four: Utilize Data for Improvement - Institutions that use the wealth of data available to improve their processes and academic outcomes are the ones that thrive. Leaders must recognize that measuring and assessing performance is essential to success and utilize data to make informed decisions about strategic plans and resource allocation.

- Lesson Five: Implement Effective Project Management - Accreditation processes involve a lot of moving parts and tight deadlines. Leaders must ensure that project management is effective, that responsibilities and roles are clearly communicated, that deadlines are met, and that all submissions are accurate and complete.

- Lesson Six: Invest in Professional Development - Institutions that are truly committed to excellence invest in professional development. Leaders must provide their staff and faculty with the space, time, and resources needed for ongoing training, workshops, and collaboration with peers and industry experts. This will keep them informed about changes and trends in education and equip them with the skills they need to comply with evolving standards.

- Lesson Seven: Engage External Auditors Early - Institutions that engage external auditors early can avoid surprises and receive valuable insight into improving compliance. Leaders should use expert guidance and insight during the testing and review of their processes and proactively work on areas needing improvement that auditors might flag.

- Lesson Eight: Foster a Culture of Ownership and Responsibility - Institutions that instill a culture of ownership and responsibility among all stakeholders thrive. Leaders must involve all faculty, staff, and students and empower them to take responsibility for accreditation requirements and outcomes.

- Lesson Nine: Promote Transparency in Decision-Making - Institutions that promote transparency in their decision-making processes build credibility and trust. Leaders must make information accessible, communicate changes and decisions to all stakeholders, address concerns, and have open feedback mechanisms.

- Lesson Ten: Celebrate Achievements - Institutions that celebrate their achievements and learn from their mistakes do better than those that don't. Leaders should celebrate accreditation successes with all stakeholders and should also have measures in place to continually improve. They should be transparent about any issues to ensure future mistakes are avoided.

Leaders at colleges and universities can learn from institutions that have had accreditation issues and take positive actions to avoid suffering similarly negative consequences. As pointed out, taking a proactive approach, nurturing a culture of change and ownership, utilizing data and external input, and celebrating successes are key to a successful accreditation process. Accreditation processes are an opportunity for institutions to reflect and improve. Leaders must take lessons learned from others' mistakes and implement them to ensure their institution's ongoing success and academic excellence.

Risks of Not Strategically Leveraging Accreditation

Accreditation is not only a requisite but also a catalyst for institutional growth and excellence. However, leaders who fail to strategically leverage accreditation may find themselves traversing a perilous path. This next section focuses on the risks of neglecting the power of accreditation and emphasizes how important it is for colleges and universities to embrace this process to unlock innovation and secure a prosperous future, and is summarized in Exhibit 1.6.

1. Accreditation Apathy: Letting accreditation fall by the wayside exposes institutions to the danger of apathy. Leaders must recognize that accreditation drives continuous improvement

Risks of Not Strategically Leveraging Accreditation

Accreditation Apathy

Waning Competitive Edge

Missed Innovation Opportunities

Compliance-Driven Mediocrity

Stunted Institutional Development

Diminished Reputation

Inadequate Resource Allocation

Missed Collaborative Networking

Institutional Inertia

Missed Opportunities for Continuous Improvement

and revitalizes institutions. Ignoring accreditation stifles the motivation for growth and jeopardizes the institution's ability to adapt to emerging trends.

2. Waning Competitive Edge: Disregarding the strategic potential of accreditation diminishes an institution's competitive edge. In a rapidly evolving educational landscape, colleges and universities that fail to leverage accreditation miss out on opportunities to differentiate themselves, attract top talents, and secure funding vital for success.

3. Compliance-Driven Mediocrity: Merely viewing accreditation as a compliance exercise restricts the institution's ability to strive for excellence. Leaders who neglect the strategic aspects of accreditation perpetuate a culture of mediocrity rather than fostering innovation, creativity, and entrepreneurial thinking.

4. Missed Innovation Opportunities: Accreditation offers a fertile ground for innovation, yet failure to strategically capitalize on this opportunity leads to missed chances for transformative growth. Institutions that overlook the potential for innovative practices within accreditation are left lagging behind, while their competitors surge ahead by embracing new and inventive approaches.

5. Stunted Institutional Development: Colleges and universities that do not strategically leverage accreditation risk stagnation in both academic and administrative areas. By neglecting the process, leaders hinder the institution's ability to reflect on its strengths and address weaknesses, ultimately impeding progress and hindering opportunities for growth.

6. Diminished Reputation: Accreditation is a hallmark of quality and credibility. Neglecting the strategic implications of accreditation can tarnish an institution's reputation, leading to

decreased public confidence and reduced enrollment. Leaders must recognize the power of accreditation as a reputation-building tool and actively harness its potential to solidify the institution's standing.

7. Missed Collaborative Networking: Accreditation reviews offer a prime opportunity for networking and collaboration with peer institutions. Leaders who fail to strategically leverage accreditation miss out on the chance to establish valuable connections, share best practices, and tap into a larger community of professionals dedicated to advancing higher education.

8. Inadequate Resource Allocation: Overlooking the strategic implications of accreditation leads to inefficient allocation of resources. Institutions that disregard the inherent potential of accreditation waste valuable time, effort, and funds, hindering their ability to invest in initiatives that enhance quality, student success, and institutional effectiveness.

9. Institutional Inertia: Neglecting the strategic leverage of accreditation perpetuates institutional inertia. Leaders who fail to embrace accreditation as a catalyst for change risk alienating faculty, staff, and students, creating a climate of resistance to innovation and hindering the institution's ability to adapt to the evolving educational landscape.

10. Missed Opportunities for Continuous Improvement: Accreditation is a process that demands self-reflection and continuous improvement. Failing to leverage accreditation strategically deprives institutions of the chance to propel themselves along a path of constant enhancement and growth. Leaders must seize this opportunity to instill a culture of proactive improvement, ensuring their institution remains responsive to the changing needs of students and stakeholders.

Leaders at colleges and universities must recognize that the risks of neglecting the strategic potential of accreditation far outweigh any short-term gains of racing through the tasks and skipping over much needed steps, such as hard decisions, building infrastructure, and fostering a positive campus culture, etc.. By strategically leveraging accreditation, institutions can unleash their full potential for growth, innovation, and excellence. Embarking on this journey requires a shift in mindset, embracing accreditation as a driving force for positive change rather than a burdensome administrative task. Leaders can navigate the precarious path of accreditation, fortifying their institutions for a future of success and continued impact.

Discussion Questions

1. How can leaders at your institution actively involve themselves in the accreditation process to demonstrate their commitment to quality assurance and academic excellence?

2. What are three potential consequences for your institution if accreditation issues are not addressed proactively and in a timely manner? How can leaders mitigate these risks?

3. In your role as a leader at your institution, how can you promote effective communication to ensure that all stakeholders are working towards accreditation goals? Name three specific strategies that can be employed.

4. What steps can leaders at your institution take to foster a culture of ownership and responsibility among faculty, staff, and students toward accreditation requirements and outcomes? Provide three examples of how leadership can actively encourage this culture.

5. How can leaders at your institution ensure transparency in decision-making processes related to accreditation and make

information accessible to all stakeholders? Name three ways in which you can enhance transparency in your leadership role.

6. In your opinion, what are three effective strategies that leaders at your institution can implement to celebrate and showcase accreditation achievements to build credibility and trust within the institution and the wider community?

7. In your view, how can leaders at your institution leverage the power of accreditation to enhance the institution's prestige and attract top talent? Provide three strategies or initiatives that can be pursued to this end.

8. Name three ways in which leaders at your institution can leverage accreditation to foster collaboration and innovation within the institution. How can accreditation be used as a catalyst for positive change and growth?

9. What steps can leaders at your institution take to ensure that the institution's strategic goals are aligned with accreditation standards and requirements? Explain how this alignment can strengthen the institution's overall performance.

10. In your opinion, what are three potential opportunities for institutional improvement and growth that can arise from leaders at your institution strategically leveraging the power of accreditation? How can accreditation serve as a catalyst for positive change and innovation?

Discover and Propel

The following resources are included for readers to continue their learning and further connections that advance their knowledge and learning:

- 1440 news – Their tagline is "All your news. None of the bias." You can subscribe to their free daily news service that delivers curated info right to your inbox. https://join1440.com/

- Chartr – Data Storytelling Newsletter https://www.chartr.co/

- Ron Hetrick – Labor Economist Extraordinaire https://www.linkedin.com/in/ronlhetrick/

- The EvoLLLution – higher ed news articles written by people who are moving the needle on student success. Subscribing (for free) to the daily news email provides a round-up of articles to your inbox https://evolllution.com/

- Seth Godin – Thought Leader and Trendsetting Freelancer https://www.sethgodin.com/

  ◊ Subscribe for daily inspiration https://seths.blog/subscribe/

- Read his amazing books https://seths.store/

Chapter 2

Political Strategy Applied to Accreditation

Jennifer E. Walsh

Accreditation reaffirmations require collaboration, participation, compromise, and agreement – all of which are familiar topics to the field of political science. This chapter leverages guiding principles and key concepts from the field of political science so that leaders of the accreditation process can think about how to strategically sequence, appeal to, and engage key stakeholders in the accreditation process for success.

At its core, the field of political science is dedicated to the study of political activities and behaviors, institutional processes, and political ideologies, with an underlying goal of making government better. Having originated as a merger of philosophy and history, it now encompasses an entire field of study on its own, with more than 50 subfields dedicated to in-depth examination of various political ideas, institutions, and processes. Defining "good government" may prove daunting, particularly when considering that political scientists study all types of government systems, including autocracies, oligarchies, plutocracies, and theocracies; yet within the context of American democracy, a description of good government is codified directly in the preamble to the U.S. Constitution:

We the People of the United States, in order to form a more perfect Union, establish Justice, insure domestic Tranquility, provide for the common defense, promote the general Welfare, and secure the Blessings of Liberty to ourselves and our Posterity, do ordain and establish this Constitution for the United States of America.

Although the U.S. Constitution was ratified more than 225 years ago and democratic societies have since become far more complex, the American understanding of *what* government ought to do remains the same: Government ought to express the will of the people ("We the People"), create a system of transparent procedural rules ("establish Justice"), protect the peace ("insure domestic Tranquility" and "provide for common defense"), preserve freedom ("secure the Blessings of Liberty"), and advance the public good ("promote the general Welfare").

Over the years, however, the collective understanding of *how* government should accomplish these things has changed considerably. Without devolving into the political debates that have consumed the modern era, it is safe to say that most political scientists would support the notion that government policies, at least in the United States, ought to reflect the needs of a diverse, pluralistic society (Manza & Cook, 2002) and that government officials ought to make decisions in a neutral fashion, without bias or prejudice (Kaufman, 1956). Political scientists would also posit that to establish and maintain a position of legitimacy, government leaders ought to follow their own regulations, thus adhering to the rule of law; that decisions should be made in the open, not in secret; and that the public should have opportunity to provide input and review through public hearings, open meetings and proceedings, or regularly scheduled free and fair elections (Goodwin-Gill, 2006). In addition to establishing a sense of legitimacy, these practices are necessary for sustainability: Instead of relying on authoritative force to achieve compliance, governments rely on voluntary adherence, either out of a sense of moral duty or out of respect for their fellow citizens (Buchanan, 2002).

Within the context of higher education, accrediting bodies function much like quasi-governmental entities. Established with the passage of the Higher Education Act of 1965, (U.S. Department of Education, n.d.) accrediting agencies, which are private organizations, serve as a functional extension of the U.S. Department of Education. In this regard, they help ensure that academic programs supported by federal financial aid funds meet established quality standards. To do this, accrediting agencies create principles, policies, and procedures for institutions of higher education (IHEs) consistent with sound educational practices. Colleges and universities that meet these standards through the accreditation review process are subsequently recognized as "legitimate" by the U.S. Department of Education. This, in turn, authorizes them to dispense federal funds to students who enroll.

The U.S. Department of Education requires adherence to a rigorous set of standards that provide lawmakers and the constituents that they represent with assurance that both the accrediting agency and the colleges and universities being reviewed are operating with the public's best interest in mind. Accreditors must support the government's commitment to "establish Justice" and adherence to the rule of law by ensuring that accreditation reviews are not discretionary or arbitrary but rather comply with published criteria and guidelines. For example, an accrediting agency must demonstrate regulatory compliance through its own self-study and review process, providing evidence that standards and procedures and operational policies align with federal law. In turn, accreditors require colleges and universities to show alignment with the accreditation criteria and standards through self-study, supporting documentation, and an onsite review.

Additionally, the federal government expects accreditors to institute criteria and policies that "create a culture of continuous improvement of academic quality at colleges and universities and stimulate a general raising of standards among educational institutions" (U.S. Department of Education, n.d.). This expectation of continuous improvement helps to reassure the public that higher educational programs supported by federal taxpayer funds are legitimate and good today and will continue to get better as the needs of students, employers, and society evolve. Indeed, in an age where the public is beginning to question the value of a college degree, having a federally monitored quality-control process could help to counter such skepticism. It can also provide tangible evidence of the government's commitment to "promote the general Welfare, and secure the Blessings of Liberty to ourselves and our Posterity." Accrediting agencies thus help to fulfill the government's promises to its citizens ensuring that IHEs are doing a good job at educating the people.

Of course, in a democracy, people have the final say in whether or not the government is doing a good job. Likewise, accreditors are empowered to determine whether colleges and universities are fulfilling their responsibility to provide their students with a sound education. In both cases, this determination is made after a rigorous review process. For most government officials, this review culminates in a popular election; for colleges and universities, the accreditation review process ends with the accrediting agencies deciding whether the institution is fit to receive federal financial aid funds.

In this way, accreditation reviews have much in common with electoral campaigns. Both involve retrospective reflection and consideration of constituent opinions. Both also provide opportunities for agenda setting, strategic planning, and coalition building. Not surprisingly, both require significant resources in the form of time, money, and personnel to be successful. Given these similarities, political science can offer some useful insights and practical suggestions to help IHEs secure accreditation victories.

Accreditation and Agenda Setting

In the modern age, mass media is understood to play a large role in shaping public opinion on just about everything, from consumer preferences to current affairs to what people are thinking (Gunther, 1998). When it comes to influencing public opinion on political issues, mass media is unrivaled. Dubbed the "fourth estate" by political scientists, the media is perceived as a pillar of American democracy because the constitutionally protected freedom of the press makes it possible to hold government officials accountable without fear of reprisal. As reflected by the slogan of *The Washington Post*—Democracy Dies in Darkness"—the media exposes the faults and foibles of government officials, while investigative journalism brings to light concerns previously unknown to the public. Research has shown that repeated press coverage of an issue elevates its importance in the minds of the public (McCombs & Shaw, 1972). This effect, known as "agenda setting," can in turn affect public policy since elected officials, who regularly consult public opinion data, are motivated to respond.

In addition to raising public awareness of an issue, media coverage can also influence what the public thinks about that issue. This phenomenon of "framing" is also linked to "priming"—how the public evaluates government leaders' response to the issue on the agenda (Scheufele & Tewksbury, 2007). Take, for example, the concern about rising student loan debt. Prior to 2010, the public largely believed that the cost of college attendance was an individual problem; students were the primary beneficiaries, so they should incur the cost (Quadlin & Powell, 2023).However, the spike in enrollment at expensive for-profit colleges following the Great Recession of 2008 resulted in extensive media coverage of this sector.

In addition, rising interest rates following the housing market crash prompted news stories about the cost of college attendance and its twin problem, student loan debt. Not surprisingly, elected officials were quick to respond; members of Congress introduced legislation to reform the federal student loan system, and in 2011, the U.S. Department of Education issued new rules tightening the regulatory oversight of for-profit colleges (Epstein, 2011). The agenda-setting, framing, and priming dynamic is depicted in the graphic in Exhibit 2.1 below.

Exhibit 2.1: Early Accreditation to Agenda Setting Dynamic

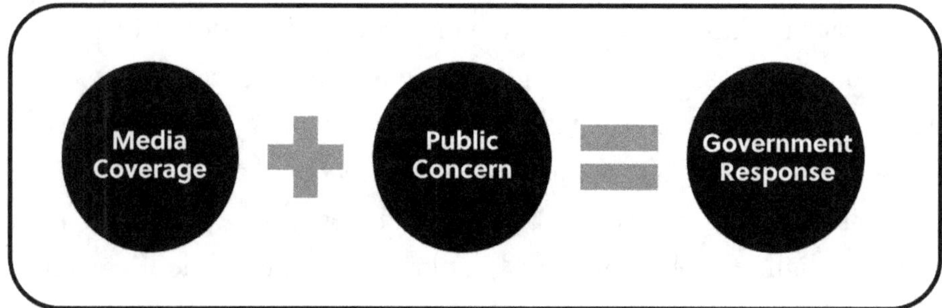

Today, this cycle could be extended to include the priorities of accrediting bodies. Standards of accreditation are not static; they are modified periodically, with each iteration reflecting the concerns of the day, as shown in Exhibit 2.2. For example, the student loan debt problem described above particularly impacted first-generation college students who dropped out before finishing their degree. With large student loan debts and no degree, they found it difficult to regain their financial footing. Concern about this population prompted accreditors to embed the provision of student success resources in their accreditation standards in order to help IHEs improve degree completion outcomes. Today, continued public concerns about the cost of college and the perceived return on investment have motivated accreditors to require IHEs to closely monitor the success of their alumni to better demonstrate the value of a college degree.

Exhibit 2.2: Current Accreditation to Agenda Setting Dynamic

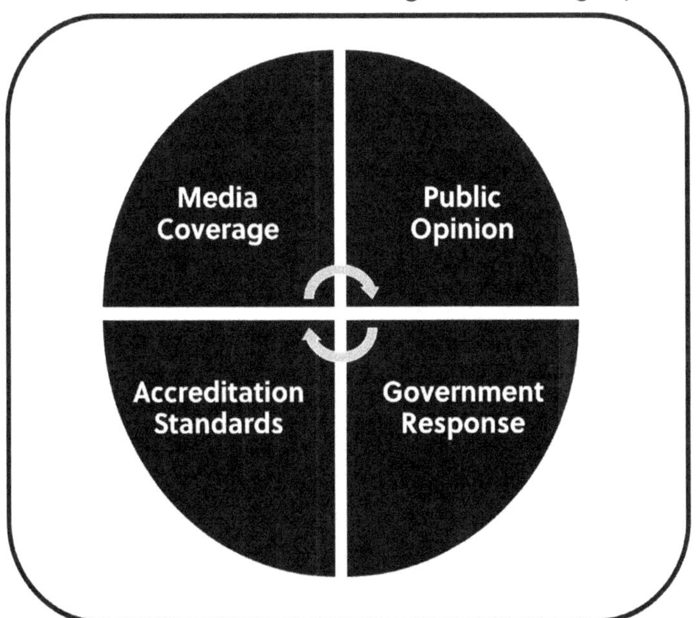

Knowing that public concerns will eventually influence policy, college and university leaders should proactively monitor media coverage of higher education in regional and/or national news. They should also monitor public opinion polling data on education-related items, especially if they are anticipating an accreditation review or starting a new strategic planning cycle. There are many polling organizations; Gallup and the Pew Research Center are good places to start.[1] Note, too, that there may be partisan differences in public opinion data that could result in the issues being framed differently across various regions of the country.

Colleges and universities can also learn from the political communication dynamics described above by engaging in their own agenda-sending and framing activities. Frequent discussion on campus about the need for and benefit of continuous improvement can reinforce the relevancy of accreditation reviews and frame the

---

1   See, for example: Brenan, M. (2023, July 11). Americans' confidence in higher education down sharply. *Gallup News.* https://news.gallup.com/poll/508352/americans-confidence-higher-education-down-sharply.aspx

process in a positive light. In fact, annual goals could be reframed as "continuous improvement" goals, with annual reports completed by division leads recapping continuous improvement accomplishments and articulating continuous improvement goals for the following year. Likewise, email summaries and newsletter entries could regularly include coverage of accreditation-related activities. Consistent with agenda-setting theories, continuous exposure to accreditation stories will elevate the importance of accreditation among members of the campus community.

IHEs should be sure to communicate their "accreditation wins" to local government officials, journalists, and the broader public as well. Campaign-related research has found that the public does respond to new information, especially if their prior knowledge of an issue is limited (Jacobson, 2015). The successful conclusion of an accreditation review provides opportunities for institutions to educate their own communities and the broader public alike on the significance of this result. Institutions should seize the occasion to explain the salience of their strategic plan to their internal and external constituents and emphasize how an accredited college or university benefits the local community and economy.

However, IHEs should be careful to use positive, not negative, messaging. Accreditation should always be framed in the context of seeking excellence and promoting the public good. Even if reviews are less than glowing, institutions can use the messaging about the outcome to reinforce their commitment to continuous improvement. "Attack ads" are common in political campaigns, but research has found that they rarely result in increased support for the attacker. They might succeed in reducing support for the target of the ad, but public support for the attacker is also reduced (Lau, Sigelman, & Rovner, 2007). Negative advertising thus becomes a "lose-lose" scenario, with both accreditors and the IHE losing credibility with the public. Accordingly, blaming the accrediting body or maligning the visiting team for a poor outcome should be avoided at all costs.

Accreditation and Enduring Coalitions

To be successful in a political campaign, candidates must build a web of support to aid them in their quest for electoral office. Political parties form the foundation of this support, providing everything from financial to tactical assistance. Described as "enduring multilayered coalitions," political parties animate significant resources to aid candidates during the election process (Hernson, 2009). These include access to party leadership for strategic direction and guidance; campaign funds for research, polling, and advertising; access to political consultants and experts; and support from outside coalitions, such as labor unions and interest groups, that can provide candidates with volunteers, additional funding, and endorsements. A spirit of cooperation binds party members together, for it is in their common interest to have like-minded political leaders elected to office. This same common interest is what makes the coalitions enduring. Incumbents are more effective at accomplishing political goals than newcomers, so working together over time improves the likelihood of political success.

Just as political candidates need the support of parties and interest groups to win elections, IHEs must align their internal and external constituencies around the need for continuous improvement in order to better position themselves for long-term success. To do this, institutional leaders should work to build enduring internal coalitions by forging cooperative alliances between the governing board, executive and administrative teams, faculty, and support staff. All must be united in their commitment to pursuing academic excellence.

At the center of a coalition is a leader who has the political clout to bring people together. In political circles, this is typically the party or organizational leader; in universities, the provost, dean of the faculty, or other centralized institutional leader, such as the Accreditation Liaison Officer. This person is responsible for cultivating relationships with others in order to accomplish the task at hand. For activities related to curriculum improvement, a coalition of faculty and administrative leaders, including Faculty Senate leadership, is required. To ensure adequate resourcing for continuous improvement projects and ongoing accreditation-related activities, the chief financial officer (CFO) must become a political ally as well. If possible, the CFO should attend accreditor conferences, participate in other accreditation-related activities, and contribute to the preparation of self-studies to gain a better understanding of the purpose and importance of accreditation.

As in political campaigns, technical expertise is also essential. Staff assigned to institutional research, student success, and admissions can provide the know-how necessary for a successful accreditation review. They should also be committed to creating a culture of continuous improvement on campus. Bringing these teams into the planning process early on helps to secure their buy-in and their long-term investment in a positive outcome.

Communication is essential to keeping the coalition focused on the goal. Key coalition leaders can form a steering committee that oversees and directs accreditation-related activities. These leaders can also broadcast the need for continuous improvement early and often, inviting other faculty and staff to contribute ideas for effecting positive change. Cooperative alliances can be animated at the start of each academic year during kick-off meetings and retreats, with targeted conversations between administrators, faculty, and staff. Follow-up conversations throughout the year can help to maintain momentum. Finally, communicating directly with students about activities underway to secure continuous improvement can engender their support as well when the institution is preparing for an accreditation review.

Off-campus or external coalitions are also vital to long-term success. Alumni have a vested interest in the strength of their alma mater and should be included in the accreditation and strategic-planning processes. Their participation could be solicited through advisory boards, alumni affinity groups, and alumni communication outlets, with specific requests tailored to the need at hand. For example, some institutions may need to present evidence of employment and professional outcomes; others may need alumni to provide testimonials about their experiences as students. Whatever the case may be, all IHEs would do well to broaden their understanding of alumni relations to include accreditation-related activities.

Colleges and universities should also work to build cooperative alliances within the community by hosting focused conversations with industry and community leaders. This could be done in traditional "town and gown" events or in town hall meetings. Advisory board discussions and career fairs provide additional opportunities for community input. Like political candidates during the run-up to an election, IHE leaders should be willing to ask the question "what can we do better?" Active listening can foster awareness of emerging concerns, and targeted follow-up actions can assure external constituents that the institution is committed to meeting community needs.

Accreditation and the Permanent Campaign

Political figures can no longer afford to allow their public-facing activities to go dormant after winning an election. In today's world of 24/7 news cycles and continuous polling of the public, elected officials must keep on doing the things that got them into office in the first place. Political scientists have dubbed this the "permanent campaign" since incumbents must court goodwill and public support throughout their term so that they can enter the next campaign period from a position of strength (Blumenthal, 1980). Staffing for election-related activities is also considered permanent, as the "election-related function" and "governing function" of the position are increasingly intertwined (Ornstein & Mann, 2000).

Similarly, colleges and universities should respond to accreditors' push for a culture of continuous improvement by adopting their own "permanent campaign" perspective; their focus and attention must not flag between accreditation review cycles. A dedicated ALO can consistently engage with faculty, staff, and administration to remind the campus community of the importance of accreditation and to periodically assess progress on the continuous improvement projects pledged by the institution during the most recent accreditation review cycle. Regular activities, such as curriculum and program reviews, should be completed with an understanding that summaries and follow-up action items will be included in the next accreditation self-study. Similarly, strategic planning and annual assessments should involve a review of accreditation standards to ensure that the institution remains fully aligned with these requirements. The governing board should be regularly apprised of the college or university's continuous improvement goals and, of course, involved in planning meetings and self-study reports prior to an accreditation review. Finally, the annual budgeting process should include dedicated funding to support ongoing accreditation-related activities. This could come in the form of funding for conference attendance, funding for assessment activities, or funding for dedicated staffing to support the ALO.

Concluding Thoughts

With the higher education landscape shifting rapidly, leaders must have a clear sense of purpose and direction. Accreditation criteria and standards serve as an anchor to prevent mission drift. Additionally, accreditation review cycles can provide a framework to keep leaders on track to achieve their long-term strategic planning goals. Colleges and universities can secure accreditation success by adopting strategies similar to those used by political candidates to win elections. By framing the accreditation process as an extension of the government's commitment to advance the public interest, aligning the accreditation goals with the institution's long-term strategic plan, and building long-lasting coalitions to secure cooperative alliances within institutions and the communities they serve, college and university leaders can create a framework for the future that results in a win.

Discussion Questions

1. What is the general perception of accreditation on your campus? Is it framed as a necessary evil or as a means to advance the institution's mission?

2. How often do institutional leaders discuss accreditation? When do they discuss it? What is the content and tone of the messaging?

3. What natural coalitions currently exist on your campus that support continuous improvement initiatives? Who could be cultivated as a political ally to further support these efforts?

4. How does your strategic planning process align with your accreditation review cycle? Is there a close relationship between them or are they considered separate and distinct?

References

Blumenthal, S. (1980). *The permanent campaign: Inside the world of elite political operatives.* Boston, MA: Beacon Press.

Brenan, M. (2023, July 11). Americans' confidence in higher education down sharply. *Gallup News.* https://news.gallup.com/poll/508352/americans-confidence-higher-education-down-sharply.aspx

Buchanan, A. (2002). Political legitimacy and democracy. *Ethics, 112*(4), 689-719. https://doi.org/10.1086/340313

Epstein, J. (2011, June 2). Ed Dept issues for-profit-college rules. *Politico.* https://www.politico.com/story/2011/06/ed-dept-issues-for-profit-college-rules-056077

Goodwin-Gill, G.S. (2006). *Free and fair elections.*

Gunther, A. C. (1998). The persuasive press inference; effects of mass media on perceived public opinion. *Communication Research, 25*(5), 486+. https://link-gale-com.hpu.idm.oclc.org/apps/doc/A21210015/ITOF?u=hono53192&sid=oclc&xid=08165493

Herrnson, P.S. (2009). The roles of party organizations, party-connected committees, and party allies in elections. *The Journal of Politics, 71*(4), 1207-1224.

Jacobson, G.C. (2015). How do campaigns matter? *Annual Review of Political Science, 18, 31-47. https://doi.org/10.1146/annurev-polisci-072012-113556*

Kaufman, H. (1956). Emerging conflicts in the doctrines of public administration. *The American Political Science Review, 50*(4),

1057-1073. https://doi.org/10.2307/1951335

Lau, R. R., Sigelman, L., & Rovner, I. B. (2007). The Effects of Negative Political Campaigns: A Meta-Analytic Reassessment. *The Journal of Politics, 69*(4), 1176–1209. https://doi.org/10.1111/j.1468-2508.2007.00618.x

Manza, J. & Cook, F.L. (2002). A democratic polity? Three views of policy responsiveness to public opinion in the United States. *American Politics Research, 30*(6), 630-667. https://doi.org/10.1177/153267302237231

McCombs, M. E., & Shaw, D. L. (1972). The Agenda-Setting Function of Mass Media. *The Public Opinion Quarterly, 36*(2), 176–187. http://www.jstor.org/stable/2747787

Ornstein, N., & Mann, T. (Eds.). (2000). *The permanent campaign and its future.* Washington, DC: American Enterprise Institute & The Brookings Institution.

Quadlin, N. & Powell, B. (2023). Who should pay? Public opinion on the funding of higher education. *Footnotes: A Magazine of the American Sociological Association.* https://www.asanet.org/footnotes-article/who-should-pay-public-opinion-on-the-funding-of-higher-education/

Scheufele, D.A. &Tewksbury, D. (2007). Framing, agenda setting, and priming: The Evolution of three media effects models. *Journal of Communication, 57,* 9-20. https://doi-org.hpu.idm.oclc.org/10.1111/j.0021-9916.2007.00326.x

U.S. Department of Education. Accreditation in the United States. https://www2.ed.gov/admins/finaid/accred/accreditation_pg2.html

PART II

IGNITING INNOVATION

This section is dedicated to highlighting how accreditation can be a catalyst for innovation in higher education institutions. Readers will discover practical strategies that can be employed to foster a culture of innovation that is nurtured by accreditation. This section also features real-world examples of institutions that have leveraged accreditation creatively to drive innovation.

Chapter 3

The Futurist Accreditation Leader: A Paradigm for Advancing Innovation in Higher Education

---

Melanie Booth

There is great value in positioning the institutional work of postsecondary accreditation within a strategic change leadership and innovation paradigm that applies futures thinking. While the administrative and transactional tasks of filing data reports, writing reports, hosting visits, and generally attending to compliance need to be done—and are not unimportant—a well-positioned and effectively resourced futurist accreditation leader can facilitate critical institutional innovations to positively impact student success, community relevance, and institutional or programmatic viability. This approach to accreditation is

> *particularly valuable in this time of rapid change in higher education sectors. This chapter introduces an accreditation leadership paradigm based on futures thinking principles and connects it to a well-regarded higher education change leadership model to promote a new way of thinking about the institutional work of accreditation. Integrating these frameworks can allow accreditation leaders to advance much-needed institutional innovations for the future of higher education and, importantly, its learners.*

It's past time for a change. The challenges facing colleges and universities in the soon-to-be second quarter of the 21st century are not insignificant. Declining traditional enrollment sources; unsustainable financial models; rapidly changing demographics; emergent powerful technologies; new educational providers and sources of competition; public and private scrutiny and mistrust; political, leadership, and staffing changes; and an imperative to demonstrate relevance, value, and return on investment are but a few of the well-documented concerns facing higher education leaders. Adding to these constraints and challenges are the ever-changing external directives from the triad—federal regulations, state mandates, and accreditors' policies. College and university leaders are recognizing the imperative for institutional innovation while also needing to maintain compliance. At times it may seem an impossible balance.

One common internal response to the call for innovation in higher education is that "the accreditors will not let us do that"—an objection sometimes grounded in reality, or at least in seemingly insurmountable bureaucratic procedures. Yet a new paradigm of accreditation leadership that includes futures thinking, combined with a framework and tools for ushering in organizational change in higher education, can create the opportunity to challenge this institutional response and help position accreditation staff to *lead* and help facilitate innovation.

In writing about the learning assessment movement in higher education, Ewell (2009) described the tensions between accountability and improvement:

> Accountability requires the entity held accountable to demonstrate, with evidence, conformity with an established standard of process or outcome. The associated incentive for that entity is to look as good as possible, regardless of the underlying performance. Improvement, in turn, entails an opposite set of incentives. Deficiencies in performance must be faithfully detected and reported so they can be acted upon. Indeed, discovering deficiencies is one of the major objectives of assessment for improvement. (p. 7)

A parallel to these tensions can be found in some forms of accreditation. While some accreditors' standards and processes have genuinely promoted continuous improvement within an institution or program, accreditation writ large is not often cited as particularly valuable for promoting institutional or programmatic innovation. As with the assessment of student learning, the incentives for maintaining accreditation compliance often do not align with those for engaging in continuous improvement, let alone innovation.

Furthermore, institutions may find themselves needing to prioritize the often transactional tasks of maintaining accreditation compliance over realizing accreditation's potential as a lever to promote genuine internal reflection, organizational learning, innovation strategy, and change on behalf of their learners and communities. However, by applying an accreditation leadership paradigm grounded in principles of futures thinking and utilizing a higher education change management framework to effectively address institutional needs and challenges, colleges and universities can better position themselves to leverage accreditation requirements and processes to help promote—and sustain—institutional innovation and change.

In this chapter, accreditation staff (e.g., accredition liaison officers) are encouraged to look beyond the day-to-day or periodic tasks of accreditation on their to-do lists—organizing self-studies, reporting and analyzing data, writing reports, hosting a visiting team, keeping informed about standards and policies and processes and consider adopting a broader view of *accreditation leadership* as a transformative opportunity for their institutions and their current and future learners. While the focus is primarily on institutional accreditation contexts, many of the principles apply to programmatic accreditation as well. Moreover, when bringing together the various staff responsible for accreditation across divisions and departments, institutions can further realize the opportunities that an accreditation leadership paradigm can afford with the right perspectives and change model in play. Ultimately, this chapter is designed to help accreditation staff leverage their important role as futures thinking leaders to promote and facilitate innovations on behalf of 21st century learners and their own institutions and programs.

The Many Jobs of Accreditation Staff

Cat Herder. Cheerleader. Traffic Cop. Cruise Director. Marriage Counselor. FBI Agent. Language Interpreter. Task Master. Field Builder. Triage Doctor. Air Traffic Controller. Orchestra Conductor. Fixer. Do-It-Yourselfer. Tapestry Weaver. Hostage Negotiator. Doula. Concierge. Gate Agent. Storyteller. Meteorologist. Train Scheduler. Coach. Event Planner. Ship's Navigator. Newspaper Editor. Learning Champion. Architect.

In my more than three decades of higher education experience, these are a few of the job titles used by the more than 100 institutional accreditation staff who have attended accreditation leadership workshops facilitated by the author over the last five years. Participants were asked to name and describe a job title (other than their actual title) that reflected their work as accreditation staff at their colleges and universities (See Exhibit 3.1).

Exhibit 3.1: The Many Jobs of Accreditation Staff

Through these titles and staff members' explanations, themes emerged about the tasks of accreditation and the myriad of roles that accreditation staff play.

- **Those Who Master Tasks and Manage People:** Some participants chose titles conveying the complex set of tasks to be completed and people to manage (Train Scheduler, Cat Herder, Coach, Air Traffic Controller). They referenced the large amount of work they have to organize and the people they need to involve, often amid other initiatives and the daily business of running an institution or program.

- **Those Who Address Problems:** While some participants selected titles that evoked involvement in a thoughtful, integrative process with a positive or even celebratory outcome (Tapestry Weaver, Orchestra Conductor, Doula), others emphasized the challenging, fraught, chaotic, or high-stakes problem-solving aspects of their role. The Triage Doctor and Fixer—and perhaps most concerning of all, Hostage Negotiator–described themselves as problem solvers working within extremely challenging circumstances (such as an accreditor's sanction) and/or with difficult colleagues.

- **Those Who Have the Knowledge:** Other participants focused on the essential knowledge they bring to the accreditation work at hand. These included the Language Interpreter, who has the always helpful ability to translate specific accreditation requirements into clear and actionable requests or responses to a colleague, and the Ship's Navigator, who charts the course of accreditation work by navigating efficient routes toward the destination while avoiding storms or other internal or external challenges. Typically, the accreditation staff member's deep understanding of their accreditor's standards, processes, procedures, and even culture were cited as particularly helpful.

- **Those With Skills Who Can Get Stuff Done:** Skills represented by participants who picked titles such as Storyteller, Trainer, Cheerleader, and Newspaper Editor reflected specific roles assigned for, or elements of, an accreditation process. Participants cited skills such as being able to synthesize multiple narrative or analytical texts; teach others about an accreditation requirement or process and its rationale; and copy edit long self-study reports. (The author admits that she was first selected to work on her college's accreditation self-study because she was recognized for designing quality learning assessment activities in her department and could pull text and data together to write a cohesive report.)

- **Those Who Can Get Stuff Done, With Caveats:** Some participants shared titles and descriptions that reflected the resources allotted for their work or, in certain cases, the size of their institution (we hear you, Do-It-Yourselfer!). Others signaled that they needed to enlist a top-down, command-and-control approach to getting the work of accreditation done. The TSA Agents, Gate Agents, and Traffic Cops reported having to pry data or information necessary for compliance out of the hands of institutional staff or putting constraints on who talked to accreditors about their requirements.

Until the time of a periodic accreditation-related event such as a team visit, report, or application for a programmatic or institutional change, the work of the accreditation staff at colleges and universities frequently goes unnoticed, underappreciated, and also, as alluded to, under-resourced. Yet, hopefully, some of the titles and descriptions shared will encourage accreditation staff to start seeing themselves differently going forward—as *accreditation leaders*—and thus to think more broadly about their roles and how they might describe their work.

Exhibit 3.2: Moving Along the Continuum in Accreditation Leadership

Maintaining Compliance → Promoting Continuous Improvement → Advancing Innovation

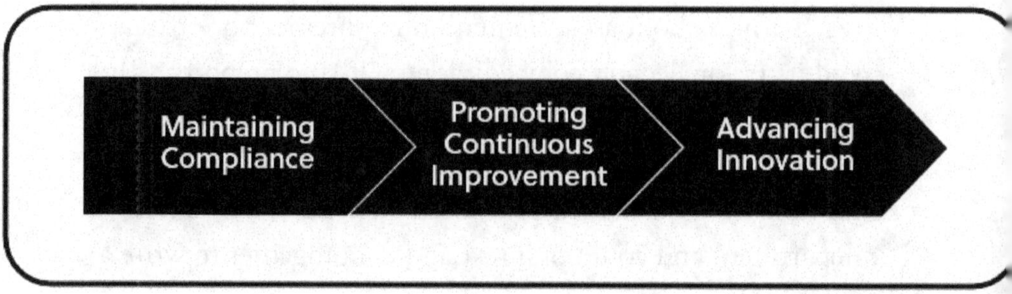

This shift toward an accreditation leadership paradigm calls for a new way of thinking about the work, as shown in Exhibit 3.2. The goal is not only to promote approaches to leading the important work of accreditation compliance and continuous improvement but also for leverage the processes for future-oriented innovations to address the needs of the institution and, ultimately, its learners. It is vital that this much-needed accreditation leadership paradigm attending to the future of higher education and the changing ecosystem in which colleges, universities, programs, and learners exist. The next section of this chapter focuses on this aspect of the paradigm: applying futures thinking.

A New Accreditation Leadership Paradigm: Futures Thinking for Leading Innovation

Beyond knowing about, tracking, and even potentially advocating for modifications to specific accreditation standards, policies, and processes, as well as building high-performing teams and fostering collaboration with colleagues to maintain compliance, an accreditation leader will be best positioned to catalyze institutional innovation and change by deepening and applying their knowledge about the rapidly evolving ecology of higher education. Therefore, this new accreditation leadership paradigm calls on leaders to learn about and pay deep attention to the current realities impacting an institution or program while also applying a futurist perspective.

Gorbis (2019) outlined five principles for futures thinking as applied to higher education that are relevant to the accreditation leadership paradigm:

1. Forget about predictions.

2. Focus on signals.

3. Look back to see forward.

4. Uncover patterns.

5. Create a community.

Applying each of these five principles both separately and in concert helps bolster the paradigm of accreditation leadership by engaging those responsible for accreditation in facilitating effective innovation to address emergent and future conditions.

Forget About Predictions

The first futurist principle is to focus less on predictions and more on observing myriad systemic changes at play, or to use Gorbis' (2019) analogy, to think beyond the waves and instead study the tides: "Waves are what we see on the surface. They are fleeting events, they come and go, appear and disappear. But there is something bigger underneath that is causing these waves. Underneath the waves is the tide, causing all kinds of disturbances of which waves are just one sign" (p. 30). For accreditation leaders, this means paying attention to multiple areas and issues outside the echo chamber of an individual college or university as well as outside the higher education sector, including but not limited to:

- National political environments that impact federal processes and outcomes (such as through negotiated rulemaking) that will impact accreditation and, therefore, institutions.

- State political and economic environments that may affect mandates or requirements, such as initiatives for measuring credentials of value, performance-based funding, or workforce education.

- Industry-specific and workforce trends, needs, and calls to action—locally, regionally, and nationally.

- Technological developments or emergent high-priority technologically related issues, such as artificial intelligence, data monetization, and individual privacy.

- Macro- and microeconomic trends and signals, including activities involving postsecondary funding but also expanding to employment and unemployment data reports, interest rate fluctuations, and global market changes.

- New or emerging models of postsecondary education, such as alternative or micro-credentials, new skills marketplaces, new curricular models, and wholly new providers.

- New or emerging models of quality assurance and consumer protection approaches.

- Media narratives about higher education and their impact on the public perception of the quality and value of higher education—and the sources of such narratives.

- Institutional and learner financial models, developments, and constraints.

- Local, regional, national, and global political and cultural forces impacting colleges and universities.

- Various governance and/or ownership models and changes

nationally or internationally.

- Demographics—local, regional, national, global—including such factors as immigration policies, affirmative action, incarceration rates, and demographically based social and economic inequities.

Practical approaches for the futurist accreditation leader to broaden their knowledge in these and other areas include subscribing to and reading newsletters and other publications, or attending convenings or conferences, that expose them to a variety of organizations outside of higher education, such as workforce development organizations, bipartisan policy groups, or advocacy associations. By becoming a student of the tides, the accreditation leader can ask such questions as: "How might this emerging development impact my institution or program? What do our learners need to know or be able to do as a result? How might this activity play out in different scenarios that we should consider? What waves might we anticipate from these national or global changes? What will we need to do to respond to, as well as advance, accreditation standards for this emergent possibility?" This is a systems thinking perspective, and combined with developing potential scenarios specific to their own university, college, or program, it can help leaders prepare for and respond with innovations on behalf of their learners and institutions.

Focus on Signals

The second futurist principle is that of focusing on signals— "developments that are on the margins. . . They are the kind of things that grab your attention and make you ask: 'Why is this happening? What is going on here?' A signal can be anything. It could be a technology, an application, a product/service/experience, an anecdote or personal observation, a research project or prototype, a news story, or even simply a piece of data that shows something different" (Gorbis, 2019, p. 31). Learning to heed such signals allows the accreditation leader to begin to sense-make from them, aggregate them, interpret them, and then help create a direction for what to do in response.

For example, many colleges and universities that have been paying attention to the indirect and direct signals from employers and industries about skills gaps and talent shortages regionally, nationally, and globally have realized the imperative for institutional redesign to better address and facilitate learners' employability development and social and economic mobility, and to better meet the needs of society. These institutions have restructured for, broadened, or are developing such offerings as internships for all learners, embedded skills-based or industry-recognized credentials, work-placed learning, employer-based faculty, non-credit to credit stackability, credit for prior learning, and redesigned wrap-around services specifically for working learners. While some of these approaches are not particularly new or innovative on their own, may, in fact, just be additive, or require accreditor approval, in aggregate some colleges and universities are in fact redefining themselves through new institutional missions, business and governance models, strategic partnerships, and programmatic offerings that often do require an accreditor's review.

Look Back to See Forward

A third and important principle for futures thinking involves looking back to see forward. As Gorbis (2019) explained, "...there is no data about the future; the only data we have is about the past. While we cannot fully rely on past data to help us see the future, there are larger patterns in history that we tend to repeat over and over again" (p. 31). For the accreditation leader helping to facilitate innovation and future direction, an understanding of the forces at play throughout the history of higher education can be instructive. A very practical approach to deepening that knowledge is to enroll in a course or read one of the many books or articles detailing historical events or changes that have resulted in current-day realities.

Additionally, interviewing retired institutional leaders can potentially reveal specific historical forces at play that may have impacted the way an institution exists today. One Catholic college accreditation leader interviewed the few remaining founding order nuns who were serving on the institution's board of trustees. Their stories helped reveal a long-held ethos of austerity that infused the college to the modern day. This knowledge became instructive to the accreditation leader in determining specific organizational change moves (see more details about organizational change moves and levers later in this chapter).

Uncover Patterns

After gaining an understanding of the historical events that have shaped change over time, the accreditation leader can then uncover any significant patterns—, the fourth principle of futures thinking—to gain insights into the collective forces shaping the future. As we sit at the cusp of an exponential explosion of artificial intelligence technologies, in addition to the patterns of unbundling and disruption that have occurred in other industries (music, television, newspapers, retail, etc.), the futurist accreditation leader may very well be the best person not only to lead institutional innovation but also to advocate for changes in accreditation requirements and processes that anticipate these future forces as well.

Create Community

Gorbis's (2019) fifth principle of futures thinking focuses on the importance of creating a collaborative community to attend to the signals, patterns, and needs that are emerging. This aligns nicely with what is required in accreditation leadership generally—to create a diverse community of viewpoints and perspectives about the relative health and quality of an institution or program. "Thinking about the future is a collaborative and highly communal affair. It requires a diversity of views. We need to involve experts from many different domains. When we think about anything, from higher education to work, we need to include people who bring different perspectives on the topic—demographics, economics, technology, artificial intelligence, organizations. We need young people in the room. A robust forecast is a collective endeavor; it's very much a product of collective intelligence" (Gorbis, 2019, p. 34). The futurist accreditation leader will wish to involve a wide variety of constituents from outside of the institution, including potential future employer groups, diverse members of local communities, and regional housing or workforce representatives, in order to broaden the forecast. What signals or patterns are they paying attention to in their unique realms that could be instructive for the college or university to monitor?

Applying these futurist principles will assist accreditation leaders in putting the needs of 21st century learners and communities at the center of innovation and change initiatives and can also support internal case-making for change. But how might an accreditation leader leverage their futures thinking skills and knowledge of accreditation requirements and processes in an institution that is steeped in tradition or inertia and that may be, in fact, resistant to real change?

Linking a Change Leadership Model to Futurist Accreditation Leadership

Now that we have considered an accreditation leadership paradigm based on futures thinking, adopting or adapting an organizational change leadership model as part of facilitating innovation can help accreditation leaders engage their colleagues and propel their institution forward. Change fatigue and failure are well documented in higher education; 70% of change initiatives were found to have failed in the implementation process (Kezar, 2018). A lack of change management expertise, including the ability to equip people with the new knowledge and new tools necessary to understand and create change, has a significant impact on this fatigue:

> *In times of pervasive implementation initiatives, agencies are impotent to build internal capacity to measure and focus on fidelity to evidence-based solutions. Many new change initiatives get off the ground, yet very few land, settle, and become deeply rooted in organizational culture and habits. One change initiative is eventually eclipsed by a new change initiative, which in turn is later overshadowed by yet a different one* (Tapia and Walker, 2020, p. 11)

Even when a culture of evidence-based continuous improvement is infused in the institution and endorsed by an accreditor, change fatigue or implementation failure can hinder true innovation.

This is where an understanding of change leadership, and utilizing a change leadership framework and tools, can help the futurist accreditation leader propel innovation. The *Change Leadership Toolkit: A Guide for Advancing Systemic Change in Higher Education* (Elrod, Kezar, and González, 2023) is a key resource. This research-based toolkit highlights the significance of deeply understanding the leadership context for a given change initiative, including institution type, governance model, culture, politics, human capital and capacity, resources, and external factors (notably accreditation requirements).

The *Change Leadership Toolkit* also describes eight "Change Leader Moves" that can help accreditation leaders, equipped with futurist perspectives, to facilitate systemic innovations effectively. These moves include:

1. creating vision for the change;

2. developing strategy and resources to enact the change;

3. fostering diversity, equity, and inclusion to ensure attention to all constituents' interests;

4. leading people and teams;

5. advocating and navigating politics;

6. communicating effectively;

7. making sense and learning from data and other sources of information to inform change strategies and outcomes; and

8. preparing for sustaining the change over the long term (Elrod et al., pp. 16-17).

(It is highly recommended that the accreditation leader download the entire *Toolkit*, engage in its exercises, and explore its application to their institutional context to gain a deep understanding of its potential impact.)

There are certainly numerous other organizational change frameworks that may be in play already at a college or university or that an accreditation leader might wish to explore in helping develop future-focused innovation strategies to benefit the institution, program, and learners. What matters, though, is that without addressing the institution's "change acumen" (Tapia and Walker, 2020), the desired outcomes for any innovations may very well fall short:

> *As intelligent change leaders, we become intoxicated by the thought of progressive change and innovation. As we start our applied implementation work, we then become sobered by the challenges of real-world change. While the trials of the real world must always sober us, we must simultaneously think, imagine, and lead with the uninhibited and intoxicated mindset of adaptive change*

and innovation. Organizationally intelligent leadership demands that both co-exist in conflict and in harmony. To abandon either mindset is to doom such leadership to ineffectiveness (Tapia and Walker, 2020, p. 16)

While the accreditation leader may have the required knowledge, skills, and abilities, along with futurist perspectives, to help advance an innovation initiative, their efforts may fall short without attention to the forces that will truly result in sustainable organizational change. An "infinite leadership mindset" focused on continual change and agility, and avoiding change enervation from failed past initiatives, will support implementation success (Tapia and Walker, 2020).

Getting Meta: Moving Toward a New Approach

Moving from a traditional model of periodic get-it-done accreditation compliance tasks to an ongoing accreditation leadership paradigm, one inclusive of futures thinking and change leadership skills and tools, can position the accreditation staff of a college or university to promote and advance innovation on behalf of 21st century learners and the institution. This perspective extends the work of accreditation well beyond managing compliance and even attending to continuous improvement toward promoting, facilitating, and sustaining institutional change, as shown in Exhibit 3.3.

Exhibit 3.3: The Accreditation Leadership Paradigm for Advancing Innovation involves knowledge of and skills for leading accreditation work, futures thinking perspectives, and change leadership

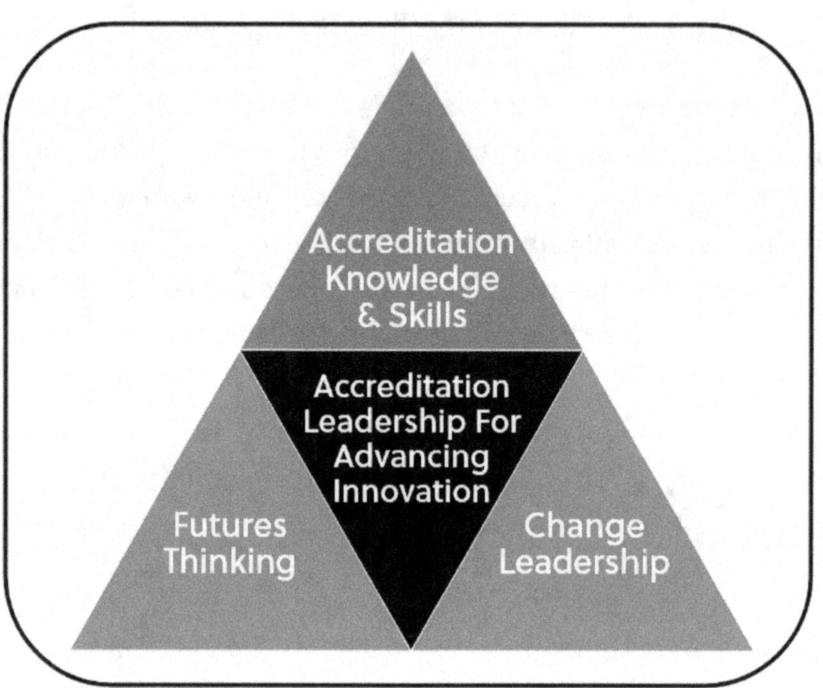

Paying particular attention to at least three shared themes across the frameworks will be essential to assuming accreditation leadership:

1. **Practice the Leadership Approach Continuously:** As Elrod, Kezar, and González (2023) conveyed in the *Change Leadership Toolkit*, attending to change is not a "one and done" event; it is a dynamic set of actions and activities best addressed in an iterative cycle over time. The same holds true for futures thinking. The dynamic nature of the 21st century and the speed of change reveal the importance of continuously thinking in this new way (Gorbis, 2019). In this regard, the accreditation leader's work facilitating innovation will never be complete; everything will be a work in progress, and it will be essential to learn to "be comfortable being uncomfortable" (Tapia and Walker, 2020, p. 16).

2. **Attend to the People:** No innovation will be successful without the engagement and commitment of the people doing the work. Gorbis (2019) contended that "futures thinking is not about predicting the future; rather, it is about engaging people in thinking deeply about complex issues, imagining new possibilities, connecting signals into larger patterns, connecting the past with the present and the future, and making better choices today" (p. 35). Likewise, innovations need to be the products of a collective approach. While this is often referred to as "getting buy-in," adopting a model of "gaining investment in" the conditions and needs for innovation instead may reap longer-term rewards. Leading the hearts and minds of colleagues before spending time on the "what" and "how" is a strategy to support colleagues' investment (Tapia and Walker, 2020). The *Change Leadership Toolkit* includes understanding culture as a lever and leading people and teams as one of the very important Change Leader Moves.

3. **Get Meta and Share Your Learning:** Futures thinking involves learning and is about transforming the ways we think (Gorbis, 2019). Likewise, critically reflecting on the processes of innovation and change can further learning, not only for accreditation leaders themselves but also, importantly, for their organizations as well as others along the path and in the field. "Real-world leadership requires a time to stop and reflect on what you have learned and to share that learning forward with others . . . Savoring the journey means that leaders have a duty to inventory our experiences so that we can see tangibly what we have learned in the infinite pursuit of organizational intelligence. It is a focus on the learning and, more importantly, the abundant sharing of that learning with other leaders and followers in our collective environment" (Tapia and Walker, 2020, p. 16).

While this model of accreditation leadership will hopefully be attractive to accreditation staff, adopting it at your institution, may require knowing which institutional levers can be pressed using several of the Change Leader Moves described in the *Change Leadership Toolkit*. In other words, helping other college or university leaders understand the rationale for moving toward this new accreditation leadership paradigm can be a great opportunity to practice the paradigm itself.

Discussion Questions

1. Which person or people are responsible for leading the work of accreditation at your institution? Is it centralized or decentralized?

   a. To what extent are the accreditation staff positioned as, or equipped for being, institutional leaders?

   b. To what extent are the accreditation staff equipped to engage in futures thinking?

3. How is the work of accreditation resourced? Is the resourcing sufficient for a futurist accreditation leadership paradigm?

4. To what extent does the work of accreditation at your institution reflect an ongoing process of reflection, data collection, analysis, and continuous improvement?

5. To what extent could the work of accreditation at your institution help promote innovation and change? What might be the barriers to this new approach?

6. What will it take to move toward a futurist accreditation leadership model at your institution? What levers will you need to push, and what Change Leader Moves might you make to promote this new approach?

7. What is the culture of change and "change acumen" at your institution? Where has innovation truly been successful, and what were the conditions that made it so? What from these successful innovations can you carry forward?

8. How might your institution be able to align its accreditation processes with its innovation initiatives?

9. What additional knowledge, skills, or abilities will you need to develop to be a futurist accreditation leader? What learning opportunities might you gain access to?

References

Ewell, P. T. (2009, November). *Assessment, accountability, and improvement: Revisiting the tension. (Occasional Paper No. 1).* Urbana, IL: University of Illinois and Indiana University, National Institute for Learning Outcomes Assessment (NILOA).

Elrod, S., Kezar, A., & González, Á. d. J. (2023). *Change leadership toolkit: A guide for advancing systemic change in higher Education.* Pullias Center for Higher Education.https://pullias.usc.edu/download/change-leadership-toolkit-a-guide-for-advancing-systemic-change-in-higher-education/

Gorbis, M. (2019, March). Five principles for thinking like a futurist. *EDUCAUSE Review.*https://er.educause.edu/-/media/files/articles/2019/3/er191102.pdf

Kezar, A. J. (2018). *How colleges change: Understanding, leading, and enacting change.* Routledge: New York.

Tapia, G.A. and Walker, A. (2020, September). The 10 essential leadership principles of implementation leadership: Real-world applications of change leadership acumen. *Federal Probation, 84*(2), 11-17.

Chapter 4

Effectively Managing the Chaos of Multiple Accreditations at the Same Time

Jillian Huot

This chapter focuses on strategies and techniques for managing and multi-purposing when a college or university has institutional and discipline-specific accreditations at the same time.

Chaos is defined as "a state of utter confusion" (Merriam-Webster, 2023). Confusion? "A state in which people do not understand what is happening or what they should do" (Cambridge Dictionary, 2023). One might reasonably assume that managing multiple accreditations would be chaotic. To achieve or maintain accreditation, a program or an institution must simply demonstrate continuous improvement and meet quality criteria.[2] However, ask anyone involved in the

---

2   The word "criteria" is used throughout this chapter to describe the expectations an accrediting agency sets for institutions. These expectations may also be referred to as "standards".

process of achieving or maintaining accreditation is simple, and most likely, their response will be no. Why might that be? Various tasks need to be completed, and often staff, students, faculty, and other stakeholders in the accreditation process don't understand what is happening or what they should be doing, thus leading to chaos.

Managing multiple accreditations doesn't have to be chaotic, though. While they may be implemented differently depending on variables such as an institution's size or organizational structure, an accreditation leader's experience, or the internal or external resources available, certain strategies for handling the accreditation process are sound and can serve to reduce or eliminate chaos. This chapter discusses those strategies most effective for institutions tackling multiple accreditations at the same time.

Overview and Types of Accreditation

According to the U.S. Department of Education, "The goal of accreditation is to ensure that education provided by institutions of higher education meets acceptable levels of quality" (U.S. Department of Education, n.d., p.1). However, it may be difficult to assume that there is just one level of quality for all institutions and all programs. Therein lies the need for different types of accreditation. This chapter includes a description of the various types of accreditation and the variability in criteria, as well as a discussion of the accreditation process and the features common to all types of accreditation.

Types of Accreditation

When researching types of accreditation, you will find hundreds of different accrediting agencies in the United States (U.S. Department of Education, n.d.). While the goal of each accrediting agency is to "ensure that education provided by institutions of higher education meets acceptable levels of quality" (p. 1), these levels of quality may differ and reflect each accrediting agency's *scope of recognition.*

For example, the scope of recognition of institutional accrediting agencies such as the Southern Association of Colleges and Schools Commission on Colleges (SACSCOC) and the Higher Learning Commission (HLC) is primarily institutional in nature, while that of, say, the Midwifery Education Accreditation Council, the Commission on Accrediting of the Association of Theological Schools, or the Commission on Massage Therapy Accreditation is more specific and narrowly defined based on discipline specific content.

Regardless of their scope of recognition, all accrediting agencies are categorized into two types, according to the U.S. Department of Education as shown in Exhibit 4.1.

Exhibit 4.1: Types of Accreditation Agencies

Institutional Accreditation	Specialized/ Programmatic Accreditation

"Institutional accreditation normally applies to an entire institution, indicating that each of an institution's parts is contributing to the achievement of the institution's objectives, although not necessarily all at the same level of quality. Specialized or programmatic accreditation normally applies to programs, departments, or schools that are parts of an institution. The accredited unit may be as large as a college or school within a university or as small as a curriculum within a discipline" (U.S. Department of Education, n.d., Accreditation in the U.S.).

The Accreditation Process

The Council for Higher Education Accreditation (CHEA) has defined accreditation in higher education as "a collegial process based on self and peer assessment for public accountability and improvement of academic quality" (Council for Higher Education Accreditation, 1998). Notice the word *process*; to achieve and maintain accreditation, there is a process. Fortunately, regardless of the type of accreditation, the general or high-level phases of the process are the same.

To successfully maintain accreditation, there are key, high-level phases that are critical in the accreditation cycle, and must be completed: the self-study and accreditation visit preparation, the peer review process, the accreditation visit, the accreditation decision, and continuous monitoring and improvement.

Exhibit 4.2: The Accreditation Cycle

It is important to note that the cycle in Exhibit 4.2 is general in nature and applies to all types of accreditations. However, the multiple actions that occur within each phase may vary based on the type of accreditation body. While the accreditation cycle can be easily summed up in just a few phases, achieving and maintaining even one accreditation involves a vast amount of tremendously important work and preparation. Therefore, it is essential to review and follow the guidance from each accrediting agency.

Benefits and Drawbacks of Managing Multiple Accreditations

Differences and Similarities in Criteria and Content

When managing multiple accreditations, there is a lot to keep track of—people, timelines, deadlines, and more. However, the most time-consuming aspect might be understanding the different criteria for the various accrediting agencies, developing the required content, and gathering evidence to show that each of the criteria have been met. It's not uncommon for each accrediting agency to have just a handful of criteria. While that might seem manageable, each criterion may have up to hundreds of components, sub-components, or some variation of additional sub-points that need to be addressed. Therein lies the complex nature of accreditation.

The differing criteria of institutional and programmatic accrediting agencies can multiply the volume of content and evidence that needs to be collected and kept track of. However, where there are differences in criteria, there are also similarities; these can be identified through cross-referencing. Overlapping criteria frequently relate to the mission or vision of the institution, institutional outcomes such as persistence and completion rates, assessment of student learning, student support services, and financial viability. Once the commonalities are identified, relevant pieces of evidence and content may be gathered and stored accordingly, helping to avoid duplicative efforts, allow for consistency of information, and reduce workload.

You Aren't Alone on an Island

The work of an accreditation leader is nonstop and ever-evolving. It can be both challenging and rewarding, and most often is done solo. At any given institution, just one person is typically tasked with being the accreditation leader, or Accreditation Liaison Officer (ALO). According to the Higher Learning Commission: the ALO is a primary contact point between HLC and the institution. They receive communications from HLC regarding policies, procedures, news, and other updates, and are responsible for coordinating efforts to ensure their institution meets its obligations of HLC membership (Higher Learning Commission, 2023).

To ensure that a college or university meets all the requirements of an accrediting agency, the ALO may need to be a part of various committees at the institution, including the assessment committee, as well as any group that oversees policy making.

While some institutions may appoint an additional person or a small team to assist the ALO, the heavy workload and responsibility will always fall to the accreditation leader. However, having a single ALO at an institution does have benefits. For example, a clear document-tracking structure can be developed. Accreditation documents such as self-studies, evaluation reports, certifications, and letters from accrediting agencies can all be tracked and managed through one person or one central office rather than through individual departments.

While an ALO may sometimes feel they are alone on an island when it comes to managing their college's or university's accreditation efforts, they aren't. Achieving and maintaining one or multiple accreditations requires the commitment of the entire institution. Discovering the accreditation-related roles and responsibilities of others at the institution will enable ALOs and accreditation leaders to see that they aren't alone in this endeavor.

Challenges and Opportunities of Managing Multiple Accreditations

You Can't Control Everything

As previously discussed, managing multiple accreditations involves multiple tasks, such as writing the self-study, gathering evidence, preparing for the site visit, communicating with stakeholders, and monitoring continuous improvement. The management and completion of these tasks pose a serious challenge to any one person. Moreover, while an accreditation leader can control a lot, they can't control everything.

Managing multiple accreditations offers an opportunity to develop or utilize an accreditation organizational structure. Hierarchal structures can be developed that assign key stakeholders or stakeholder groups within the institution a clear role in contributing to the accreditation process, and aim to divide large accreditation responsibilities into manageable tasks. These structures may or may not align with the institution's current organizational chart, as shown in Exhibit 4.3.

Exhibit 4.3: Accreditation – Organizational Structure Alignment

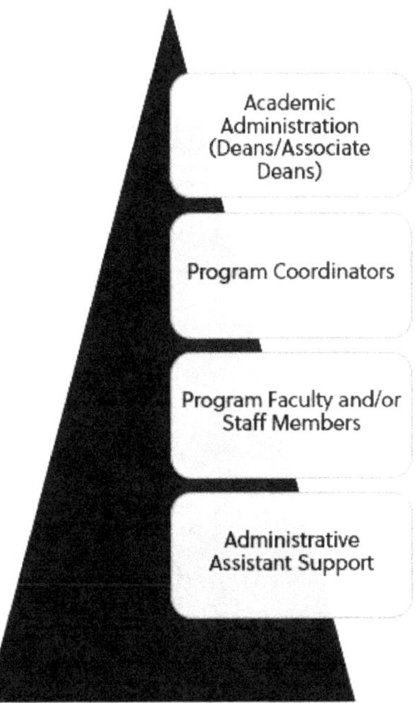

Accreditation leaders must remember that they *can't control everything*, but they can develop a structure and a team to assist in managing one or multiple accreditations.

Build Relationships…Get Things Done

Accreditation leaders often have to ask faculty and staff who don't report to them to perform tasks or furnish information. This can pose a challenge, especially when there is a looming deadline. So, how do you tell someone to do something or ask them to provide you with something when they don't report to you? Build relationships.

ALOs must nurture existing relationships with stakeholders at their institution and also build new ones based on trust and common understanding to get what they need.

Strategies and Techniques for Effectively Managing Multiple Accreditations
Get the Little Things Right

It can be overwhelming to try to focus on the little things that matter amongst the monstrous amount of work that needs to be done to achieve and maintain multiple accreditations. From adhering to different criteria, meeting the requirements of each individual accrediting agency, and following timelines and schedules that may not be in sync to communicating effectively with the appropriate stakeholders and keeping track of thousands of pieces of evidence, the work may seem never-ending.

Consider the task of completing a jigsaw puzzle. With a six-piece puzzle, the pieces are large and the pictures on them clear. Completing the puzzle requires no strategy and little effort. Compare that to the task of putting together a 1,000-piece puzzle. The puzzle box is opened to reveal pieces of different sizes, some stuck together, some upside down, some right side up. Needless to say, it's *chaotic*. However, there is a strategy to follow: find the corners and straight edges to create the border, then find any faces, similar colors, or patterns, and complete small sections of the puzzle. Place the small, completed sections within the larger frame and fill in the rest. When the focus of a strategy is on doing the little things right, the monstrous task of completing the puzzle suddenly becomes less daunting, less chaotic.

The same goes for accreditation: Get the little things right, and the chaos of managing multiple accreditations will subside. The next section provides several 'little things' that are crucial to have in place.

Create an Accreditation Tracking Spreadsheet

The main purpose of the accreditation tracking spreadsheet is to track high-level accreditation activities for academic programs. The spreadsheet can also be used to ensure that the institution's website features up-to-date accreditation information and that proper documentation has been collected and filed. Consistently gathering and maintaining just a few pieces of information on this tracking spreadsheet helps eliminate confusion and chaos. The spreadsheet should be reviewed at a minimum annually. See Exhibit 4.4 for examples of spreadsheet content.

Exhibit 4.4: Examples of Content that Could be Included on the Accreditation Tracking Spreadsheet

Program Name & CIP Code	The Accrediting Agency Name and Contact Information	Initial Accreditation/ Approval Date	Last Accreditation/ Approval Start Date	Length of Full Accreditation/ Approval	Accreditation/ Approval End Date	Current Status/ Citations
Ex: Nursing						
Ex: Physical Therapy						
Ex: Culinary Arts						

Other information that could be added to the tracking spreadsheet includes:

- Name of the program coordinator and/or program administrator(s).

- Whether the accrediting agency information is listed on the institution's main accreditation webpage and the program's individual webpage.

- If applicable, whether the pass rates are included on the program's webpage and/or the institution's main accreditation webpage.

- Whether the accrediting agency is recognized by CHEA.

- Whether the program has been issued a sanction, been put on probation, or been subject to an adverse action, including denial or withdrawal of accreditation.

- Whether the most recent letter of accreditation has been received and filed.

- Whether the most recent self-study has been received and filed.

Create a Naming Convention for Evidence

It is not uncommon to gather hundreds if not thousands, of pieces of evidence when preparing for accreditation. Keeping that evidence organized and relevant is the key to minimizing chaos. Therefore, creating and establishing a naming convention is crucial. This ensures consistency and can be especially useful for multi-purpose institutional documents such as the strategic plan, which must be provided to each accreditor. The naming convention should be applied to each piece of evidence, facilitating organization, access, and sharing. It is important that the naming convention be specific to the institution. For example, employing acronyms already familiar to stakeholders is preferable to adopting those in use elsewhere. A clear filing system mirroring the naming convention should also be established.

What does a naming convention look like? Most often, institutions will organize evidence by each accrediting agency's standard or criterion, the title of the document, and the year in which the document was created. This may look something like the following:

2.A.III._Academic Catalog_2023-24

3.B.2._Committee Meeting Minutes_08.2023

IV.A.1._Academic Integrity Policy_10.05.2022

1.C.5a._Clery Report_032122

This is certainly a foolproof way to ensure that evidence is properly identified for each standard or criterion of one individual accrediting agency, visit, or evaluation. However, when managing multiple accreditations simultaneously, and potentially dealing with multiple accrediting agencies with varied criteria, using this type of naming convention may present challenges. Consider an alternative: a naming convention that organizes evidence according to the organizational structure of the institution. The examples above might be modified as follows (OAA is the acronym for Office of Academic Affairs; OSA, Office of Student Affairs):

OAA_ Academic Catalog_2023-24

OSA_ Committee Meeting Minutes_08.2023

When using the organizational structure as the basis for a naming convention, the focus is on what the piece of evidence *is* rather than what standard or criterion the piece of evidence *meets*. Therefore, a single piece of evidence may easily be used for multiple accreditations.

The specificity of the naming convention is endless but should align with the needs and organizational structure of the institution. There may also be varying levels within the naming convention. In the examples below, ARC stands for the Academic Resource Center, which is a part of the Office of Academic Affairs, and CS for Career Services, which is a part of the Office of Student Affairs.

OAA_ARC_ Academic Catalog_2023-24

OSA_CS_Committee Meeting Minutes_08.2023

Lastly, no matter what naming convention is created, a glossary of acronyms should be developed and shared with key stakeholders.

Don't Underestimate the Power of Effective Communication

The ability to communicate effectively is one of the most important skills leaders and managers can possess. In any industry, it can improve outcomes, enhance messaging to constituents and stakeholders, foster collaboration and the exchange of ideas, and reduce confusion. On the other hand, a lack of effective communication can hinder the progress of any project, decrease team productivity, and create confusion, frustration, and even chaos.

When managing multiple accreditations at the same time, it's imperative that communication be clear, consistent, and effective. Regardless of institutional resources such as an established communication department, communication originates with the accreditation leader. It will be up to this person to determine *what* information needs to be communicated, as well as *when, to whom, and how.*

Remember the definition of chaos? A state of utter confusion. The definition of confusion? A state in which people do not understand what is happening or what they should do. Think about that: a situation in which people *do not understand what is happening or what they should do*. What better way to help people understand what is happening or what they should do than to communicate effectively with them? While there are techniques upon techniques, methodologies, and best practices for effective communication, just a couple are of importance to an accreditation leader.

Be Consistent and Continuously Communicate

Change is inevitably imminent throughout the accreditation process. To make certain that stakeholders are aware not only of the process and steps involved in accreditation but also of any changes that might occur, it's important to share news, information, and resources consistently and continuously. One way to ensure consistency is to utilize resources your institution already has in place, such as its public website or an internal webpage or portal.

The use of collaboration software, such as Microsoft Teams, should be considered as well. Such platforms can be quickly updated and are excellent tools not only for sharing pertinent information but also for fostering collaboration between specific stakeholders for a specific task, whether it be writing the self-study or assurance argument or gathering evidence.

Adapt to Your Audience

An accreditation leader must work and communicate with stakeholders ranging from employees and students to the board of trustees and even community leaders. All are important in the accreditation process, but each is a different audience. While having a consistent message is imperative, an accreditation leader may have to adapt and convey that same message differently to various audiences to ensure that it is understood. For example, when there is an upcoming accreditation visit, all stakeholders must be informed, but since each will play a different role, the message must be modified accordingly. Whereas the board of trustees and administration of the college may need to know the full itinerary of the visit, a few relevant details will suffice for students. Part of knowing what needs to be communicated and to whom is understanding the roles and responsibilities of each of the stakeholders in the accreditation process.

Know Your Role…and Others' Too!

The process of managing multiple accreditations could involve dozens, hundreds, or even thousands of people. Therefore, it is essential to clearly define the roles and responsibilities of these stakeholders. It is not advisable to list every single one; instead, focus on identifying those groups or individuals that are crucial to the accreditation process and determining their respective roles, responsibilities, and level of involvement.

From there, consider using a simple table shown in Exhibit 4.5, which can be completed with the stakeholder information you've gathered. The table can then be used as a tool to inform others of the importance of each key stakeholder or stakeholder group in the accreditation process.

Exhibit 4.5: Stakeholder Information

Stakeholder	Role/Responsibility	Level of Involvement

Don't Reinvent the Wheel

Whether you are new to accreditation or have been around the block once or twice, it's important to remember that others have been in your role, may have had more or different experiences than you, and most likely will be willing to share their experiences. They have probably documented accreditation processes or provided resources to help others learn about best practices. *Don't reinvent the wheel.* Reach out, search, and gather those experiences, documented processes, and resources.

Where should you start? If there is someone at your current institution with prior accreditation experience, they might be your best bet. However, don't be afraid to go beyond the campus gates. One of the best resources to learn more about achieving and maintaining accreditation is directly from the source: the appropriate accrediting agency.

As discussed earlier, there are different agencies for each type of accreditation, whether it be institutional or programmatic. It's those accrediting agencies that will provide you and your institution with expectations, timelines to adhere to, criteria/standards to meet, resources such as webinars and conferences to access, and an agency contact to reach out to should you have questions.

Utilize Project Management Tools and Techniques

Project management has been practiced for thousands of years. However, "It's not until the 1950s that organizations have started to apply systematic tools and techniques to complex projects" (Seymour & Hussein, 2014, p. 233). Project management principles, methodologies, and tools and techniques have evolved over the decades and are now in broad use.

Project management is often associated with large-scale projects in industries such as construction, manufacturing, engineering, healthcare, and information technology. But what if the tools and techniques of project management were used to lead both large- and small-scale projects in higher education and, dare I say, *accreditation*? In recent years, the *project economy* has emerged, and the increasing need for project managers in *all* industries has become apparent.

Let's face it: achieving and maintaining multiple accreditations is a major undertaking that involves juggling the routine tasks of managing the schedule, communications, resources, and stakeholder engagement while ensuring that quality standards and criteria are being met. Fortunately, common project management tools and techniques such as a work breakdown structure (WBS) and a responsibility assignment matrix (RAM) can make it easier to complete those tasks and coordinate one or multiple accreditations, thus minimizing confusion and chaos. According to the Project Management Institute's *Guide to the Project Management Body of Knowledge* (PMBOK), 7th Edition, a WBS is "a hierarchical decomposition of the total scope of work to be carried out by the project team to accomplish the project objectives and create the required deliverables." (Project Management Institute, 2021). Essentially, it's a chart that begins with high-level information about a project, which is then divided into smaller and smaller pieces, starting with deliverables and moving into work packages.

WBSs are used every day, often times in our own personal lives. Consider baking a cake, for example. There's a lot more to it than just mixing ingredients and having the proper bakeware. The ingredients must be bought, measured, and combined in a specific order. Eggs must be cracked, butter softened, and flour sifted. If there's decorating involved, the work breakdown continues. A work breakdown structure is just that: a way to break down the work that needs to be done from the biggest steps to the littlest ones.

Cann and Brumagim of the University of Scranton demonstrated the application of this tool in preparing for and maintaining accreditation. They noted that meeting the requirements of an accrediting agency can create a complex, chaotic situation and suggested that excellent organizational skills and proper sequencing of deliverables would lead to successful accreditation. "Trying to keep track of what has been accomplished and what has not becomes very difficult without some kind of mechanism to organize the effort" (Cann & Brumagim, 2008, p. 37). According to their research, the use of a tool such as a WBS can provides a clear, visual overview of the entire accreditation effort.

Exhibit 4.6 and 4.7 are examples of work breakdown structures. Exhibit 4.6 is general in nature and includes just some of the deliverables that need to be completed in order to achieve or maintain accreditation. This could be used to help communicate to stakeholders the steps involved in preparing for accreditation.

Exhibit 4.6: Accreditation Structure Breakdown

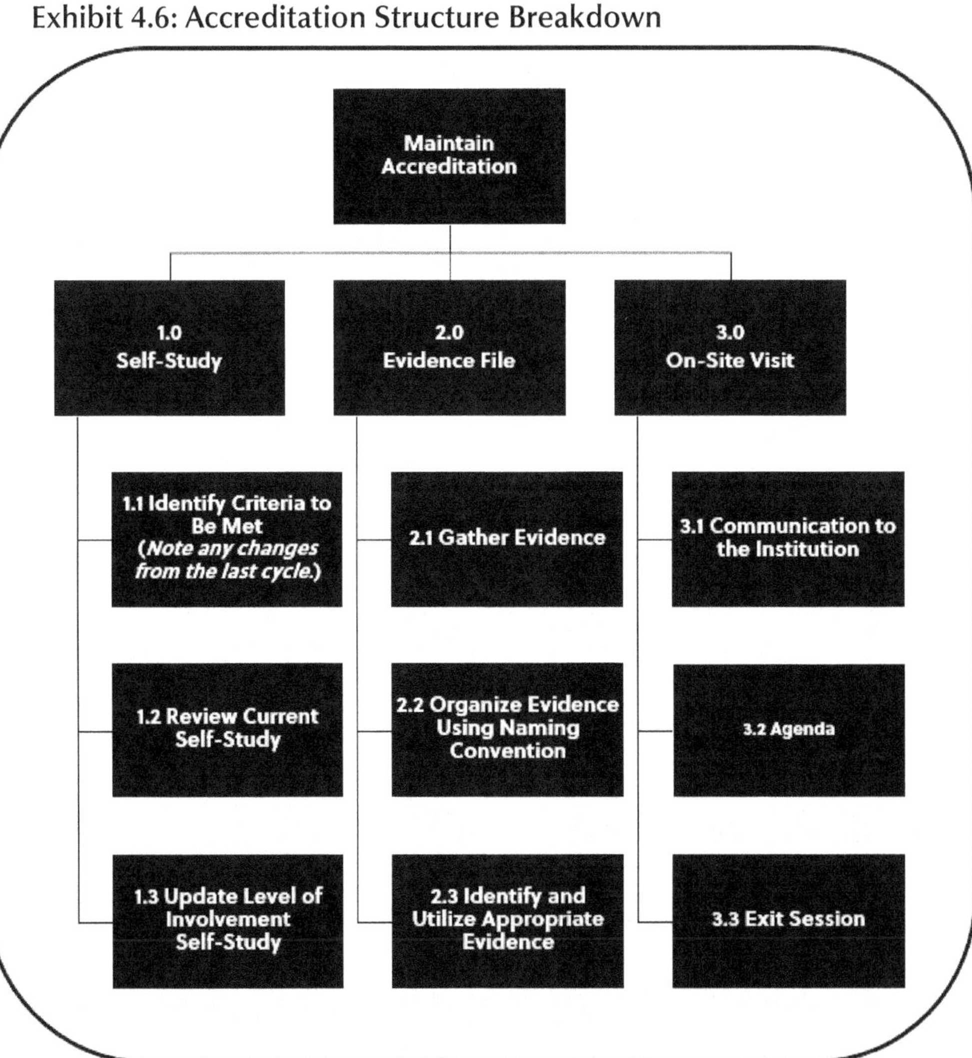

Exhibit 4.7 is specific to an accrediting agency's criteria. While this type of WBS doesn't include all actions required to maintain accreditation, it does provide an easy way to break down the criteria that need to be addressed and assign each one to a key stakeholder or stakeholder group in a responsibility assignment matrix.

Exhibit 4.7: Accreditation Structure Breakdown – Accreditation Body Specific

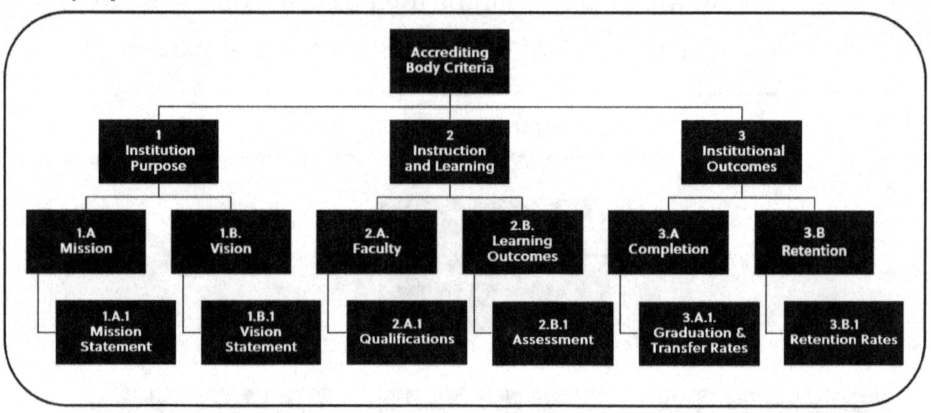

Once a WBS has been created, it's time to turn to the second tool mentioned above: a responsibility assignment matrix. According to the Project Management Institute's *Guide to the Project Management Body of Knowledge* (PMBOK), 7th Edition, a RAM is "a grid that shows the project resources assigned to each work package" (Project Management Institute, 2021). "The responsibility assignment matrix lists all the detailed deliverables from the WBS on one axis and lists the names of the persons responsible for completing the deliverable on the other axis. This arrangement enables accountability and understanding of who is responsible for each deliverable" (Cann & Brumagim, 2008, p. 38).

The RAM example in Exhibit 4.8 below aligns with the Accrediting Body Criteria WBS above and can be used to indicate, by means of a simple X, which key stakeholder or stakeholder group is responsible for each criterion. A more detailed type of RAM known as a RACI chart (Exhibit 4.8) shows "stakeholders who are responsible I, accountable (A), consulted (C), or informed (I) and are associated with project activities, decisions, and deliverables" (Project Management Institute, 2021).

Exhibit 4.8: Accrediting RAM

	Key Stakeholder or Stakeholder Group	Key Stakeholder or Stakeholder Group	Key Stakeholder or Stakeholder Group	Key Stakeholder or Stakeholder Group	Key Stakeholder or Stakeholder Group
1	X				
1.A	X				
1.A.1	X				

Concluding Thoughts

In conclusion, this chapter provides valuable insights and practical strategies for institutions dealing with the daunting task of managing multiple accreditation reviews. The chapter emphasizes the importance of establishing a clear naming convention and filing system to keep evidence organized and accessible. It also highlights the need for institutions to adapt their naming convention and acronyms to align with their unique stakeholders and not adopt those used elsewhere. Additionally, the chapter stresses the significance of effective communication, preparation, and organization in successfully navigating the chaos of multiple accreditations.

By implementing the recommendations outlined in the chapter, institutions can create a more streamlined and efficient accreditation process. The use of an Accreditation Tracking Spreadsheet and a Work Breakdown Structure allows for better tracking of activities and responsibilities, ensuring that no critical steps are overlooked. Furthermore, the chapter underscores the importance of aligning management structures and leadership styles with the demands of chaotic situations, promoting effective communication and collaboration among key stakeholders. Overall, this chapter serves as a valuable resource for institutions aiming to successfully manage the complexity of multiple accreditation reviews and minimize the chaos surrounding them.

Discussion Questions

1. Knowing that your institution will have to manage multiple accreditation reviews simultaneously, what are the first steps you will take to prepare for them?

2. Reflect on a time when a situation felt chaotic. What management structure and leadership style were present during that time? What management structure or leadership style would you have implemented to effectively manage the chaotic situation?

3. What strategies discussed in this chapter could you implement to ensure consistency across multiple accrediting bodies' standards and requirements?

4. What role does communication play in managing the chaos of multiple accreditations? How could accreditation-related communication be improved at your institution?

5. How can your institution ensure that it is meeting the unique requirements and expectations of each accrediting body?

6. What steps can your institution take, and how can key stakeholders be leveraged, to streamline the accreditation process and minimize duplication of efforts?

7. How can project management techniques be leveraged to automate and simplify the management of multiple accreditations?

8. How can institutions stay up to date with changes and updates
    to accrediting bodies' standards and requirements to ensure
    ongoing compliance, thus streamlining accreditation processes?

Discover and Propel

1. U.S. Department of Education

    ◊   https://www2.ed.gov/admins/finaid/accred/index.html

        Provides an overview of accreditation, the history
        and context of accreditation in the U.S., and lists of
        institutional and programmatic accrediting agencies.

2. The Higher Learning Commission (HLC)

    ◊   The Leaflet https://www.hlcommission.org/News-
        Reports/leaflet.html

3. WCET – WICHE Cooperative for Educational
    Technologieshttps://wcet.wiche.edu/

4. Institution for Effectiveness in Higher Education

    ◊   Website https://instituteforeffectiveness.org/

    ◊   LinkedIn https://www.linkedin.com/company/iehe/

5. Council for Higher Education Accreditation (CHEA)

    ◊   Website https://www.chea.org/

    ◊   LinkedIn https://www.linkedin.com/company/chea/

    ◊   List of institutional and programmatic/specialized
        accrediting agencies https://www.chea.org/search-
        accreditors-results-table?search_api_fulltext=&field_
        accreditor_type=All

References

Cambridge Dictionary. (2023). https://dictionary.cambridge.org/us/example/english/utter-confusion

Cann, C. W., & Brumagim, A. L. (2008). How project management tools aid in Association to Advance Collegiate Schools of Business (AACSB) international maintenance of accreditation. *Journal of Education for Business*, 9. https://eric.ed.gov/?id=EJ814406

Council for Higher Education Accreditation. (1998, February 1). *What is accreditation?* Council for Higher Education Accreditation https://www.chea.org/what-is-accreditation

Higher Learning Commission. (2023, March). *Accreditation liaison officers: Welcome to the role.* Higher Learning Commission: https://download.hlcommission.org/ALOFactSheet_INF.pdf

Merriam-Webster. (2023). https://www.merriam-webster.com/dictionary/chaos

Project Management Institute. (2021). *A guide to the project management body of knowledge (PMBOK): Seventh edition.*

Seymour, T., & Hussein, S. (2014). The History of Project Management. *International Journal of Management & Information Systems, 18*(4), 233-240. https://www.clutejournals.com/index.php/IJMIS/article/view/8820/8811

U.S. Department of Education (n.d.). *Accreditation in the United States.* Retrieved December 2023 from U.S. Department of Education: https://www2.ed.gov/admins/finaid/accred/index.html

PART III

CAPACITY CATALYSTS

This section emphasizes the importance of leadership in embracing the potential of accreditation in institutions. It explores practical ways that institutional leaders can use accreditation to amplify their leadership and capacity-building skills. The section also provides guidance on how to engage stakeholders meaningfully, establish partnerships, and leverage accreditation to build internal capacity.

Chapter 5

Creating People-Centered Colleges and Universities

Rebecca Hong

This chapter focuses on leveraging accreditation to create more student-centered, faculty-centered, staff-centered, and community-centered colleges and universities, thereby elevating the institution's effectiveness.

Mention the word "accreditation" to college and university stakeholders, and you're met with a wide variety of responses. These range from exasperated sighs acknowledging the impending workload needed to prepare for an accreditation report and team visit to eager and urgent expressions from a new leader looking to leverage this opportunity to catalyze change at the institution. There is no doubt that accreditation impacts every critical corner of a college or university. The U.S. Department of Education states, "The goal of accreditation is to ensure that institutions of higher education meet acceptable levels of quality," and how quality is measured is articulated through standards and criteria outlined by accrediting agencies and verified by peer evaluators (College Accreditation in the United States, n.d., p. 1).

According to the Western Association of Colleges and Schools' Senior Colleges and University Commission (WSCUC), "Accreditation aids institutions in developing and sustaining effective educational programs and assures the educational community and the general public that an accredited institution has met high standards of quality and effectiveness" (WSCUC, 2023). One can find similar statements around the purpose of accreditation across other accrediting agencies. There is no other process in higher education that examines every part of the institution simultaneously and invites every constituent to demonstrate quality, effectiveness, and continuous improvement. Accreditation requires an all-hands-on-deck mentality and approach. Rarely is a call for this extent of heightened engagement across an institution is required.

The WSCUC Standard 3 for accreditation examines investment in human, physical, fiscal, technology, and information resources within appropriate organizational and decision-making structures (WSCUC, 2023a). A similar standard can be found across other accrediting agencies. At question is whether colleges and universities have sufficient people and qualified personnel to carry forward the roles and responsibilities to support the institution's educational structure and mission. If you've written, read, or reviewed an accreditation report, you know that it's not unusual to find sections of a self-study report highlighting the recent hiring of a chief diversity officer to address campus climate issues or a dean of strategic initiatives to lead the university's strategic plan. This is a common tactic leaders use to demonstrate investments made in physical, fiscal, and technological infrastructures. However, if a college or university is to be and remain effective, it must not take an isolated, singular, or siloed approach to investing in people. It must not rely on mere tactics. What is required is a paradigm shift in how we view people in our institutions? What is required is for institutional leaders to adopt a people-centered strategy?

What Does it Mean to Be People-Centered?

Higher education institutions are complex by nature. While colleges and universities vary across mission, size, location, and status (non-profit or for-profit, private or public), one foundational attribute they all share is people. Administrators, faculty, staff, and students are central to the existence and effectiveness of an institution—arguably more so with the rapid speed of technological advances. What, then, does it mean to center people in an organization?

The notion of a people-centered organization is grounded in human-centered design (HCD), which originated in the field of engineering and was popularized by innovators and designers in product development. Stanford University's Hasso Plattner Institute of Design, founded by David Kelley and known as the d.school, can be credited for the increasing popularity of this methodology (McCarthy, 2022). At the heart of human-centered design lies a deep empathy for people and the idea that meeting their needs fuels creativity.

HCD combines three core elements: empathy, creativity, and business needs. Its goal is to find solutions to people's problems by understanding their needs, wants, and desires and ultimately improve their lives. Human-centered design starts with people and threads their needs throughout its phases: empathize, define, ideate, prototype, and test, with the goal of implementation, as shown in Exhibit 5.1.

Exhibit 5.1: Human-Centered Design Model

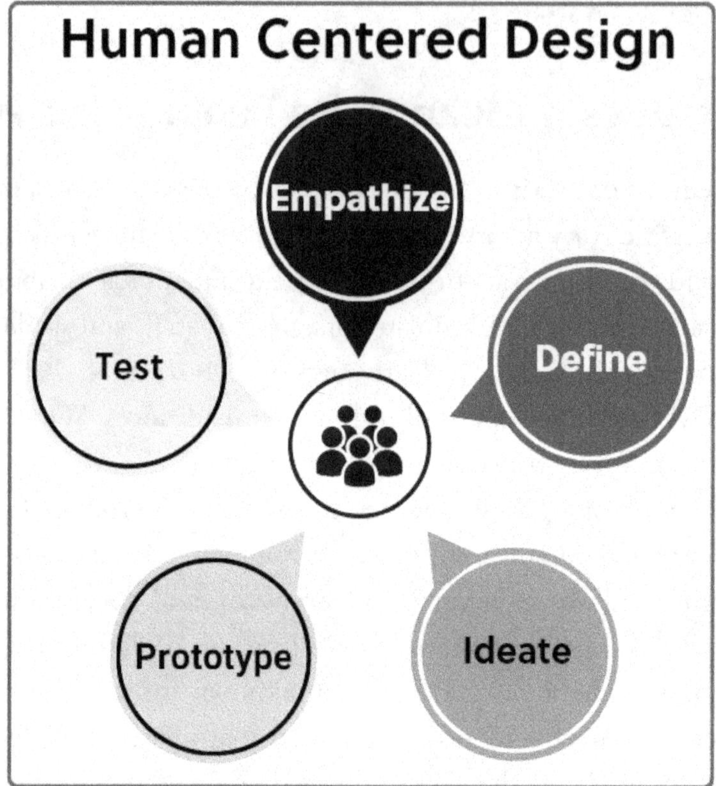

Define

In this phase, you seek to learn about the people for whom you are designing by gaining a better understanding of who they are. Foundational research approaches in this phase include observations, interviews, focus groups, surveys, and listening sessions. It is critical to acknowledge one's own biases and assumptions in order to engage with your users and appreciate their experiences and realities. Ensuring this phase is inclusive, open, and bias-free increases the possibility of creative approaches to design.

Ideate

This phase draws upon findings from the design phase and brings what has been learned about users to the surface. Through a process of meaning-making of data collected, you begin to map out themes and insights that inform ideas and opportunities for design. In this brainstorming and prototyping phase, it is critical to keep in mind that psychological safety is vital to creativity in collaborative design. This is a judgment-free zone. If you're finding yourself making judgments about what you're hearing and learning from users in this phase, it may be helpful to pause and check your personal biases and assumptions.

Prototype and Test: Iterate

In this phase, an idea is chosen and taken into rapid prototyping and testing. The prototype is a quick, low-cost version of the design created to gain feedback from users and test whether the product meets their needs and addresses pain points. Key to this phase is flexibility and iteration—giving yourself the opportunity to fine-tune the design before it goes into production.

Bringing All the Phases Together to Implement

While a product is never really finished and opportunities for improvement are ongoing, this phase takes the product to market to test it out in the real world with a wider audience of users. Keep in mind that understanding the needs of people requires flexibility, nimbleness, and adaptability because people are dynamic. A commitment to learning and listening is part of the process.

Design Thinking vs Human-Centered Design

Perhaps you've heard of design thinking and are wondering how it differs from human-centered design. "Design thinking" is a term, and more recently a buzzword, that was popularized and widely adopted over the past decade thanks to Stanford's IDEO, though the roots of design thinking are global and can be traced back decades. According to Tim Brown, CEO of IDEO, "Design thinking is a human-centered approach to innovation that draws from the designer's toolkit to integrate the needs of people, the possibilities of technology, and the requirements for business success" (IDEO Design Thinking, n.d.). There is no singular approach to design thinking; it is a lens through which to seek creative solutions to wicked and complex problems.

So, is there a difference between design thinking and human-centered design? While empathy lies at the heart of both, the timing in which you use them differs. Design thinking typically provides the direction in which you are developing a new product, initial prototype, or feature, while HCD serves to iterate and improve an existing design or product. One key difference is that design thinking is generally employed in the discovery phase when learning about user needs and challenges assumptions and hypotheses, while HCD focuses on improving the overall human experience through an iterative approach.

HCD has mostly been used for product design, but the notion of empathy for users and the approach of designing for people and with people in an iterative fashion can transcend disciplines and fields.

Characteristics of People-Centered Colleges and Universities

In the recent technology drama around ChatGPT creator OpenAI and the dismissal (and later reinstatement) of its CEO, the company's Chief Technology Officer (CTO) wrote on X, "OpenAI is nothing without its people" (Muratai, 2023). This led to a wave of key leaders and employees at OpenAI posting the same statement and backlash from hundreds of OpenAI employees threatening to quit and join the ousted CEO at Microsoft (Roush, 2023). The sequence of events surrounding this pivotal moment for the company is layered and sure to be included in business school case studies for years to come.

However, the statement "OpenAI is nothing without its people" is significant and the collective response from numerous OpenAI employees unprecedented. While many leaders today would likely echo the same sentiment about the people in their organizations, amidst the internal and external pressures facing higher education, it is worthwhile and timely to ask ourselves, "What would colleges and universities be without their people?" If leaders say their organizations are about their people, what does that mean in practice? How do we adopt the principles behind human-centered design and apply them to our colleges and universities? The characteristics of institutions which are truly people-centered are depicted in Exhibit 5.2.

Exhibit 5.2: Characteristics of People-Centered Colleges and Universities

Know Your People

The first step in human-centered design is to learn about the people you are designing for through such methods as surveys, listening sessions, focus groups, and observations. Since people are by nature complex and dynamic, so too are the organizations they compose. People-centered colleges take a consistent, methodical, and systematic approach to understanding and knowing their people by collecting data about people's experiences in the institution. Leaders of people-centered organizations are aware of their own biases and assumptions and embody a posture of curiosity and openness to understanding what their students, faculty, and staff are experiencing. They listen to learn and then reflect back what's been said to ensure that the people who work and learn in their institution feel heard.

Being Empathetic

The past four years in higher education have been unlike any other time. As institutions shifted to emergency remote working and learning during the height of the pandemic, the national racial reckoning; financial challenges leading to mergers, acquisitions, and closings of campuses; and loss of jobs, coupled with stranded college students, churn in university leadership, and tensions on campuses around free speech escalated by the Israel and Palestine conflict, have caused a rise in disengagement among students, faculty, and staff (Young, 2023). While the compounding effects of these events are seen in headlines in higher education news, the sub-surface effects of the rate of change and tensions on campuses require increased empathy for and understanding of the people who serve and are served by the institution. This requires a recognition that employees are more than cogs in the university machine and students are more than consumers of higher education's product.

Leaders of people-centered colleges and universities invite their staff, faculty, and students to be co-designers and collaborators in creating a more hospitable place to work and learn. They start with the presupposition that people should have regular forums where their voices are heard, where their ideas are considered, and where shared ownership and collaboration are considered the lifeblood of the institution.

Being Innovative

Leaders of people-centered institutions use what they've learned to develop policies and practices that address the needs of staff, faculty, and students. They seize opportunities to test ideas, get feedback, and iterate to fuel innovation. Their approach to innovation is grounded in a culture of psychological safety. According to Edmonson, team psychological safety is a shared belief among team members that risk taking, expressing ideas and concerns, asking questions, and admitting mistakes do not result in negative consequences but are welcomed as part of the process of continuous learning and improvement (Gallo, 2023). A snapshot of a psychological safety assessment is displayed in Exhibit 5.3.

Exhibit 5.3: Psychological Safety Assessment

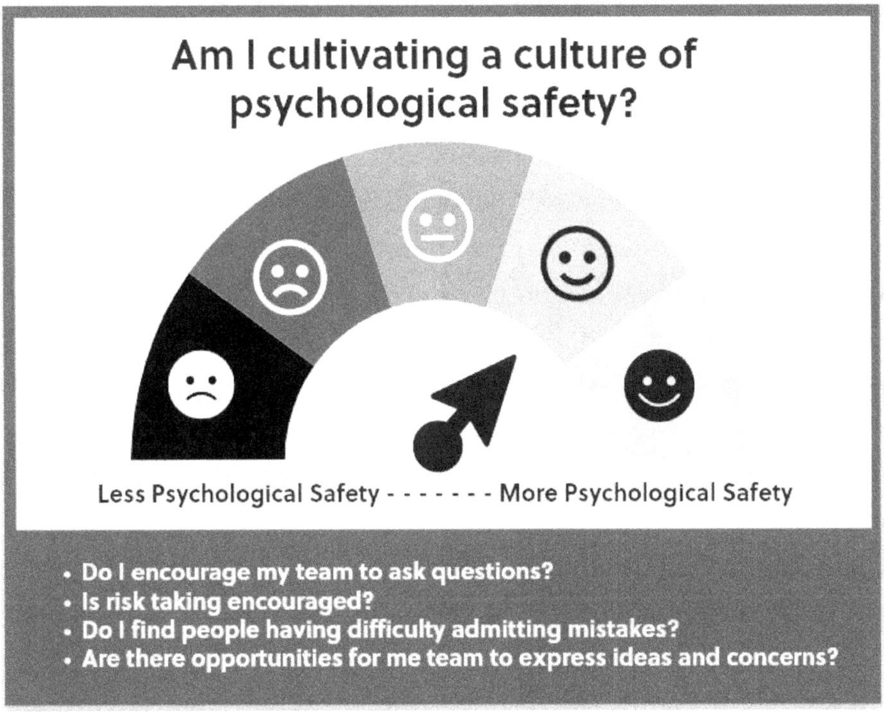

For organizations to be innovative, they need to be resilient. Resilient organizations make psychological safety a strategic priority.

Innovation vs Efficiency

The COVID-19 pandemic proved that colleges and universities, historically notorious for hewing to tradition, have the capacity to be innovative in the way they deliver teaching and learning, student support services, and business processes. This occurred at the height of the global pandemic, when leaders were facing unprecedented levels of uncertainty. As the pandemic phase transitions into the endemic stage of COVID-19, institutional leaders have taken different approaches. Some have called for a "return to normal," discontinuing flexible work modalities and online teaching and learning and chalking up the changes enacted during the pandemic as temporary practices (Edelman, 2023). Others have leveraged what has been learned through the emergency pivot to remote learning and working and accelerated innovation. Four common ways that colleges and universities have changed as a result of the pandemic are: 1. Expanded virtual services, 2. A shift in mindset, 3. Improved career pathways, and 4. A renewed focus on equity (Baston, 2021).

Leaders may easily recall pandemic-era innovations that increased efficiencies through new technological capabilities. However, people-centered colleges and universities are careful to avoid conflating efficiency with innovation. Innovation can often result in efficiencies; for example, software technologies have optimized administrative tasks such as scheduling meetings. To maximize profit, businesses prioritize eliminating waste to increase efficiencies and outperform competitors. Leaders of people-centered colleges and universities, on the other hand, may increase efficiencies in their short-term goals through new technological adoptions or outsourcing but are cognizant that efficiency is not the end goal when innovation is central to the long-term sustainability and resilience of the institution.

The fallacy in efficiency-focused organizations is the goal of reducing routine labor as an expense to be minimized, which results in a lack of investment in people and skill development (Martin, 2021). This type of organization views its people as cogs in the wheel rather than individuals who play a key role in institutional innovation, infrastructure, and resilience.

Colleges and universities are at a critical inflection point as they emerge from a pandemic that has disrupted traditional teaching, learning, and business practices. Their leaders are faced with creating value-driven academic programs and market-driven credentials to boost student enrollment in the face of the impending demographic cliff and re-examining their business model in order to generate new revenue. These are real and critical issues that must be addressed by people within the institution. If leaders subscribe to the belief that their colleges and universities are truly nothing without their people, what people-centered strategies can they adopt? The first step is to understand how to leverage the best abilities of their people in concert with the best of what technology has to offer their institution.

Strategies for Becoming a More People-Centered College or University

Humans in the Loop

In machine learning and artificial intelligence (AI), human-in-the-loop (HITL) is an approach where humans are interactive and provide iterative feedback to the model to improve its output accuracy. Human-in-the-loop approaches demonstrate the need for and value of collaboration between humans and technology, rebuffing fears that robots will be taking over the world. The benefits of HITL in interactive AI systems include gains in transparency, incorporation of human judgment, shifting pressure away from building perfect algorithms, and enabling more power systems (Humans in the Loop: The Design of Interactive AI Systems, 2019).

When designing a system with the HITL approach, each step that requires human interaction also requires humans to understand the system before making a decision around the current or next step. Transparency of the system and design are essential if humans are to provide feedback. Such transparency not only gives humans agency but also leads to greater clarity and less ambiguity in the overall process and design.

HITL systems embed humans in the decision loop, allowing them preferences and giving them voice in effective ways—a reminder that technological advances, in AI or otherwise, are meant to help humans, not replace them. HITL design strategies seek to outperform both fully automated and fully manual systems. They represent a shift away from the dichotomous and fear-based thinking that either preserves inefficient manual processes or adopts automated systems that eliminate the need for people The alternative proposed is a thoughtful and intentional integration of human skills with technology to improve models and systems.

So how can higher education leaders adopt the HITL approach in their own institutions? Just as there is no a single approach to adopting the HITL strategy in machine learning AI, there are various approaches to adopting an HITL strategy in creating human-centered and effective colleges and universities. However, a few general design principles to consider include:

1. Foreground human agency.

2. Start small.

3. Recognize the difference between efficiency and effectiveness.

Human Agency

Successfully designing an HITL strategy for an institution requires transparent systems that intentionally harness human preferences, values, and judgement. Making transparent how the institution operates, the flow of communication, how decisions are made, and where people are included, involved, and heard in the decision-making process is vital. Strategic decision-making in people-centered colleges and universities means inviting people's active involvement and elevating transparency and clarity among stakeholders. People have a voice in the system and feel valued for their contributions to the institution. With technological adoptions accelerating workflow and efficiencies in higher education, it is increasingly crucial for leaders of people-centered institutions to elevate human agency. What are people capable of doing that technology and AI are not, and to what extent are people aware of these differences?

Differentiating Between Efficiency and Effectiveness

The bias toward efficiency has been precipitated and heightened by the growth of AI and technology tools and exacerbated by the pursuit of cost-saving measures. Undoubtedly, costs are easier to measure than benefits, and cutting measurable costs is a common (and often preferred) strategy undertaken by institutional leaders facing financial constraints. People-centered college and university leaders recognize the difference between efficiency and innovation, as previously mentioned; they also recognize the difference between efficiency and effectiveness. While understanding that new systems, interfaces, and technology tools can be a gateway to innovation and efficiency, they are also keen to emphasize that such changes are meant to expand the effectiveness of the institution by using HITL strategically rather than taking humans out of the loop. Examining unintended consequences of decisions made solely to increase efficiency is a regular practice, and these types of decisions are never made in haste.

Efficiency is never the end goal in people-centered colleges and universities; effectiveness is. While efficiency may play a part in increasing effectiveness, a people-centered leader asks, "How might we be more effective as an institution as a result of this decision? How will we know if we are effective in carrying out our mission?" Answers to these questions involve people in co-constructing the process and response, which may require time. The answers may not be easily evident on a spreadsheet in the short term. This process does, however, emphasize that colleges and universities are nothing without its people.

Start Small

Creating or becoming a people-centered college or university does not need to be a massive undertaking or an all-or-nothing approach. You don't need to boil the ocean. Start small. Shift the focus away from big, splashy, silver bullet–type changes to seeing granularity as a virtue, breaking up tasks to incorporate human interaction. Avoid the lure to make seismic shifts when trying to become more people-centered. Instead, consider simple tasks that engage people in your department or unit and invite their feedback. Listen with a posture to learn from people, whether they are students, faculty, or staff. Be specific about what you are asking of them and why their engagement is critical to what is being developed or iterated. Additionally, embed people's interactions systematically in the process when appropriate and ensure psychological safety by valuing their contributions as part of the continuous improvement and learning posture of the institution.

Concluding Thoughts: People-Centered Colleges and Universities in the Context of Institutional Effectiveness

College and university leaders are acutely aware of how seminal it is to articulate how their institution is achieving its mission and goals and to demonstrate its effectiveness in doing so. Internal and external pressure from stakeholders is increasing as belief around the value of higher education continues to wax and wane.

This chapter proposed a people-centered approach to building institutional capacity and effectiveness. It challenges leaders to reflect on how teaching and learning is designed in their colleges and universities and how students, staff, and faculty are involved as collaborators in the design process. Opportunities to strategically center people in everything from the design, feedback, and delivery of teaching and learning to the execution of support services and business processes are yet to be realized as leader seek to increase institutional effectiveness.

Examining where humans are in the loop is a great starting point to improve institutional effectiveness. In the teaching and learning environment, it is worthwhile to ask, "Where are students in the loop?" Consider opportunities to give students a voice in teaching, learning, and assessment, and engage them as partners in designing and iterating toward a student-centered environment. Additionally, examine institutional structures, including committees and task forces, and take note of where students are excluded from key places where decisions that directly impact them are made. With the shifting demographics in higher education, "it is more salient now than ever to ensure that students have a voice and seat at the table where critical conversations and decisions are made about their educational experience" (Hong, 2020). Given the heightened focus from accreditors around student success and student-centeredness, strategically ensuring that students are in the loop is germane to the effectiveness of an institution.

The advancement of technology to optimize processes and efficiencies in colleges and universities continues to shift workloads and alter the work environment. The increased interest in the adoption of technology tools on campuses presents college and university leaders with a chance to examine where humans, particularly staff and faculty, are in the loop. For example, if a new early alert system is being considered to address student retention issues, they must ask, "How does this tool address the pain points of staff and faculty in supporting student needs? Where are there opportunities to provide feedback on the effectiveness of the early alert system and chances to iterate in order to truly meet the needs of those involved in supporting students and the students themselves?"

Further, it is critical to communicate how these new systems leverage the best of what technology can provide around data and decision-making, and concurrently, how they open up an opportunity for increased human agency through thoughtful integration with human skills, thereby improving institutional effectiveness, capacity, and educational quality. Leaders should take a thoughtful and strategic approach to examine whether an institutional job strategy has been conceived and an investment in staff and faculty learning and development considered in order to improve educational effectiveness in unanticipated and valuable new ways.

When preparing for an accreditation self-study report and visit, a people-centered institution takes an empathetic approach toward its review team. Consider how your self-study report is prepared and what assumptions you're making about the reader's knowledge and context. It may be tempting to upload hundreds of documents and links to demonstrate how well prepared the institution is to meet accreditation standards, unintentionally creating information overload for the reader.

Similarly, steering committees might be tempted to provide countless Tableau dashboards and reports to show how the institution is using data. Rarely are these approaches people-centered as little consideration is given to the pain points of those volunteering their time to serve on the review teams. Consider how you can prepare for accreditation with a people-centered strategy that does not trade effectiveness for efficiency. Leverage the accreditation process as an opportunity to design, iterate, and innovate with internal and external stakeholders as partners and collaborators.

Cultivating a people-centered college or university is the bedrock of innovation and resilience, both of which are desperately needed at this time in higher education if institutions are to be effective in carrying out their mission. Now more than ever, with the acceleration of technological progress and artificial intelligence, leaders will need to prioritize collaboration and co-design with students, faculty, and staff, positioning themselves to listen, empathize, learn, fail, and iterate.

Discussion Questions

1. How can your institution benefit from a people-centered approach to improving institutional effectiveness?

2. Where can you best bring humans (students, faculty, staff) in the loop in your institution?

3. What opportunities do you foresee in ensuring that humans are in the loop in your college or university to improve human agency while collaborating with technology?

4. Colleges and universities have found ways to improve efficiencies in business processes and services. What unintended consequences have you witnessed when trading effectiveness for efficiency and as a result abandoning a people-centered approach?

5. What would it mean for your college or university to say that it is "nothing without its people?" What would need to change? Evolve? Improve?

6. How can you create an environment that embodies psychological safety as a key component of being a people-centered institution?

References

Baston, M. A. (2021, November 4). COVID has spurred four positive changes on campuses (opinion). *Inside HigherEd.* https://www.insidehighered.com/views/2021/11/04/covid-has-spurred-four-positive-changes-campuses-opinion

College Accreditation in the United States, (n.d.). https://www2.ed.gov/admins/finaid/accred/accreditation.html

Edelman, J. (2023, February 9). A return to the 'Normal-Normal': Colleges ready to adjust to end of pandemic emergencies. *Diverse: Issues in Higher Education.* https://www.diverseeducation.com/covid-19/article/15306616/a-return-to-the-normalnormal-colleges-ready-to-adjust-to-end-of-pandemic-emergencies

Gallo, A. (2023, February 15). What is psychological safety? *Harvard Business Review.* https://hbr.org/2023/02/what-is-psychological-safety

Hong, R.C. (2020). Student assessment scholars: Cultivating and empowering student voice in assessment. In N.A. Jankowski, G.R. Baker, E. Montenegro, & K. Brown-Tess (Eds.), *Student-focused learning and assessment: Involving students in the learning process in higher education* (pp. 99-120). Peter Lang Publishing. 10.3726/b16909

Humans in the loop: The design of interactive AI systems. (2019, October 20). Stanford HAI. https://hai.stanford.edu/news/humans-loop-design-interactive-ai-systems

IDEO Design Thinking. (n.d.). IDEO | Design Thinking. https://designthinking.ideo.com/

Martin, R. L. (2021, June 9). Our obsession with efficiency is destroying our resilience. *Harvard Business Review.* https://hbr.org/2019/01/the-high-price-of-efficiency#the-high-price-of-efficiency

McCarthy, S. J. (2022). Design thinking? Thank an engineer. *Dialectic (Ann Arbor)*, *3*(1). https://doi.org/10.3998/dialectic.14932326.0003.102

Muratai, M. (2023, November 20). *OpenAI is nothing without its people* [Tweet]. Twitter. https://twitter.com/miramurati/status/1726542556203483392

Roush, T. (2023, November 20). More than 700 OpenAI employees threaten to quit—and join Microsoft—unless board resigns. *Forbes.* https://www.forbes.com/sites/tylerroush/2023/11/20/more-than-500-openai-employees-threaten-to-quit-over-sam-altmans-removal/?sh=191cd0694ebc

WSCUC. (2023a, October 20). *2023 Handbook of Accreditation – WSCUC.* https://www.wscuc.org/handbook2023/#standards-of-accreditation

Young, J. R. (2023, January 10). How instructors are adapting to a rise in student disengagement. *EdSurge.* https://www.edsurge.com/news/2023-01-10-how-instructors-are-adapting-to-a-rise-in-student-disengagement

Chapter 6

Mentoring for Accreditation Success

Lori Williams

It takes a 'village' to achieve accreditation. There are several critical institutional roles in the accreditation process. Learning by mentoring is a hallmark of succession planning. This chapter focuses on mentoring strategies and techniques for mentoring key roles in accreditation.

The concept of mentoring first appears in Homer's ancient Greek epic the Odyssey. When the hero, Odysseus, heads off to fight in the Trojan War he leaves his son, Telemachus, in the care of his friend Mentor (Homer, 725 BCE/1999, p. 100). In current usage, the concept generally describes a trusted friend or advisor with more experience than the person being mentored. In work settings, a mentor often assists a less experienced colleague in professional development. It is this type of professional mentoring relationship that this chapter addresses, specifically with respect to accreditation work. Developing promising leaders through mentoring is essential to successful and continued compliance with accreditation standards as outgoing leaders must be replaced with new ones who are fully capable.

This chapter explores the value of mentoring in accreditation, the roles of mentor and mentee, key roles in accreditation, and mentoring techniques for those key roles. It concludes with discussion questions to prompt mentoring-related thinking and planning at academic institutions.

The Value of Mentoring

There are many reasons why mentoring can be an important aspect of successful accreditation work. All those who play key accreditation roles in an academic institution can benefit from mentoring, including but not limited to the accreditation liaison officer (ALO), president, chief academic officer, deans, board (and especially board chair), institutional research department lead, assessment staff, and faculty. Several of these positions play particularly vital roles and may or may not have experience with the accreditation process. They may need assistance from others with relevant experience and in the specific roles needed for maintaining compliance with accreditation standards.

Some staff, such as the ALO and the institutional research staff, will see the connection between accreditation and their day-to-day work more easily than others. Some, including board members who work outside the academy and staff new to their roles, may not have had any experience at all with accreditation. Others may be somewhere in the middle of these two ends of the continuum, having held different roles at earlier times in their careers but now need to participate in a comprehensive review or ongoing documentation of quality assurance progress. Mentoring all of those individuals will help them better understand the connection between day-to-day work and accreditation, the need for continuous improvement, and the need to comply with accreditation standards.

In general, succession planning is imperative for all key roles at institutions of higher education, and accreditation is a critical component of that planning, particularly for the president, provost, institutional research leader, and accreditation liaison officer. When people in these roles leave the organization, their replacements need to effectively ensure accreditation standards compliance and navigate the changes in accreditation expectations and processes. Succession planning may involve grooming internal staff to acquire the skills and competencies to achieve higher-level positions or seeking talent outside the organization (Rothwell, 2016).

Human resources (HR) professionals generally take responsibility for succession planning for most key roles at academic institutions. One role that may pose a challenge to HR is the accreditation liaison officer. To identify staff within the institution who may be mentored to serve as ALOs, the ALO might first look to the assessment staff, if there are designated roles for those responsibilities. If there are none, the ALO may look to the faculty, program chairs, and deans who express a keen interest in and appreciation for assessment and program review.

Mentoring plays an important part in succession planning when preparing staff either to take on a more senior role or make a lateral move. A current ALO may identify a staff member to mentor to take over their role. This may be a faculty member currently serving as a peer evaluator on review teams. It may be a faculty or staff member who has demonstrated a keen interest in accreditation. Another potential ALO mentee might be a staff member serving in a strategic planning leadership role. Whether it be a retirement, a move to another organization, or a promotion that results in a vacancy, mentoring others to serve as ALOs provides positive professional development with important benefits. Mentoring prepares individuals to develop dispositions of continuous improvement, ensuring measures of that improvement in response to accreditation requirements. With so much focus on the return on investment of public tax dollars for higher education, measures of improvement are important not only to the students who complete programs better prepared for the jobs they fill but also to demonstrate fiscal responsibility.

When there are no appropriate staff to be mentored to take over as ALO, a replacement must be sought outside the institution. Consider attending an accreditation or assessment conference to network with those who work at peer institutions. It may also be worthwhile to let the accreditation leader assigned to support your institution know that you are seeking a replacement in case they know of a promising candidate at another institution to consider. If someone is identified, a relationship might be formed with that person to see if they are willing to explore the option of moving to a new institution. The roles of mentor and mentee is depicted in Exhibit 6.1.

The Roles of Mentor and Mentee

Mentoring can take place informally or formally. Informal mentoring occurs naturally and voluntarily, whereas formal, structured mentoring takes place when mentors and mentees are purposefully paired and the relationship is monitored for progress in some way. In either case, the mentoring relationship is intentional such that the mentor assists the mentee in professional growth toward a deliberate aim. The most successful mentoring relationships are reciprocal as depicted in Exhibit 6.1. Mentoring is a generative activity whereby the mentee gains important knowledge and skills through the mentor's coaching and modeling, serving both parties' professional development needs. The value to the institution of higher education extends beyond the mentor and mentee.

Exhibit 6.1: The Reciprocal Mentor-Mentee Relationship

The Reciprocal Mentor-Mentee Relationship

Coaching and modeling is a professional development opportunity for the mentor.

Mentor

Mentee

The mentee gains important knowledge and skills.

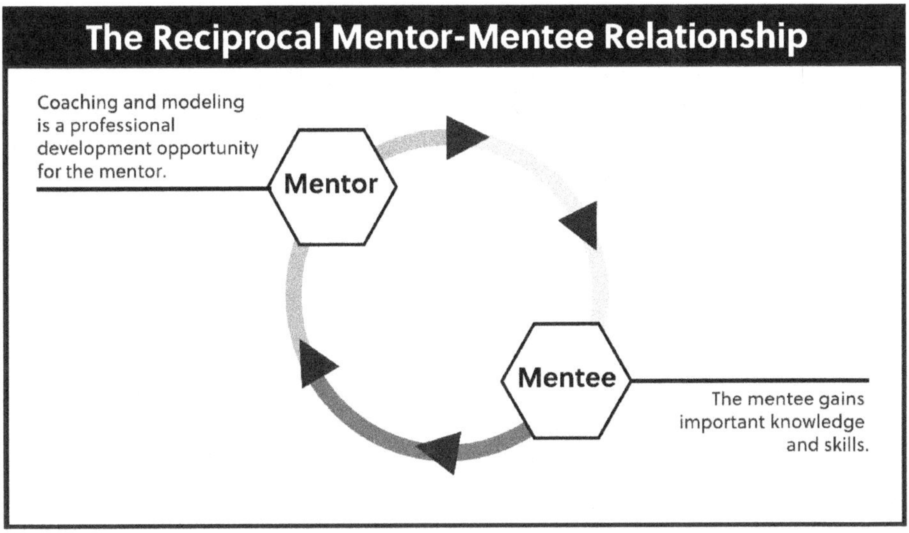

The research on mentoring in higher education is largely confined to faculty mentoring junior faculty and students, especially graduate students to prepare them for roles in academia (Ard & Beasley, 2022; Meda et al., 2023). The literature on faculty mentoring of other faculty, especially those traditionally underserved (Eliasson, et al., 2000; Jernigan, et al, 2020) is extensive, yet the accreditation context is most often missing.

Effective mentors possess specific skills and behaviors that when demonstrated successfully assist their mentees in developing those competencies themselves. Determining whether the mentee has acquired the competencies involves assessment. In the early 1970s, McClelland (1973) began the work of job competence assessment. McClelland argued that to determine the potential for future success in a particular job, the best measure of a person's capability is to learn the behaviors and characteristics of high performers in the role and then administer standardized tests of those competencies (Klemp, Jr., 2001). McClelland and the research associates who worked with him at McBer and Company devised a method (Klemp, Jr., 2001) to determine job competence called the Behavioral Event Interview (BEI). The BEI seeks to identify the specific behaviors exhibited by those who are most successful in their roles. The interviewer can get a full picture of how successful and unsuccessful performers carry out their jobs by asking questions that prompt interviewees to describe their actual behaviors, including actions, thoughts, and feelings. The competencies required for a particular job type are then determined by comparing the characteristic behaviors of the most and least successful performers (Williams, 2008).

Effective mentors can coach others in the competencies and skills needed for accreditation work, which are similar to those generally required for success in an academic career. These mentors serve as advocates for their mentees and sponsor their development. They provide mentees with challenging assignments—"stretch assignments," so to speak—that require practicing new skills and competencies, with developmental goals and with appropriate advice and support. These capacities include an achievement orientation, good verbal and written communication skills, strong organizational abilities, knowledge of accreditation standards, trust and open communication, and an understanding of how best to document compliance.

Key Roles in Accreditation and the Need for Mentoring

Successful compliance with accreditation standards (particularly when preparing annual data submissions and midcycle reports on progress and when conducting a self-study review for a comprehensive visit) involves engagement from several key roles across the institution, as shown in Exhibit 6.2. Depending upon their level of experience and competencies, individuals in these roles may benefit from mentoring. The most obvious accreditation role is the ALO. Large universities with institutional and multiple programmatic accreditations have a staff person whose role is primarily responsible for ensuring accreditation compliance and often also for assessment

Key Roles in Accreditation

President
Reviews the report to ensure it includes examples and is accurate, succinct, and complete

Accreditation Liaison
Holds overarching responsibilities for accreditation

Provost or Chief Academic Officer
Expected to understand data on the success of all academic programs

Chair of the Board
Ensures all Board members take responsibility for oversight of the institution.

Head of the Faculty Governing Body
Respond to questions about the role of faculty in shared governance

Director of Institutional Research
Contributes narratives and data to a self-study review report

Deans and Faculty Chairs
Share data on the success of their academic programs

Enrollment Management Leaders
Work closely with academic affairs to ensure goals are met

Chief Financial Officer
Demonstrates evidence of strong fiscal health and management

Legal Counsel
Ensures that the institution meets applicable laws and regulations

Communications Staff
Ensure that all institutional staff and faculty understand the schedule during the accreditation period

Human Resources Leaders
Leads succession planning of key positions.

documentation. This individual must take on overarching responsibilities for accreditation, with full understanding of the requirements for compliance, key annual requirements, requirements for adhering to rules when major changes take place at the institution, and how institutions are expected to comply with self-study reviews and their accompanying comprehensive visits at the end of an accreditation period.

Other roles that may benefit from mentoring for successful accreditation compliance are the president, the chair of the board of trustees, the provost or chief academic officer, the head of institutional research and data analytics, the head of the faculty governing body, deans and faculty chairs, enrollment management leaders, the chief financial officer, legal counsel, communications staff, and human resources leaders. While the provost, ALO, head of institutional research, and others may contribute large portions of the narratives and data to a self-study review report, the president takes primary responsibility for the whole of the academic institution and so must review the report carefully to ensure it includes key examples and is accurate, succinct, and complete. Most comprehensive visits include separate time for a review team with the president. Preparation for that time is essential, as it will ensure that the president can speak to the issues likely to be raised by a review team, including previous reviews and the potential deficiencies that surfaced, challenges since the last review, and any major changes at the institution in service to openness and transparency.

The provost or chief academic officer takes responsibility for all academic affairs and must work in lockstep with all of the other academic leaders, including deans and program chairs. The provost and all academic leaders are expected to be knowledgeable about key data on the success of their academic programs, including enrollment, persistence, and graduation rates. They should also be able to tell the story that the data represent. Working collaboratively with key institutional research staff will help ensure that all agree on program success measures and improvements over time.

During a comprehensive visit, faculty are often asked to spend time with review teams separately from their deans and academic leaders. They will be expected to respond to questions about the role of faculty in shared governance of the institution, issues of academic freedom, and how well they are able to ensure learning outcomes for all students, including those traditionally underserved. This may require mentoring to assist faculty in seeing that their roles extend beyond disciplinary research to the scholarship of teaching and learning.

The chief financial officer must demonstrate evidence of strong fiscal health and management to the accreditor, generally through regular annual financial audits and preparation to respond to questions about financial challenges. Enrollment management staff are expected to work closely with academic affairs leaders to document that institution policies are followed, that students are admitted per school admissions requirements, and that goals for enrollments, persistence, and graduation rates are met, and not only for the majority of students but also for all those traditionally underserved. Accreditation staff and review teams expect enrollment management staff to share the mitigation efforts used to meet challenges in achieving those goals and specify which were more or less effective.

Although they may seem tangential to the primary accreditation roles described above, communications staff are essential to accreditation as well. They work closely with the ALO to ensure that all institution staff and faculty understand the schedule of events during the accreditation period and especially in the time leading up to a self-study review and comprehensive visit. Communications staff work with the ALO on the dissemination of key information, including how the accreditation steering committee will work to engage the entire college or university in the self-study period and then later assemble the components of the resulting report. They also use the institution's website and other communication channels including email and social media to share key information about the status of the institution's accreditation and seek input from the larger community as part of a comprehensive revie w.

Mentoring Techniques for Key Roles

Each of the key roles described above may benefit from mentoring. Mentoring a new or less experienced ALO is most important, and the main responsibilities of the role to a large extent dictate the competencies needed for success. The ideal situation for mentoring a new ALO is when the existing ALO is planning to retire or move to a new role long in advance of the change. If an institution is fortunate enough to have this time, the existing ALO can mentor and groom the person who will take over the role. The mentor can assess the new person's skills and competencies and then tackle any deficiencies.

The Process

The process of mentoring a new ALO is shown in Exhibit 6.3. Initially, the mentor should come to an agreement with the mentee on the purpose of the relationship, the goals the mentee seeks to achieve, and the way they will work together and communicate. Specifically, the mentor should ensure that the mentee wants to assume the AOL role and make clear that the mentoring relationship is intended to prepare the new ALO for success. The mentor and mentee also need to agree explicitly on the areas for development and improvement and how to address them.

Following initial meetings on these foundational aspects of the ALO mentoring relationship, the mentor should perform the ALO work with full openness and transparency, involving the mentee in meetings, email correspondence, and calls with the accreditor staff and explaining to others that this person is being mentored to take

Exhibit 6.3: Mentoring an Accreditation Liaison Officer

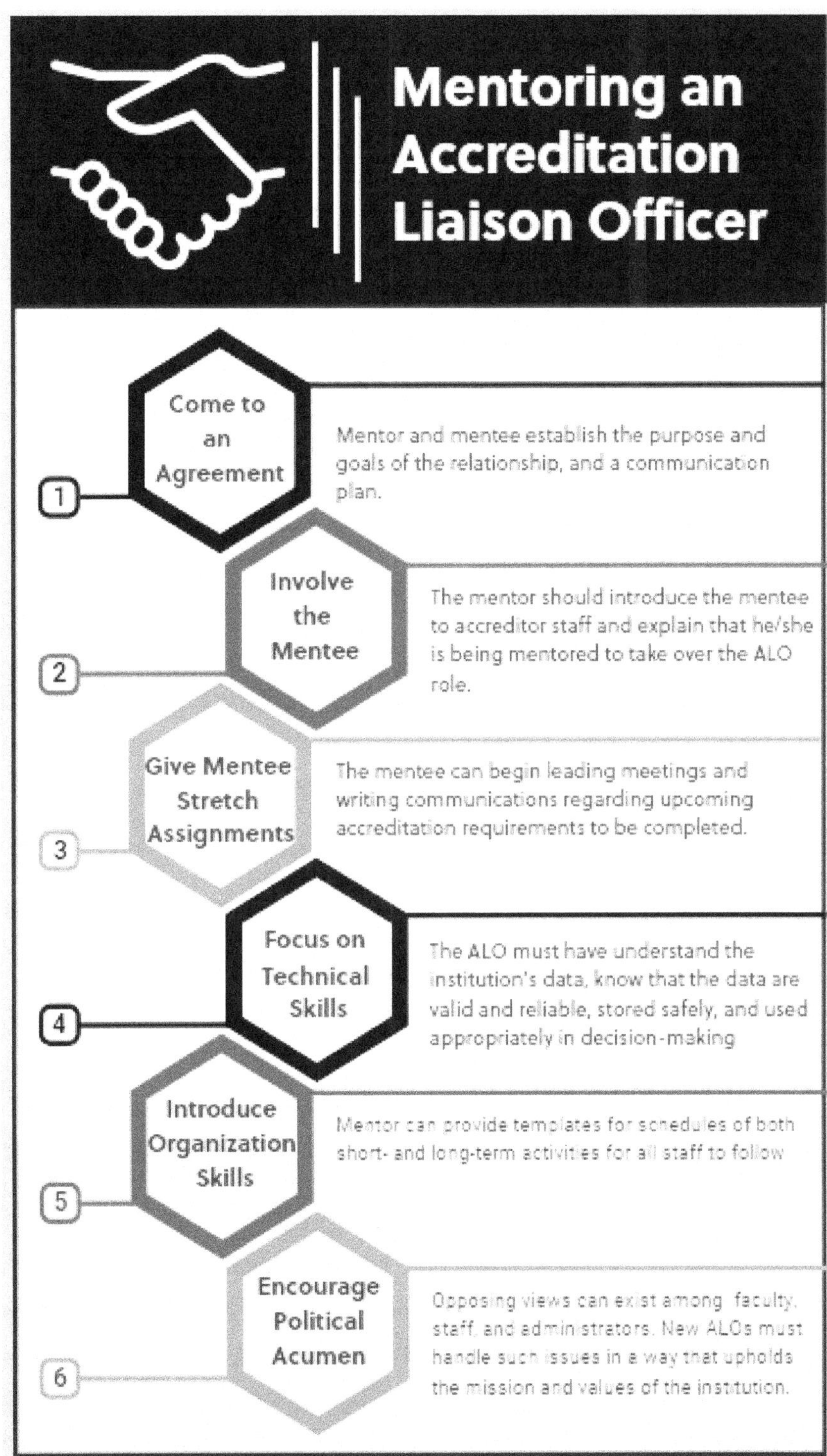

over the role at a future date. In time, the mentor can begin to give the mentee stretch assignments, such as leading meetings and writing communications to the college's or university's key roles regarding upcoming accreditation requirements to be completed. Support in these assignments can take the form of previous communications, agendas for past meetings, and one-on-one meetings to practice verbal communication in town halls and other forums.

Some areas of focus for those mentoring new ALOs include technical skills, organization skills, project management, and political acumen. With respect to technical skills, working closely with institutional research staff is essential given that these individuals maintain data on learning outcomes achievement, program review, enrollment, persistence, and graduation rates. Data literacy, data management, and data architecture responsibilities often rest with institutional research and information technology staff. The ALO must have sufficient knowledge of the institution's data along with assurance that the data are valid and reliable, are stored safely, and are used appropriately in decision-making. In addition to spending time with institutional research and information technology staff learning more about their college's or university's data, ALOs can enhance their knowledge by taking courses in data science degree programs or certificate programs and through formal training provided by the Association for Institutional Research (more below).

Planning for a Self-Study Review with Mentors and Mentees

Planning for a self-study review and associated site visit should begin 18 to 24 months before the visit. Mentors can assist mentees in gaining the organizational skills needed to prepare for the review by providing previously used templates for schedules of both short- and long-term activities for all staff to follow. Mentees should be trained in the effective use of accreditation and assessment software to organize staff, materials, and documentation of compliance with standards and requirements. Adherence to a schedule for measuring achievement of the goals associated with the institution's strategic plan is another key accreditation area of focus requiring strong project management and organizational skills.

Developing Political Acumen

Developing political acumen is also important for future ALOs. There may be challenges or issues at the institution that elicit controversial or opposing views among administrators, faculty, and staff. Experienced accreditation staff will recognize that some issues are ever present at colleges and universities and will not necessarily give more weight than is warranted to those who express opposing views. Still, it is important for the ALO to have enough political acumen to be able to speak openly and honestly about controversial issues yet also present a balanced view of opinions and ensure that a minority view does not have an outsized voice in site-visit meetings. Good mentors will coach new ALOs on how to handle such issues in a way that upholds the unique mission and values of the academic institution. Building trusting relationships with all those in key roles across the college or university is an important competency for ALOs and comes with time and experience. Mentors can remind new ALOs that even in the event of personality clashes, ensuring respect and focusing on common goals can still foster positive relationships.

When an Experienced ALO Isn't Available

In those cases where it is not possible for an established ALO to mentor a successor, institutions must seek outside assistance. The accrediting body can provide good sources of mentoring for new ALOs, whether they are being actively mentored by a previous ALO or not. Some accreditors provide face-to-face, online, or hybrid training for their accredited institutions' ALOs. Other options include webinars on specialized topics such as substantive change. These trainings may take place in conjunction with an annual conference. Attending sessions by peer institutions at accreditation conferences or during instructive webinars can help ALOs learn new ways to innovate in the context of demonstrating continuous improvement.

Mentoring Up

Those who serve in such higher-level executive roles as president or chief academic officer may need to be mentored by someone in a more junior position with more experience in accreditation. In addition to imparting key accreditation information and skills, reverse-mentoring (when younger staff or faculty mentor older, more senior staff) can increase retention of millennial-age staff, improve digital skills, drive culture change, and promote diversity (Jordan & Sorell, 2019). A strong ALO can mentor the president or provost through helpful preparation, which might include writing draft email messages on their behalf, creating talking points for meetings, and reviewing key information ahead of meetings with the accreditor. When an accreditor announces new standards, rules, or processes, the ALO can mentor, or manage up to presidents and provosts by sending these along with a brief executive summary of what these changes will mean for the institution in practice.

To ensure appropriate mentoring of presidents and provosts, the ALO and other leaders should insist that these individuals attend the accreditor's annual conference and any special sessions intended for college and university presidents or provosts. Presidents and provosts who are new to accreditation or unfamiliar with an institutional accreditor can also gain valuable experience through serving on peer evaluation teams for reviews of other academic institutions. Each accrediting body provides essential training for its peer evaluators who serve on review teams, and the review process itself provides structure over a set period for learning about the standards of accreditation and the timeframes for meeting key milestones. When a president or provost finds it difficult to heed the advice of a more junior colleague, it may be helpful to enlist the assistance of key board members. The chair of the board or the chair of the academic affairs committee of the board may be able to provide guidance and mentoring to a president or provost when managing up is not welcomed or successful. Other potentially helpful sources of mentors for presidents and provosts are experienced peer provosts and presidents or the accreditor staff person assigned to serve that school.

Institutional Research as a Mentor Focus

The head of institutional research is another key role that has a lot to gain from mentoring. When preparing for annual data reports, for example, a new head of institutional research may benefit from being mentored by the ALO, others who hold this position at peer institutions, or even from the vice president at the accreditor assigned to support the institution. While accrediting bodies are increasingly seeking disaggregated data to show how, for example, specific student types are meeting learning outcomes, persisting, and graduating, providing too much data will not be helpful without sharing the key insights to be drawn from those data and detailing the efficacy of the actions taken to improve on key metrics to demonstrate standards compliance. It is therefore important to mentor those responsible for data management on choosing a few key metrics in alignment with the accreditor's requirements and spanning a period of at least a few years to demonstrate a focus on continuous improvement. Telling the story in the data are key—explaining how actions taken or unexpected events led to changes in the data over time, and that decision-making by institutional leaders was driven by insights obtained from the data.

An additional competency for the head of institutional research is building trust in the department and its data as the single source of truth for the college or university. If multiple leaders share differing answers to common questions about students and program health, they may be using data with differing data definitions from different data sources. Mentors can coach institutional research staff on establishing reliable data sources that can be demonstrated over time and building trust in the department's ability to produce reliable and valid data reports.

Mock Reviews for a Successful Accreditation Visit

One of the best techniques for mentoring all key roles in accreditation is to hold a mock review ahead of an actual accreditation site visit. To stage a mock review, the ALO should obtain from the accreditor the exact schedule of activities for the real site visit to know with whom the review team plans to meet and how long each session is likely to last. The next step is to schedule as exact a simulation as possible. For the mock review to be most effective, participants should treat the time and effort seriously and plan not only to attend sessions specific to their roles but also to be "on call" for any impromptu requests for interviews or additional documentation. Mock reviewers must be selected as well; potential candidates include retired former senior leaders, former board members, and accreditation consultants. Preparation for each session of the site visit should include selecting a leader for each session, brainstorming questions that the reviewers are likely to ask, and determining who will be responsible for producing any additional data or documentation.

Ahead of each mock review session, the mock reviewers should scrutinize questions created by the accreditation steering committee and refine them to be as authentic as possible. The questions ought to be tough enough to simulate an actual site visit but also be realistic and fair. Each session's selected leader can be mentored to respond broadly to questions and then "pitch" them to others who can provide more detail. This technique allows the session's experts in a particular functional area to take a few minutes to collect their thoughts and consider carefully how to respond with specific examples. For example, in a session with faculty, the chair of the faculty senate might respond to questions about faculty voice in governance with descriptions of the structure, how elections are held, and interactions with administration. Then individual faculty members may share specific examples of their experiences with faculty governance in the context of policy changes.

The mentor for each session should collaborate with their mentees as colleagues in a team dynamic. They can emphasize the need for participants to stay in their roles, addressing the mock reviewers as though they are actual review team members and waiting until the practice session is over to debrief and talk about what went well and what could be improved. At a final debrief session of the mock review, the mock reviewers can provide feedback to session leaders regarding the strengths and challenges that arose, with advice on how to coach participants to improve their active listening and speaking skills. Some may need to listen more carefully to the questions posed, slow down, not talk over others, or only share pertinent examples. Effective mentors in the debrief session can generate enthusiasm, excitement, and confidence in the accreditation work all are engaged in, building on the strengths of those who participated, which is essential to demonstrating both compliance with accreditation standards and continuous improvement.

Concluding Thoughts

Mentoring for accreditation success involves more than compliance with accreditation standards and succession planning. It requires passionate professionals who believe in the positive value of accreditation to graduate students who have benefitted from the institution's focus on continuous improvement and innovation.

Through active planning to mentor talented professionals, institutions can ensure that rising leaders are entirely competent to take on accreditation challenges.

Discussion Questions

1. Why is it important for the mentor and mentee to agree on the skills and competencies to be developed in the mentee?

2. Which specific skills and competencies are most important for a mentor to develop in an ALO?

3. Are promising leaders mentored by those leaders, staff, and faculty most experienced with accreditation at your institution? If not, what can be done to ensure that they are?

4. What steps and activities should be included in a project plan to stage a mock review visit? Who might need to be prepared for such a mock review and in what way?

Discover and Propel

The sources that follow can assist those engaged in accreditation work in maintaining momentum both in mentoring and in their professional development.

Assessment Training Programs

- Higher Learning Commission (HLC) Assessment Academy Experience https://www.hlcommission.org/Programs-Events/assessment-academy-experience.html

- Northwest Commission on Colleges and Universities (NWCCU) ALO Institute https://nwccu.org/programs_and_events/educational-programming/alo-canvas-course/

- Western Association of Schools and Colleges Senior College & University Commission (WSCUC) Assessment Leadership Academy https://www.wscuc.org/educational-programs/accreditation-leadership-academy/

Accreditors to Follow on LinkedIn

Follow specific institutional and specialized accreditors for your institution on LinkedIn. Some offer the ability to subscribe to their email messages through their websites. Some of these accreditors include:

- Distance Education Accrediting Commission (DEAC) https://www.deac.org/

- Higher Learning Commission (HLC) https://www.linkedin.com/company/hlcommission/

- Middle States Commission on Higher Education (MSCHE) https://www.linkedin.com/company/mscheorg/

- Southern Association of Colleges and Schools Commission on Colleges (SACSCOC) https://www.linkedin.com/company/southern-association-of-colleges-and-schools-commission-on-colleges-sacscoc-/

Organizations to Follow on LinkedIn

- American Council on Education https://www.linkedin.com/company/american-council-on-education/

- United States Department of Education https://www.linkedin.com/company/usedgov/

- Higher Education: Assessment of Student Learning Outcomes & Continuous Process Improvement – largely posts by Calvin Yu https://www.linkedin.com/groups/1171287/

Professional Associations

Professional associations offer resources for accreditation professionals through annual conferences, webinars, membership benefits, and email lists to follow news and announcements:

- Association for the Assessment of Learning in Higher Education (AALHE) https://www.aalhe.org/

- National Institute for Learning Outcomes Assessment https://www.learningoutcomesassessment.org/

- Council on Higher Education Accreditation (CHEA) https://www.chea.org/

- Indiana University – Purdue University Indianapolis (IUPUI) Center for Leading Improvements in Higher Education Assessment Institute https://assessmentinstitute.iupui.edu/overview/clihe.html

- Association for Institutional Research (AIR) https://www.airweb.org/

Mentoring

- International Mentoring Association (IMA) https://www.mentoringassociation.org/

- American Institutes for Research's Mentoring Research Resources https://www.air.org/our-work/human-services/mentoring

- International Journal of Evidence Based Coaching & Mentoring https://radar.brookes.ac.uk/radar/items/b6bb9783-f20a-44f6-9e07-f9bdf4437eb1/1/ (This is an open source journal that requires no fee.)

References

Ard, N. & Beasley, S. (2022). Mentoring: A key element in succession planning, *Teaching and Learning in Nursing*, 17, pp.159-162.

Eliasson, M., Berggren, H., & Bondestam, F. (2000). Mentor programmes—A shortcut for women's academic careers? *Higher Education in Europe, XXV*(2), pp.173-179.

Homer (1999). *The Odyssey* (R. Fagles, Trans.). Penguin Classics. (Original work published approx. 725 BCE)

Jernigan, Q.A., Dudley, M.C. & Hatch, B.H. (2020). Mentoring matters: Experiences in mentoring black leaders in higher education. *New Directions for Adult & Continuing Education*, pp. 167–168. DOI: 10.1002/ace.20397

Jordan. J. and Sorell, M. (2019). Why reverse mentoring works and how to do It right. *Harvard Business Review*. https://hbr.org/2019/10/why-reverse-mentoring-works-and-how-to-do-it-right

Klemp Jr., G.O. (2001). Competence in context: Identifying core skills for the future. In J. Raven & J. Stephenseon (Eds.), *Competence in the learning society* (pp. 129- 147). New York: Peter Lang.

McClelland, D.C. (1998). Identifying competencies with behavioral-event interviews. *Psychological Science, 9*(5), 331-339.

Meda, L., Mohebi, L., El Sayary, A. and Karaki, S. (2023). A mutually enriching inclusive education teacher professional development program: Mentors' and mentees' reflections. *International Journal of Evidence Based Coaching and Mentoring, 21*(2), pp.51-62. DOI: 10.24384/fv45-1467 (Accessed: 20 November 2023)

Raven, J. (2001). The McClelland/McBer competency models. In J. Raven & J. Stephenson (Eds.), *Competence in the Learning Society.* (pp. 225- 235). New York: Peter Lang. https://www.researchgate.net/publication/242566220_The_ McClellandMcBer_Competency_Models

Rothwell, W. (2016). *Effective succession planning: Ensuring leadership continuity and building talent from within.* Redstone Arsenal, Alabama: AMACOM

Tomlinson, H. (2004). *Educational leadership: Personal growth for professional development.* London: Paul Chapman Publishing.

Williams, L. (2008). *Mentoring online adult undergraduate learners* [Doctoral dissertation]. Union Institute & University.

Chapter 7

Strategic Engagement of Faculty in Institutional and Programmatic Accreditation

Mary Ann Coughlin and Valerie Martin Conley

This chapter delves into the strategic engagement of faculty in institutional and programmatic accreditation processes, offering insights into how leaders can leverage the expertise and involvement of faculty members to enhance accreditation outcomes and promote academic excellence.

Historically, accreditation has been viewed as a compliance requirement. Whether institutional/regional or programmatic/disciplinary,[3] accreditation allows a college or university to reflect

---

3   We use the terms "institutional accreditation" and "regional accreditation" interchangeably throughout the chapter. Further, the adjectives "specialized," "disciplinary," "professional," "programmatic," and "program- level" are also used interchangeably with regard to accreditation.

on, plan, and gain critical external feedback on its programs and processes. Even more importantly, it provides the institution with the opportunity to engage key stakeholders—faculty, staff, and students—-in this review, which increases their knowledge of the institution and further connects individuals from across the campus.

Accreditation has traditionally had two main purposes: assurance and quality. It delivers external assurances that the institution or academic programs are meeting their stated mission and goals and also serves to improve the quality of the institution's offerings. Faculty provide the curricular and disciplinary expertise for our academic programs. Thus, if the objective is to assure external stakeholders and improve the quality of our academic programs, then faculty engagement and participation in accreditation is critical.

It is important to note the differences between institutional and disciplinary accreditation. Throughout this chapter, we will highlight both similarities and differences between faculty engagement in these two forms of accreditation. The basic framework is similar for institutional and disciplinary accreditation. Both include a self-study, an on-site evaluation or post-COVID virtual site visit, public notification, an evaluative report, an opportunity for the program/institution to respond to the team's report, and a notification of final actions taken by an authorizing authority. In the case of institutional accreditation, the authorizing authorities are the commissions of regional accreditors and national faith- or career-related boards. For program accreditation, the authorizing authorities are the boards of professional organizations and associations.

The primary differences between institutional and professional accreditation relate to the standards being evaluated and the level of the review being undertaken (i.e., the unit of analysis, the institution, or the academic program). Historically, faculty are more familiar with and more motivated to participate in professional accreditation. Often, they view institutional accreditation as the responsibility of the administration.

It is incumbent on institutional leaders not only to establish
an expectation that faculty participate in the process but also to do
so in a way that conveys the importance of faculty engagement.
Accreditors expect engagement on the part of faculty, who play a key
role in curricular processes and delivery. Further, these expectations
are similar in both institutional and professional accreditation. This
chapter will thus provide insights into the important role of faculty
in the accreditation process (both programmatic and institutional),
the benefits of faculty engagement (for the faculty and for the
institution), and mitigating challenges and roadblocks that prevent
faculty engagement.

The Role of Faculty in Accreditation

Accreditation has a long history in U.S. higher education. It emerged
in the late 1800s and early 1900s to distinguish the curricula of
institutions as providing an education beyond the secondary level. As
the stakes got higher (accountability, eligibility for Title IV funding)
and the process/standards became more complex, professionalization
of accreditation led to lessening faculty engagement, especially in
institutional accreditation. Over time, as the focus of accreditation
and assessment shifted from inputs to outputs and outcomes, the role
of faculty in accreditation processes became more vital. The American
Association of University Professors (AAUP) encourages faculty
participation in institutional accreditation. Faculty engagement
requires faculty to have knowledge of accreditation standards and any
initiatives the institution is undertaking to meet those standards, not
just inside the classroom but outside the classroom and off-campus.

This section offers practical suggestions for improving faculty
engagement in both professional and regional accreditation processes.
Later in the chapter, we will provide suggestions on removing barriers
and educating faculty on accreditation standards. All these practices
need to be part of the process of engaging faculty in accreditation.

While many means of engaging faculty are similar in institutional accreditation and professional accreditation, we will also explore some fundamental differences.

Institutional Accreditation

Institutional accreditation is vital to colleges and universities if for no other reason than that it provides them with access to federal financial aid programs through Title IV funds. Beyond the fiscal impact, the Department of Education and the Office of Postsecondary Education, through the Accreditation Group, have the important role of providing public assurance of the quality of institutions of higher education (U.S. Department of Education, n.d.). Thus, institutional accreditation is viewed as a high-stakes process for colleges and universities.

The various regional accreditors define their role in this process. Each of them has the autonomy to create its own processes and expectations for meeting its standards and review procedures. Yet they all call for widespread participation in the accreditation process and emphasize faculty engagement. For example, the Higher Learning Commission has as its mission to "advance the common good through quality assurance of higher education as the leader in equitable, transformative and trusted accreditation in the service of students and member institutions" (Higher Learning Commission, n.d., p.1).

The New England Commission of Higher Education (NECHE) states that it is:

> a voluntary, non-profit, self-governing organization
> having as its primary purpose the accreditation of
> educational institutions. Through its evaluation
> activities, the Commission provides public assurance
> about the educational quality of degree-granting
> institutions that seek or wish to maintain accreditation.

Institutions of higher learning achieve accreditation
from NECHE by demonstrating they meet the
Commission's Standards for Accreditation and comply
with its policies. (NECHE, 2021, p. 1)

Each of the regional accrediting agencies stresses the importance
both of the institution's self-study and the participation of the entire
community—faculty, staff, and students from across all levels of
the institution—in that process. Therefore, defining and managing
the self-study process is critical to engaging faculty and stakeholder
engagement.

Strategies for Creating Working Groups

One key but simple approach to defining the self-study process is to
create working groups that align with the accreditation standards. For
example, NECHE has nine standards for accreditation:

1. Mission and Purposes

2. Planning and Evaluation

3. Organization and Governance

4. The Academic Program

5. Students

6. Teaching, Learning, and Scholarship

7. Institutional Resources

8. Educational Effectiveness

9. Integrity, Transparency, and Public Disclosure.

One possibility would be to form a working group to evaluate the institution's performance relative to each of the standards. Yet while the alignment and simplicity of this approach make sense, not all standards are equal in complexity or in terms of the work necessary to complete the evaluation. As a result, when constituting the working groups, it is wise to consider combining standards with less content (e.g., Mission and Purposes with Planning and Evaluation) or increasing the number of individuals on those working groups assigned to more complex standards (e.g., the Academic Program).

The selection of working group members is key to faculty engagement. When we were relatively new to accreditation, we were brought into the planning process by academic leaders responsible for the self-study at our respective institutions. After attending a workshop on the self-study process, we sat down and discussed how to select and appoint members of our working groups. Several important factors emerged. Years later, when leading accreditation, we relied heavily on these suggestions in building our self-study process.

The first was the value of asking faculty to serve as co-chairs with administrators for each of the working groups. Having a faculty co-chair signals to the faculty the importance of their role in this process and provides the faculty member with an opportunity to demonstrate their leadership skills. Having an administrative co-chair helps to minimize the administrative burden on the faculty co-chair.

Using faculty governance leaders in key areas to support communication and shared governance was another consideration. For example, you may wish to appoint the current faculty senate or council president to serve as a co-chair for a standard related to organization or governance or the current chair of your curriculum committee to serve as a co-chair of the Academic Program standard. Yet another suggestion was to invite faculty who have experience with disciplinary accreditation to serve as members of working groups. That way, individuals who are knowledgeable about accreditation processes can help guide the work. Exhibit 7.1 depicts strategies for recruiting participants for accreditation working groups.

Exhibit 7.1: Strategies for Recruiting Participants for Accreditation Working Groups

Strategically placing students in working groups can also increase faculty engagement. Although accrediting agencies strongly encourage having students as working group members, students often become overwhelmed in these settings and withdraw from the process. Consider asking students who are connected to one or more of the faculty members on the committee. This provides the student with a connection to the committee and has the added benefit of tapping into faculty members' motivation to support their students. If your institution has a graduate program in higher education or student affairs, you may want to consider engaging students as part of a practicum.

Including junior faculty in working groups is also important. Not only does this provide an opportunity for these faculty to gain a larger view of the college or university, but it also builds institutional knowledge for future accreditation reviews. Having had the opportunity to co-chair one of the working groups for our institution's reaffirmation of accreditation as junior faculty members, we can attest to the value of the experience and insight gained—not only into the institution but also into ourselves as leaders.

A final and critical suggestion was to be sure to mix faculty representation across divisions and schools. This assists with faculty engagement as it allows faculty to network with individuals from across the institution.

Creating working groups is just the first step in ensuring faculty engagement in institutional accreditation. We have all been on committees where one individual dominates the discussions or committees that never seem to get anything done and are constantly circling around issues and not accomplishing their tasks. Therefore, once the working groups have been formed, faculty and working group participation must be facilitated. In leading these processes, we have found that participation can be enhanced through positive communication and leadership. And it starts with the invitation to serve. This invitation should come from the president or senior leadership to indicate the importance of their service to the institution.

Key Strategies While the Working Groups Are Working

Positive communication continues with the leadership of the self-study. We have found it helpful to create a steering committee chaired by key members of the president's leadership team (the provost with perhaps a co-chair) and include the co-chairs of each of the working groups. Regular meetings with the steering committee with a set agenda to guide the process and keep the timeline and process on track, provide the co-chairs with a structure they can follow in leading their working groups.

Supporting the working groups is critical to their success. Institutional self-study processes should rely heavily on the institutional research (IR) department or function to provide data to working groups or perhaps conduct surveys to collect data for them. Many times, while reviewing the standards, working groups will want to collect their own data, which can be extremely problematic. Working groups collecting data can distract the committee from the important tasks of reviewing standards and assessing evidence. Further, the committee may seek out data that might be biased or not represent all aspects of the institution. Be sure to engage institutional data sources. Doing so will not only spare the working group the burden of collecting data but also ensure that the self-study draws on verifiable institutional data. After all, the focus of the working group should be on reviewing its assigned standard(s), evaluating evidence to determine the extent to which the institution meets the standard(s), and writing a narrative about the standard(s).

It is important that academic leaders facilitating the process be available to co-chairs and that they consistently check in with each of the working groups. At some point in time, one or more of the working groups will fall behind in their work or have difficulties with one or more of their members who are not participating fully. Expect those interruptions to occur, and be prepared to intervene. Maybe a faculty member is having family or medical issues and can no longer participate; you need to talk these issues through with your co-chairs and consider replacing that individual or providing additional support to the working group.

We have also found that giving working group members the opportunity to celebrate their accomplishments builds community and assists with the process. Encourage working groups to plan a meeting with lunch, or consider getting all working group members together over pizza for an update on the process This type of social interaction allows for further networking and contributes to a sense of community and belonging.

Faculty engagement is more than just participation in the self-study process. Once the self-study document is written, there should be an opportunity for community review. Inviting faculty to review the self-study and holding open forums for them to discuss the document will generate valuable input. Be sure to build in the time needed for this stage of the process.

Just holding an open forum will not ensure faculty engagement. We all know faculty who are great reviewers or even some who are critics of the process. Consider drawing those individuals into the review process. You may wish to engage the assistance of your academic deans or department chairs. Have them encourage faculty to review various sections of the self-study document and ask the faculty to lead parts of the open forum. While opportunities for input can bring out issues and disagreement, having this type of candid review is exactly what accrediting bodies encourage. Moreover, the visiting team will also be evaluating awareness of and participation in the self-study process, which these activities promote. .

Disciplinary Accreditation

When students think about accreditation, they are often thinking about an individual program of study. The role of disciplinary accreditation is to ensure the quality of an academic program within a specific discipline/field of study and for professional fields to ensure graduates will have the knowledge, skills, and ability to perform (i.e., be prepared for practice). Although the agencies that review and accredit specialized programs are national in scope, licensure requirements may vary by state. Regardless, graduating from an accredited program streamlines the process for licensure and is sometimes a prerequisite for licensure in a professional field of practice. Some states require that graduates complete accredited programs to be eligible for licensure. Employers may not consider hiring someone who did not graduate from an accredited program.

For these reasons, specialized accreditation is often considered necessary for a program to be competitive—or even viable.

For example, the Commission on Collegiate Nursing Education (CCNE) "ensures the quality and integrity of baccalaureate, graduate, and residency/fellowship programs in nursing. CCNE serves the public interest by assessing and identifying programs that engage in effective educational practices" (American Association of Colleges of Nursing, n.d.). "The mission, goals, and expected program outcomes are consistent with relevant professional nursing standards and guidelines for the preparation of nursing professionals" (American Association of Colleges of Nursing, n.d.), and the level of nursing practice being evaluated (e.g., baccalaureate and graduate, entry to practice, or practitioner fellowship). Simply put, CCNE provides assurance that the public can trust that nurses who graduate from CCNE-accredited programs are qualified to do the job of providing a prescribed level of care.

Similarly, the Council for the Accreditation of Educator Preparation (CAEP) accredits teacher education programs. CAEP's mission is to advance "excellence in educator preparation through evidence-based accreditation that assures quality and supports continuous improvement to strengthen P-12 student learning"(Council for the Accreditation of Educator Preparation, n.d.).

As noted, the process for disciplinary accreditation generally mirrors that of institutional accreditation. Given that faculty are responsible for the curriculum, it is natural that they hold primary responsibility for programmatic accreditation. Indeed, faculty expect to play a significant part in conducting the self-study for programmatic accreditation and sometimes even feel complete ownership of the process. This sense of ownership is tied to their identification with the discipline/profession. Faculty in accredited professional programs sometimes even maintain professional licensure themselves.

From a leadership perspective, it is important to maintain

active engagement and communication with faculty facilitating these processes. Sometimes, there are multiple accredited programs within an academic unit. According to the Council for Higher Education Accreditation (CHEA, 2023), there were 66 "recognized" programmatic accreditors in 2020. Acknowledging the contributions of faculty through workload reductions, stipends, and service credit is critical. Also, saying "Thank you" goes a long way. In addition to recognizing the work involved, these incentives create a mechanism for accountability to ensure adequate planning and resource allocation.

Even with the best-laid plans, outcomes from accreditation reviews are not always positive. In some cases, these findings lead to programs being placed on probation or receiving conditional accreditation. While this is not a situation anyone hopes for, important leadership lessons can be derived from the experience. We inherited such a situation in one of our leadership roles.

Historically, two specialized accrediting bodies reviewed educator preparation programs in the U.S.: the National Council for the Accreditation for Teacher Education (NCATE) and the Teacher Education Accreditation Council (TEAC). These two agencies merged in 2013 to form CAEP. The organization was recognized by the Council for Higher Education Accreditation (CHEA) in 2014. Soon after, one of the first programs in the nation to undergo a CAEP site visit received conditional accreditation from CAEP, including stipulations related to one of the new standards—Standard 4: Program Impact. Specifically, one of the components of Standard 4 required that programs demonstrate that completers "(a) effectively contribute to P-12 student-learning growth and (b) apply in P-12 classrooms the professional knowledge, skills, and dispositions the preparation experiences were designed to achieve" (Council for the Accreditation of Educator Preparation, 2022).

The focus on program completers was a marked shift from previous standards, which focused on teacher candidates during their culminating clinical field experiences. Realizing that it would not be possible for programs to demonstrate that they met this standard right away, CAEP modified the expectation to require that the program demonstrate that they had a plan for meeting the standard.

We had two years to remove the stipulations and develop a plan, which provided a clear timeline for demonstrating that we met the standard. A transparent, collaborative process was key to our success. The process undertaken to remove the stipulations and receive unconditional accreditation from CAEP illustrates the important role faculty play in disciplinary accreditation. The first question we had to answer was: Were these the right outcomes to serve as an assurance of the quality of our program? Given the newness of the standards, we spent time ensuring that we understood the definitions and the intent (i.e., outcomes) of the standard. We needed buy-in from the faculty that the performance of graduates of our programs was associated with P-12 student learning growth. In other words, the impact of our programs could/should be measured by the learning that took place in P-12 classrooms where our completers (e.g., graduates) were teaching and the degree to which new teachers were applying what we had taught them.

This step was critical because it established *why* we were seeking CAEP accreditation in the first place. We were not doing anything because CAEP required it. We were developing a plan for building a process to demonstrate the quality of our programs through their impact in P-12 classrooms because we believed it was the right thing to do.

Another key consideration was the involvement of faculty from across the college, not just in the department where the educator preparation program was housed. Although the institution was a comprehensive college encompassing programs not directly related to educator preparation (e.g., counseling, human services, research, and leadership), the quality of educator preparation programs reflected on the campus as a whole. Additionally, some programs in the college were accredited by other specialized agencies (e.g., the Council for Accreditation of Counseling and Related Educational Programs, or CACREP). We wanted to ensure our plan could be executed in such a way that it would allow us to demonstrate the quality of programs overall. Additionally, substantial resources had to be devoted to developing and implementing the plan, so we wanted to ensure we had college-wide support for it as a priority.

Considering External Support

A question often asked is: Should we hire a consultant to write the self-study (or in this case the plan to demonstrate that we met the standard)? There are several considerations when making this decision. An obvious one is budget. If resources are available to hire a consultant to support the process, then doing so can be an effective strategy. Another consideration is expertise—knowledge of the program and familiarity with the standards. Retirees may be a good resource.

Ultimately, we did hire an external consultant to help us develop the plan, but not to serve as its primary author. This individual was not a retiree or affiliated with the institution. Given the newness of the CAEP standards, we felt it was important to identify a consultant who had experience with, and an understanding of, the unmet standard specifically. We also recognized the value of cultivating expertise in-house and saw this as an opportunity for professional development, so we identified a faculty member who could work closely with the external consultant and serve as the primary author of the plan.

A final consideration was time available to devote to the task. The faculty member was provided with several course releases and received the college's outstanding service award for their contributions. Hiring an external consultant gave us much-needed breathing room, reducing anxiety for faculty who were already stretched way too thin; we were simultaneously launching the college's first two undergraduate degrees. Hiring an external consultant allowed us to engage the faculty strategically in reviewing the plan, evaluating evidence to determine the extent to which it would demonstrate that the program met the standard, and endorsing the plan and the narrative about the standard.

One of the biggest challenges was the availability of data, or lack thereof, to provide evidence that we were meeting the standard. Establishing a process to collect the data was a key component of the plan. This was particularly onerous in the state where the institution was located due to strict privacy laws that made it necessary to develop individual memoranda of understanding (MOUs) with school districts to share data on the performance of our graduates and the learning outcomes of the students in their P-12 classrooms.

Faculty relationships with P-12 teachers, principals, HR, and district-level personnel were instrumental in establishing these MOUs. The relationship with Institutional Research was also critical. IR facilitated focus groups and provided subsets of institutional data relevant to our student population. In addition, we began to participate in external assessments (e.g., EdTPA) and satisfaction surveys, which gave us comparative data about other programs. Over time, we leveraged existing infrastructure to provide opportunities to reflect on the results internally and with our district partners. Faculty engagement in the planning and execution of events such as an annual partnership breakfast allowed stakeholders to come together as a community to review results and identify areas for improvement.

There is a happy ending to this story. We submitted our plan by the deadline and received notification that the stipulations were removed, resulting in accreditation without conditions. This was a successful outcome! However, the real success was the full participation of the faculty and the establishment of processes contributing to a sustainable cycle of continuous quality improvement for the college. By building an inclusive culture of using data to support decision-making, we established an environment of trust, transparency, and increased collaboration, enhancing our reputation both on and off campus.

Benefits of Faculty Engagement

Most academic leaders who have led an institutional or programmatic accreditation process will agree that if they had just "closed themselves in their office," they could have produced the self-study document in about a quarter of the time required for the participatory processes described above. We have documented that accrediting bodies require broad participation in the process, but we have not yet articulated the benefits of faculty engagement in accreditation. As we do, it is important to view them through two lenses—benefits for the faculty and benefits for the institution.

Benefits for the Faculty

As described above, faculty are more motivated to participate in programmatic accreditation processes than in institutional accreditation processes. This is a natural trend as faculty have greater internal motivation to support their academic programs than to support larger institutional efforts. We thus need to consider both intrinsic and extrinsic motives for participation, as shown in Exhibit 7.2.

Some benefits to the faculty are more obvious than others. Faculty have many responsibilities, which at most institutions include teaching, research/scholarship, and service. The pressures to produce scholarly work and be effective educators can limit the time that a faculty member has to provide service to the institution. As a result, one obvious extrinsic motivator can be allowing the faculty member to use their participation in a self-study working group as a service activity in their annual evaluation and tenure or promotion portfolio. Another obvious extrinsic motivator can be compensation in the form

Exhibit 7.2: Benefits of Faculty Participation in the Institutional Accreditation Process

What are the Benefits of Faculty Participation in the Institutional Accreditation Process?

There are both intrinsic and extrinsic motives for faculty participation in the institutional accreditation process.

EXTRINSIC MOTIVATORS

- Use participation as a service activity in the annual evaluation and tenure or promotion portfolio
- Offer compensation in the form of stipends or course releases
- Provide college apparel or other "swag"

INTRINSIC MOTIVATORS

- Gain institutional knowledge
- Build relationships with faculty and staff from across the campus
- Receive professional development that can tie back to program assessment and strategies for exploring teaching effectiveness
- Provide input on issues of importance to you

of stipends or course releases. This is best reserved for individuals who are devoting extraordinary amounts of time to the process (e.g., the lead author of the self-study). We caution against establishing a culture of expectation for additional compensation.

A final obvious extrinsic motivator for faculty participation is college apparel or other "swag.". Certainly, for some individuals, these types of rewards are valued, but they are less effective for many. At the outset of Mary Ann's first institutional self-study process, she entered the room to discover very nice bags branded with the year, self-study, and institutional logo on each chair. The more senior faculty member walking in with her uttered, "Well, that's not good" when they picked up their bag. I turned and asked, "What do you mean?" and they replied, "The nicer the gift, the more work we have to do!" I chuckled but subsequently learned that they were correct! Later in both of our careers, when we were leading self-study efforts, we chose not to use these simple extrinsic rewards, opting instead to build more opportunities for intrinsic and extrinsic motivation into our protocols.

Obvious intrinsic motivators include gaining institutional knowledge and having the opportunity to build relationships with faculty and staff from across the campus. Faculty often have a limited view of the institution or their program when they are only engaged in teaching certain courses. Participation in programmatic or institutional accreditation will provide these individuals with a much broader perspective.

Additionally, faculty often complain that they do not know what is going on at the institution and do not understand how or why certain decisions are reached. Learning how the sausage is made can not only be an intrinsic motivator for faculty to participate but also makes them better campus citizens, which benefits the institution—more on that later! Finally, having the opportunity to build relationships with faculty from across the campus can lead to future academic or research collaborations.

One less obvious motivator for faculty is receiving professional development on assessment that could tie back to their program assessment and strategies for exploring teaching effectiveness. Given the emphasis in accreditation processes to document programmatic and institutional effectiveness, the work of many self-study working groups is to review outcomes assessment reports. These efforts allow faculty to review assessment procedures and various forms of evidence from across a variety of courses and programs. Often, this review provides faculty with ideas and practices that they can incorporate into their assessment efforts for their own courses and programs.

When the institution uses accreditation as an opportunity for truly candid assessment, this creates another, less obvious benefit for faculty: an opportunity to provide input on issues of importance to them. For example, if a college or university makes the accreditation process part of its strategic planning, then projections from the self-study could include plans to address faculty workload concerns or make recommendations for resources needed for programs or research support. These, as well as other outcomes, are all future benefits that a faculty member can reap by participating in the accreditation process.

Benefits for the Institution

As mentioned above, when done correctly, effective accreditation processes require an investment of institutional resources, including the time of faculty, staff, and academic leadership. Just as it would be easier to shut your office door and write the accreditation report yourself, it might also be easier not to fully engage faculty in these processes. Hence the question: What is the benefit of faculty participation for the institution? The answer is that there are many benefits, some more obvious than others.

The most obvious benefit to the institution is that faculty engagement in accreditation will strengthen the quality of academic programs. Faculty are responsible for the curriculum and bring disciplinary expertise to the process. Their active engagement brings out and ensures their commitment to continuously improving their programs. Said another way, if accreditation is viewed as the responsibility of the administration, then making the appropriate changes and adjustments to the curriculum suggested by this process becomes much more difficult, if not impossible, to carry out.

Other obvious institutional benefits include having faculty with a broader and larger view of the college or university's issues and priorities and producing an accreditation document that is stronger and meets the requirements of the accrediting bodies. As mentioned earlier, faculty can have a limited view of their program and department/school. Accreditation processes can provide an opportunity to broaden their horizons and break down silos by creating networking opportunities and exposing them to larger institutional issues. Creating faculty who are stronger and more participatory citizens of their community is of true benefit to any college or university.

Less obvious benefits for the institution include improving the quality of academic programs and fostering collaborative bonds between faculty and staff from across different divisions. As stated previously, faculty who participate in accreditation processes bring back expertise that can be used to leverage change in academic programs. As academic leaders manage accreditation cycles, they should be constantly focused on leveraging the process to improve the quality of our academic programs, which will only occur through strong faculty engagement. Having led many accreditation reviews, we have heard one consistent theme in feedback from faculty who have engaged in the process: that they have thoroughly enjoyed interacting with other faculty and staff from across the campus. Over the years, we have seen faculty who first interacted through accreditation later collaborate to develop new initiatives, many of which led to grants, new programs, or research opportunities.

As we end this section, we wanted to share one of our favorite expressions: "Be careful what you ask for. You just might get it!" At some point in their career, every academic leader can relate to this expression. Fully engaging faculty in accreditation can make the process "messier." Candid assessment can lead to true airing of dirty laundry and identify issues that the institution needs to address. However, exposing those issues and seizing the opportunity to tackle them is to the ultimate benefit for the institution, as festering problems inevitably grow. Further, trying to cover up those issues can lead to trouble later in the accreditation process when related concerns are shared with a visiting team. It is better to address problems head-on and work through them, even if doing so is time-consuming and difficult.

Mitigating Challenges and Roadblocks to Faculty Engagement

As academic leaders are planning accreditation processes, they should place substantive emphasis on ensuring and facilitating faculty engagement. Even with the best-laid plans, issues can arise, and processes can fall apart. Thus, we suggest spending some time thinking about potential challenges and roadblocks to faculty engagement, as shown in Exhibit 7.3. This will better equip you both to plan the process and to adjust it throughout to allow for positive faculty engagement.

Exhibit 7.3: Mitigating the Challenges of Faculty Participation in the Institutional Accreditation Process

Leadership is critical to mitigating the challenges and roadblocks that keep faculty from participating fully in the accreditation process. For larger accreditation processes, leadership must begin several years before self-study reviews and should be ongoing. Academic leaders can bolster the accreditation process on an ongoing basis by encouraging faculty to become members of professional and regional accrediting review teams and by supporting continuous efforts for academic program review. As faculty develop an interest in accreditation, whether it be through their regional accreditor or through a professional organization, academic leaders should encourage and reward their participation.

As academic leaders, when we learn of a faculty member who is interested in accreditation, we offer to recommend them to our regional accreditor as an evaluator. If a faculty member is named to a review team, we send them an email and thank them for their service. Additionally, when we work on our self-study with a faculty member that we think has promise, we ask them if they might be interested in serving on a review team for our regional accreditor. Providing a faculty member with positive affirmations that they are a solid contributor and have skills in this area goes a long way toward supporting their future engagement. Accreditors are always looking for qualified volunteers and provide great professional development to peer reviewers as part of their training. When a faculty member returns to your campus after serving as an evaluator, they have a much better understanding of the self-study process.

Leading accreditation efforts cannot be thought of as something that an academic leader does once every 5 or 10 years; it should be part of your annual work plan. If you wait until a year or so before the review to put prepare for a self-study, your review will be destined to fail. Academic programs must be improved on an ongoing basis. Whether accredited by an external professional association or not, they should undergo an external review process every three to five years. Outcomes for all programs should be reviewed annually.

Things that we review and evaluate improve. Closing the assessment loop leads to change, which is then evaluated and hopefully results in enhanced student learning. If you, as an academic leader, do not champion the value of these evaluation processes, then the reports become just one more piece of paperwork that faculty need to fill out. Encourage deans and department chairs to be involved in the assessment process; message the importance of this work to your faculty; and, most importantly, when program review recommendations come to you, find ways to support the initiatives put forward. Doing so will not only make your academic programs stronger but also motivate your faculty to engage in these processes.

In sum, we advocate for a more ideal model of assessment and program review that involves faculty using real-time assessments (Maki, 2017) in their classes to evaluate student learning and also ties those assessments to program outcomes so that the assessment is authentic and integrated in the day-to-day work of the faculty. Further, the program review must return the feedback about the program outcomes to the faculty to ensure that changes are happening in the delivery of instruction. After all, faculty are the content experts and must be engaged in defining and refining the curriculum. These are critical opportunities to bridge understanding and leverage insights gained to inform continuous quality improvement and ultimately improve our academic programs. These practices engage faculty and provide them with a clear role and responsibility in accreditation processes.

Institutional leaders can help faculty see and understand the critical role they play in accreditation by developing and articulating an integrated framework for using the data and information collected for self-studies to support strategic planning, budget allocations, and decision-making at the institution. By doing so, institutional leaders may mitigate one of the most significant challenges to faculty engagement: relevance.

One such framework is Burke's (2005) Performance Loop model. This model is an example of a comprehensive framework for institutional effectiveness that links departmental, school/college, and institutional performance. Important elements include shared indicators and feedback loops to link departmental and school/college aspirations and accomplishments with institutional goals and priorities. It is by using such frameworks that academic leaders can support strategic planning and be intentional in bridging the work of the self-study process to quality improvement. Ultimately, this establishes the relevance of this work to faculty.

Perhaps the most critical challenge to engaging faculty in accreditation is an enduring one, namely the belief that the more things change, the more they stay the same—or even more cynically, that nothing ever changes, and so it is all just a waste of time. This is a roadblock for faculty and institutional leaders alike. In its most successful form, accreditation can be a mechanism for change. As projections and recommendations are made in the accreditation process through self-study, it is essential that the institution mobilize the resources to support them and commit to following through on them. The onus is on academic leadership to be clear about commitments and to ensure follow-through.

Put simply, academic leaders need to deliver on promises for change. Adopting a change management model, which considers both data and culture, may be an effective strategy for combatting inertia and cynicism. Facilitating conversations with institutional and faculty leaders about change management will provide opportunities to work collaboratively to meet objectives and accomplish goals. Using accreditation as a tool to inform the institution's overall change management strategy will make its relevance clear to the entire campus community, in turn encouraging faculty to participate in the process. Ultimately, faculty will want to take part in accreditation if they believe that doing so will truly make a difference.

Discussion Questions

1. Which 2-3 strategies discussed in this chapter can you utilize to effectively engage faculty in either institutional or

programmatic accreditation processes?

2. What challenges and roadblocks do you foresee as you engage faculty in accreditation processes? How can these be overcome?

3. What role does your leadership play in fully engaging faculty in accreditation? What changes and strategies might you adopt to further engage your faculty?

4. What steps can your institution take to maximize faculty engagement in both institutional and programmatic accreditation processes?

5. What processes could be put in place to better align faculty engagement across both institutional and programmatic accreditation at your institution?

Discover and Propel

- For Private Not for Profit Institutions – Consortium of Independent Colleges (CIC). Sign up for CAO Listserv.

- For Public Institutions – The American Association of State Colleges and Universities (AASCU).

- AAC&U for assessment resources and resources to support Core Curriculum.

- AAUP's 1968 statement The *Role of the Faculty in the Accrediting of Colleges and Universities.*

References

Alstete, J.W. (2007). A brief history of college accreditation. In

College accreditation: managing internal revitalization and public respect. Palgrave Macmillan, New York. https://doi.org/10.1057/9780230601932_2

American Association of Colleges of Nurses. (n.d.). *CCNE Accreditation.*https://www.aacnnursing.org/ccne-accreditation

Brittingham, B. (2009). Accreditation in the United States: How did we get to where we are? *New Directions for Higher Education. (145)*, 7-27.

Burke, J. C. (2005). Closing the accountability gap for public universities: Putting academic departments in the performance loop. *Planning for Higher Education. 34*(1), *19-28.*

Council for the Accreditation of Educator Preparation (2022). Standard 4: Program impact.https://caepnet.org/standards/2022-itp/standard-4

Council for Higher Education Accreditation (n.d.). Almanac of External Quality Review.https://almanac.chea.org/accrediting-organizations-types-and-operation.

edTPA. (n.d.). *Educative teacher performance assessment.*https://www.edtpa.com/

Higher Learning Commission. (n.d.). *About the Higher Learning Commission.*https://www.hlcommission.org/About-HLC/about-hlc.html.

Kelchen, R. (2017). *Higher education accreditation and the federal government.* Urban Institute: Washington, DC.https://www.urban.org/sites/default/files/publication/93306/higher-education-accreditation-and-the-federal-government.pdf.

Maki, P. (2017). Real-time assessment. Routledge, New York.

New England Commission of Higher Education. (2021). *Standards for accreditation*.https://www.neche.org/standards-for-accreditation/

Perley, J.E., Tanguaymm D.M., Scholtz, Gerber, L. G., Henry, M. & Henry, E. (2008). Faculty involvement in accreditation: Three reports. *Academe, 94*(2), 88-110.

U.S. Department of Education. (n.d.). History and context of accreditation in the United States.https://www2.ed.gov/admins/finaid/accred/accreditation_pg2.html.

Chapter 8

The Power of Collaborating and Leveraging Multiple Institutional Groups: Strategies for Effective Accreditation Liaisons

Sundra D. Kincey

In this chapter, leaders explore the importance of collaboration and effective liaison roles in accreditation processes, offering strategies on how to leverage multiple institutional groups to ensure successful accreditation outcomes and foster a culture of continuous improvement and compliance with accreditation standards.

Accreditation is essential for ensuring the academic quality, credibility, and reputation of higher education institutions and facilitating student mobility, transfer of credits, and access to financial aid. Yet, it is not a straightforward process. It requires significant time, resources, and coordination among various stakeholders within and outside the institution. It also involves multiple challenges and roadblocks, such as changing standards and expectations, competing priorities and demands, limited resources and support, resistance to change, and communication gaps. Therefore, a successful outcome depends on effective leadership and management from an accreditation liaison, the primary contact between the institution and the accrediting agency.

The accreditation liaison is crucial in facilitating the accreditation process and ensuring its success. The accreditation liaison also catalyzes institutional change and improvement by fostering a culture of assessment, accountability, and excellence. However, one individual cannot accomplish these tasks alone. The accreditation liaison must collaborate and leverage the institutional groups with a stake in the accreditation process and outcome. These include faculty, staff, administrators, students, alumni, board members, external partners, and other constituencies. By collaborating with and leveraging these institutional groups, the accreditation liaison can enhance the quality and credibility of the self-study report, increase the engagement and buy-in of the campus community, mobilize the resources and support needed for the accreditation process, address the challenges and roadblocks that may arise along the way, and foster a shared vision and commitment for institutional improvement. This chapter highlights the value of including multiple groups in the accreditation process, identifies the key institutional groups with whom the accreditation liaison should collaborate, provides strategies for leveraging each institutional group effectively, and suggests ways to mitigate challenges and roadblocks.

Accreditation is essential in higher education institutions as it serves as a mechanism designed to ensure that they meet specific criteria of quality and effectiveness and that students receive. It provides external validation to students, parents, and other stakeholders that an institution's programs, processes, and outcomes have credibility and deserve their trust. Accreditation also helps institutions identify areas for improvement and promote a culture of continuous assessment and enhancement. Additionally, it allows institutions to access federal funding, attract students, and facilitate the transfer of credits between institutions (Eaton, 2012). Because accreditation is so critical for colleges and universities, the importance of accreditation liaisons cannot be overstated. But what is an accreditation liaison? What purpose does this position serve?

As defined by most accrediting agencies, the accreditation liaison is the primary contact and coordinator between the institution and the accrediting agency. This role facilitates communication, collaboration, and compliance among various institutional groups and stakeholders involved in the accreditation process, such as faculty, staff, administrators, students, alumni, board members, external partners, and community members. The accreditation liaison also oversees the preparation and submission of accreditation reports and documents, organizes site visits and follow-up activities, and monitors and implements institutional accreditation activities on an ongoing basis (Southern Association of Colleges and Schools Commission on Colleges, 2020).

As the title suggests, accreditation liaisons are the conduit between the institution and the accrediting body, facilitating communication, organizing data, and ensuring compliance. However, the success of accreditation liaisons does not solely rest on their shoulders. By collaborating and leveraging institutional groups, accreditation liaisons can enhance their effectiveness and streamline the accreditation process. This chapter explores the value of including multiple groups in the accreditation process and provides strategies for leveraging each group. It also addresses potential challenges and roadblocks that may arise during the process. Additionally, the chapter encourages leaders to discover and propel their institutions toward a culture of continuous improvement and compliance with accreditation standards. It presents a case study of how an accreditation liaison at a public university successfully collaborated with and leveraged various institutional groups to achieve a positive accreditation outcome. The chapter concludes with questions for discussion and reflection to help accreditation liaisons discover and propel their strategies for effective collaboration and leverage.

Value of Including Multiple Groups in the Accreditation Process

According to the American Library Association (2017), "accreditation has two purposes: 1) to ensure that postsecondary educational institutions and their units, schools, or programs meet appropriate standards of quality and integrity, and 2) to improve the quality of education these institutions offer." Accreditation is also viewed as a public seal of approval and a quality guarantee. Academic programs that secure and maintain accreditation status do so by engaging in a rigorous internal and external review process and meeting defined criteria for educational excellence. However, this process has become increasingly complex with the proliferation of agencies that accredit academic programs over the years (UCSF, 1999).

The same applies to institutional accreditation because the stakes are incredibly high. Maintaining access to federal financial aid depends upon an institution's having continuous national or what is known as "former regional" accreditation (U.S. Department of Education, 2021). Consequently, accreditation can be a complex and multifaceted process that involves various aspects of a college's or university's operations. Because of the high stakes, effective accreditation liaisons must learn to galvanize and harness the strengths of multiple internal and external constituents to thoroughly evaluate institutional processes and requirements to determine compliance with the respective accrediting agencies' requirements. In doing so, liaisons must employ diverse perspectives and expertise to bring depth and richness to the accreditation process. Of course, this is easier said than done as accreditors often have many requirements that institutions must be keenly aware of to maintain ongoing compliance. The makeup of the different institutional groups thus becomes critical.

Each group, such as faculty, staff, students, administrators, or external stakeholders, may offer diverse perspectives and unique insights, knowledge, and expertise. Engaging multiple institutional groups promotes transparency, inclusivity, and shared ownership of the college's or university's goals, helping to create a culture of continuous improvement and institutional effectiveness. By harnessing the collective wisdom of these groups, leaders can gain a thorough understanding of the institution's strengths and areas for improvement. Further, utilizing different viewpoints and skills from multiple groups aids accreditation liaisons in conducting a more detailed evaluation of an institution's programs, policies, and practices. Marshaling the skills and abilities of diverse groups also promotes a sense of shared responsibility and contributes to a more comprehensive understanding of an institution's strengths and areas for growth. This approach further enhances the depth and breadth of the evaluation and ensures that all relevant stakeholders have a voice in the accreditation process.

In most instances, employees have specific knowledge about their unit within the college or university. However, by collaborating on a large-scale project with colleagues outside of their unit, they can develop a more holistic view of the institution. For instance, accreditors typically have standards related to an institution's finances. Who better than the chief financial officer (CFO), who has the most intimate knowledge of the administration of finances across an institution, to serve in this role?

Webb (2017) states that not all stakeholders contribute equally to the process. Therefore, the internal team members must be keenly aware of institutional policies and procedures related to their respective areas. Yet for individuals who may be less engaged in campus-wide initiatives, participating in projects outside their own unit could broaden their institutional knowledge and understanding of institutional policies, which will be beneficial for maintaining accreditation in the future.

In the initial stages of team collaborations, it is recommended that the accreditation liaison set a goal to develop buy-in from all members of the college or university. One method to galvanize the internal stakeholders is to establish broad engagement and shared governance across like standards for the accrediting agency. This would require the liaison to open lines of communication and be able to answer the "why" of the accreditation process (Webb, 2017). According to Brown (2024), when different groups can contribute and have their voices heard, they may be more likely to be invested in the outcomes and committed to the continuous improvement initiatives that arise from the accreditation process. Collaborating in this manner may also lend itself to expanded cross-functional teamwork, interdisciplinary approaches, and innovative solutions to address accreditation standards more effectively.

Key Institutional Groups

As accreditation liaisons work to establish their internal teams, it is essential that they assess the role of each collaborating unit or member. This section provides an in-depth analysis of the institutional groups that play vital roles in the accreditation process. Each group will be discussed individually to highlight its unique contributions and perspectives. To establish their internal teams, it is essential that they assess the role of each collaborating unit or member. This section provides an in-depth analysis of the institutional groups that play vital roles in the accreditation process. Each group (shown in Exhibit 8.1) will be discussed individually to highlight its unique contributions and perspectives. To establish initial accreditation or maintain continuing accreditation, institutional groups may include senior-level administrators, faculty, staff, students, and, when applicable, board members and alumni. The importance of each group are discussed in the next sections.

Exhibit 8.1: Key Institutional Groups

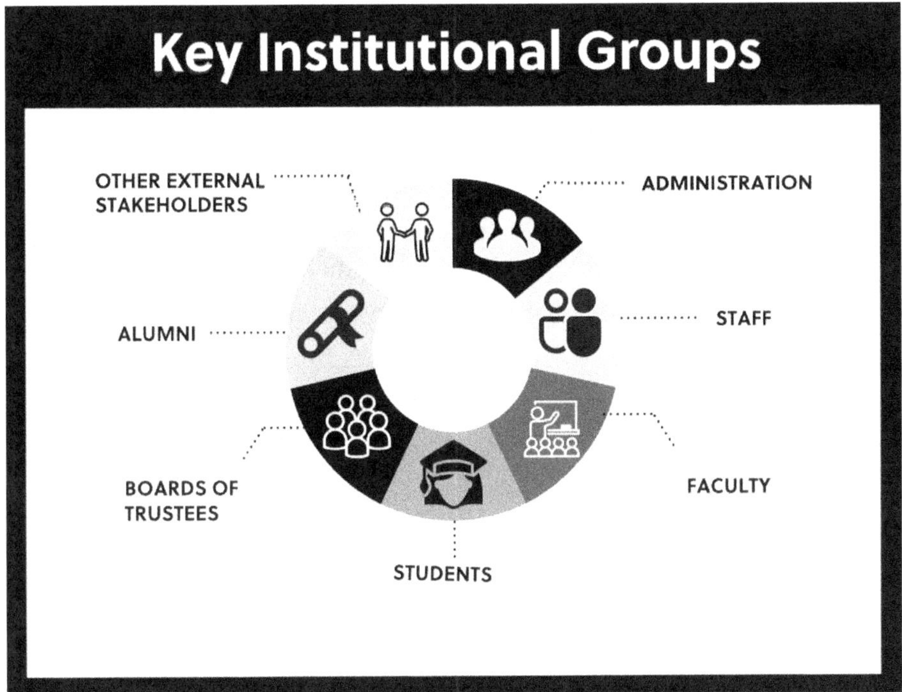

Administration

Administrators are often responsible for implementing changes to meet accreditation standards and ensuring ongoing compliance. Their strategic vision, guidance, and support are vital for effective collaboration and leveraging institutional groups in the accreditation process. In their respective roles, administrators facilitate communication between their staff, establish clear goals for the unit, and set the tone for day-to-day operations, which may include shared responsibility and varying levels of accountability. Leaders at colleges and universities, such as department chairs, deans, chief officers, and cabinet executives, typically have a thorough understanding an institution's policies, procedures, and strategic initiatives. They can thus provide valuable information during the accreditation process, particularly with respect to governance, finance, institutional planning, and effectiveness. They can also articulate the vision and mission of the college or university and how these align with the types of students served.

Faculty

Faculty members, like students, are at the heart of any educational institution. Their expertise and insight are invaluable in developing curricula, assessing student learning outcomes, and demonstrating compliance with accreditation standards. They are beneficial in outlining the requirements of standards related to academic program approval, quality and integrity of the curriculum, program length, and assessment of student learning outcomes, all of which are common to many national/regional accreditors. Involving faculty in the accreditation process ensures compliance and fosters a sense of ownership and commitment to improving the quality and integrity of the curriculum.

Staff

The staff in various administrative and support roles contribute significantly to the daily operations of an institution. Therefore, their involvement is essential for evaluating and improving student support services and institutional effectiveness. They may also provide keen insights into student experiences as they are often in front-facing positions and meet with students frequently.

Students

Without students, there is no college or university. Students are the primary beneficiaries of the education provided by institutions. Their perspectives, experiences, and feedback offer valuable insights into the effectiveness of educational programs. By engaging students, accreditation liaisons can ensure that their voices are heard and that the institution is demonstrating its commitment to student success. As the leader guiding a college or university to initial or continuing accreditation, one must remember that an institution's quality and effectiveness directly impact students. Their feedback, through surveys, focus groups, or interviews, helps identify areas of strength and improvement alike. Their perspectives can inform improvements and ensure that institutional goals align with their needs and expectations.

Boards of Trustees

Trustees and governing boards provide oversight and strategic planning for the institution. In some states, college and university presidents report to a local board of trustees. By having a voice from this organization, the institution can showcase its commitment to excellence and demonstrate effective governance and fiscal oversight.

Alumni

College and university graduates have great affection for their alma maters. Within the accreditation process, they can provide a voice for the quality of the education they received and its impact on career opportunities after graduation.

Other External Stakeholders

Accreditation processes often involve external stakeholders such as employers, professional associations, and community partners. Engaging these stakeholders could provide evidence that the institution's programs and services align with industry needs and community expectations. Academic units will usually engage local or regional employers as they work to develop a new degree. Using this type of documentation as proof that a college or university values external stakeholder input can be valuable to meet specific standards related to the educational programs.

According to Cotton et al. (2023), working with regional, national, or international organizations is also a way to identify external partners and build a network of peers who can provide guidance based on their experiences with accreditation. Experience with other accreditation liaisons is among the most valued aspects of engaging external stakeholders. Peers in this profession are eager to share their experiences and provide advice to colleagues who have proven helpful in reaffirmation reports at their institutions.

Strategies for Collaborating and Leveraging Each Institutional Group

According to Castañer and Oliveira (2020), collaboration, coordination, and cooperation lie at the core of interorganizational activities and are more effective in combination than in isolation. However, it should be noted that collaboration addresses difficulties while at the same time introducing its own set of challenges (Cotton Atwood, & DeRose, 2023). Therefore, as a leader charged with bringing together large groups and producing effective outcomes, it is important to have pre-defined strategies and a roadmap for success.

One key strategy to effectively manage institutional groups is establishing clear roles and responsibilities so that everyone understands their contribution to the accreditation process. This clarity helps organize large groups with different personalities toward a common goal (Aaron Hall, 2023) and reduces ambiguity. For example, in a committee with faculty and senior-level administrators, the faculty members may be responsible for curriculum assessment and writing reports on student learning outcomes and the administrators charged with writing governance and fiscal responsibility standards.

Another strategy is to immediately develop a collaboration,

respect, and engagement culture among the group members to foster dialogue, open communication, and trust. This can be achieved through frequent meetings, workshops, and retreats where different groups share ideas and experiences. From professional experience, off-campus retreats seem to bring people together, providing them with an opportunity to escape their typical setting and use new places to energize and brainstorm. At off-campus locations, leaders can organize team-building activities to promote camaraderie and appreciation for each member's role and the expertise they bring to the group. By incorporating frequent opportunities for collaboration and engagement, accreditation liaisons can build trust and respect among the team. Trust is generally built on a foundation of honesty and transparency, while respect is earned by valuing the opinions of others. Both are critical to this process.

A third strategy is training. Initial training is vital to the success of groups with diverse perspectives to ensure that all members have the knowledge and skills necessary to contribute effectively to the accreditation process. This may include workshops on standards, academic writing, data collection and analysis, overcoming writing blocks, or other topics. By investing in the training, leaders can maximize time spent on different tasks and the quality of content provided to the accreditation process.

Lastly, in today's environment, one cannot forget the use of technology and its value for accessing relevant data, publishing necessary reports, and storing documents. Centralized systems can provide real-time updates and allow for simultaneous collaborative writing . Many colleges and universities already have systems such as SharePoint, Google Drive, or Microsoft Teams in place. The key is to find one that will help the accreditation liaison organize documents in a central location where team members can work effectively and collaboratively.

One key element that must not be overlooked in coordinating institutional groups is the power of establishing clear communication channels. As the leader, one must regularly set the tone and direction of how information will flow from and to the team. Firsthand experiences at the author's current institution revealed a similar process as the university underwent its 10-year reaffirmation process. Monthly meetings were established at the outset. As the teams moved closer to the finish line for submitting the report to the accrediting agency, bi-weekly meetings were set. Within the last three months, weekly meetings occurred as the team worked to finalize the document and review final edits. Throughout the process, periodic updates were also provided to the senior leadership team. As the process evolved, team members who did not usually work together daily grew closer. Over time, camaraderie grew noticeably as individuals gathered in smaller subgroups to brainstorm how to approach a particular standard.

Mitigating Challenges and Roadblocks

Collaboration inevitably brings its own challenges and roadblocks (Aaron Hall, 2023). These may include resistance to change, conflicting priorities, and time constraints. Recognizing and addressing these challenges when coordinating institutional groups can be critical to ensuring successful accreditation outcomes. Cotton et al. (2023) state that breaking down barriers begins with establishing connections across campus units. They note that interacting with units with differing goals and values is challenging and rewarding. The author of this chapter surmises that to be an effective accreditation liaison, it is essential to establish relationships with campus partners and colleagues to achieve continuing institutional accreditation. Cotton et al. (2023) also suggest a common strategy when working with campus members: finding a champion for your cause. This could be any influencer on campus. For example, faculty members of programs with discipline-specific accreditation may serve as influential figures in the institutional accreditation process. Similarly, academic program coordinators may also function as influential individuals, given their access to all departmental faculty members and their extensive knowledge of the curriculum.

Additional practical solutions that leaders may implement to mitigate challenges are shown in Exhibit 8.2.

Exhibit 8.2: Strategies for Mitigating Challenges and Roadblocks

Challenge or Roadblock	Mitigating Strategy to Overcome Barriers
Resistance to Change	Clarify the rationale for change and engage stakeholders in decision-making processes. Highlighting the positive impact of collaboration on institutional improvement and student success can help overcome resistance and build a shared sense of purpose.
Communication Barriers and Organizational Silos	In large groups with diverse members, effective communication can be challenging. Leaders must ensure clear, consistent, and transparent communication strategies accommodating different communication styles and preferences. Additionally, institutional groups operating in silos can impede collaboration. Breaking down these silos through interdepartmental communication, cross-functional teams, and shared goals can enhance collaboration and foster a culture of continuous improvement.
Differing Perspectives and Personalities	Large groups will inevitably have varying perspectives and personalities. To overcome this challenge, leaders are encouraged to acknowledge the strengths of different personalities and actively work towards creating a shared vision and common goals.

Conflicting Priorities	Recognize that different groups may have competing priorities and responsibilities. Effective conflict management strategies should be implemented to address and resolve conflicts within collaborative teams. This ensures that disagreements and differences of opinion do not hinder progress or damage relationships (Aaron Hall, 2023).
Trust	Trust within teams is crucial for effective collaboration. Establishing trust through transparency, reliability, and mutual respect helps to overcome challenges and build strong working relationships (Aaron Hall, 2023).
Insufficient Time and Resources	Accreditation processes can be time-consuming and require significant resources. Leaders should ensure institutional groups have the time and resources to engage in the accreditation process fully. This may involve prioritizing accreditation-related activities, reallocating resources, and providing necessary support. It is recommended that institutions begin preparing for the decennial review at least two to three years before submission.
Lack of Mechanisms for Ongoing Improvement	Emphasize the importance of areas of growth and improvement throughout the accreditation process. Encourage institutional groups to reflect on their practices, identify growth areas, and implement improvement strategies.

Concluding Thoughts

Achieving and maintaining accreditation is neither straightforward nor simple. Anyone involved at least minimally in the process understands that it requires significant time, resources, and coordination among various stakeholders within and outside the institution. No matter how one may try to craft the perfect pathway, it is highly likely that multiple challenges and roadblocks, such as changing standards and expectations, competing priorities and demands, limited resources and support, resistance to change, and communication gaps, will be experienced along the way. Therefore, accreditation requires effective leadership and management from the accreditation liaison, the primary contact between the institution and the accrediting agency. A liaison able to leverage multiple internal and stakeholders can benefit the process to a degree that cannot be overstated.

This chapter outlined critical strategies to guide new and experienced accreditation liaisons alike toward successful outcomes:

- Establishing clear and open communication lines with institutional groups. Communication is essential at all levels. Frequent status updates about the process are helpful as well. Also, conducting pulse checks to determine how team members are feeling helps to keep them engaged and alleviates confusion during the process.

- Defining clear roles and responsibilities at the outset. This is critical so all team members understand their roles, contributions, and deadlines.

- Providing necessary training and professional development opportunities for institutional groups involved in the accreditation process. Remember, not everyone knows the criteria and standards as well as the liaison does. Accreditation liaisons often live and breathe accreditation as their primary responsibility. Training team members equips them with the necessary knowledge, skills, and tools to effectively contribute to accreditation requirements and standards.

- Encouraging collaboration and forming cross-functional teams to leverage different institutional groups' collective expertise and experience. This provides added value by creating an environment of synergistic problem-solving and sharing of best practices.

If implemented fully, these strategies can help leaders and liaisons leverage institutional groups to create a consistent culture of continuous improvement and compliance with accreditation standards. Effective leaders understand the importance of collaboration in achieving organizational goals and recognize that cultivating a collaborative environment requires intentional effort (Aaron Hall, 2023). This process allows them to galvanize large groups with different personalities toward a common goal. By collaborating and leveraging these institutional groups, the accreditation liaison can enhance the quality and credibility of the self-study report, increase the engagement and buy-in of the campus community, mobilize the resources and support needed for the accreditation process, address the challenges and roadblocks that may arise along the way, and foster a shared vision and commitment for institutional improvement. Through effective leadership, institutions can achieve successful accreditation outcomes and propel themselves toward excellence in education and a culture of continuous improvement.

Discussion Questions

The following thought-provoking questions will allow liaisons to facilitate further exploration and engagement among accreditation stakeholders. These questions can be used for individual reflection or group discussions.

1. What mechanisms can ensure effective communication and collaboration between different institutional groups?

2. What is the most effective process for hosting regular and meaningful meetings for different groups?

3. Which online platforms are easy and efficient to use for institutional accreditation?

4. What strategies can leaders use to overcome resistance to change?

5. In what ways can institutions foster a culture of transparency and collaboration between faculty, students, and accreditation bodies to enhance the quality and accountability of our academic programs?

6. How can technology be leveraged to enhance collaboration and information sharing among institutional groups?

7. How can the involvement of external stakeholders be maximized to enhance the accreditation process and strengthen institutional partnerships?

8. What type of training is most important, and who will conduct that training?

9. How can institutions align their institutional goals with the evolving standards of accreditation to ensure continuous improvement and excellence in education?

10. How will senior-level administrators be kept abreast of the outcomes?

Discover and Propel

To illustrate the power of collaborating and leveraging institutional groups, let's consider a case study of how one institution of higher education brought together large groups and produced a successful 10-year reaffirmation of institutional accreditation.

Case Study

Friends of the Sky University embarked on a comprehensive accreditation process to reaffirm its institutional accreditation for another 10 years. First, the accreditation liaison engaged multiple institutional groups in the process. Two essential committees were formed: (1) an internal Accreditation Leadership Committee, comprised of a handful of representatives from key institutional groups with experience in institutional or discipline-specific accreditation, student teaching, institutional effectiveness, and administration; and (2) a lead writers committee that included faculty, administration, staff, and students. A technology team was also added to support compiling the report using a central repository. The Accreditation Leadership Committee was responsible for overseeing the entire accreditation process, ensuring alignment with accreditation standards and requirements, and coordinating the efforts of different groups. To organize large groups with different personalities towards a common goal, the Accreditation Leadership Committee initially focused on defining roles and responsibilities for each institutional group.

Second, the accreditation liaison provided comprehensive training on the standards required for reaffirmation to enhance understanding of those standards; the data collection and analysis methods needed to demonstrate compliance; and strategic planning, mission, and vision. This investment in professional development empowered each group to contribute effectively to the accreditation process. Third, the liaison gave specific tasks, timelines, and expectations to each group with the belief that this level of specificity and clarity would help mitigate any confusion and aid in developing a sense of shared responsibility and accountability.

Next, the accreditation liaison at Friends of the Sky University implemented a technology platform as a central repository for all accreditation-related documents, reports, and data to facilitate collaboration and information sharing. This platform allowed institutional groups to access and contribute to the accreditation process in a transparent and streamlined manner. Face-to-face and virtual meetings facilitated group communication and collaboration. Each group submitted regular progress reports highlighting achievements, challenges, and proposed solutions. These reports served as a basis for meaningful dialogue and informed potential solutions to fill any identified gaps.

The institution's commitment to collaboration and leveraging institutional groups paid off when Friends of the Sky University received a successful 10-year reaffirmation of institutional accreditation. The collaborative efforts of faculty, administration, staff, and students resulted in a comprehensive self-study report demonstrating the institution's commitment to continuous improvement and compliance with accreditation standards. This case study exemplifies how collaboration and effective liaison roles can lead to successful accreditation outcomes. By leveraging multiple institutional groups' expertise and diverse ideas, higher education leaders can foster a culture of continuous improvement and ensure institutional compliance with accreditation standards.

References

American Library Association. (2017, July 18). *The role of accreditation. Education & Careers.* https://www.ala.org/educationcareers/accreditedprograms/standards/ap3/overview/roleofaccreditation

Accreditation Commission for Community and Junior Colleges (ACCJC). (2023, April). *Accreditation Liaison Officer (ALO) Guide*. ACCJC - Accrediting Commission for Community and Junior Colleges. https://accjc.org/wp-content/uploads/Accreditation-Liaison-Officer-ALO-Guide.pdf

Brown, W. (2024). *How can executive coaching improve facilitation techniques*. Coaching4Companies. https://coaching4companies.com/how-can-executive-coaching-improve-facilitation-techniques/

Castañer, X., & Oliveira, N. (2020). Collaboration, coordination, and cooperation among organizations: Establishing the distinctive meanings of these terms through a systematic literature review. *Journal of Management, 46*(6), 965-1001. https://doi.org/10.1177/0149206320901565

Cotton, P. B., Atwood, T. P., & DeRose, C. (2023, October). Connecting fragmented support on campus: Growing research data services programs through collaboration data services programs. https://digitalcommons.du.edu/cgi/viewcontent.cgi?article=1496&context=collaborativelibrarianship.

Eaton, J. S. (2012). Accreditation in the United States: A historical perspective. In J. C. Smart (Ed.), *Higher education: Handbook of theory and research* (Vol. 27, pp. 363-383). Springer.

Filerman, Gary L. The influence of policy objectives on professional education and accreditation: The case of hospital accreditation." *Journal of Health Administration Education* (Fall 1984): 409-418.

Hall, A. (2023, August 14). *The power of collaboration: Building trust, overcoming challenges, and effective techniques*. aaronhall.com.

https://aaronhall.com/insights/the-power-of-collaboration-building-trust-overcoming-challenges-and-effective-techniques/

Southern Association of Colleges and Schools Commission on Colleges. (2020, September). *The Accreditation Liaison.* www.sacscoc.org. https://sacscoc.org/app/uploads/2019/08/accreditation-liaison.pdf

University of California, San Francisco Center for the Health Professions Task Force on Accreditation of Health Professions Education. (1999, June). Strategies for Change and Improvement. Healthforce Center at UCSF. https://healthforce.ucsf.edu/sites/healthforce.ucsf.edu/files/publication-pdf/10.%201999-06_Strategies_for_Change_and_Improvement_The_Report_of_the_Task_Force_on_Accreditation_of_Health_Professions_Education.pdf

U.S. Department of Education. (2021, March 28). *Federal financial aid: Institutional eligibility.* FSA Partner Connect. https://fsapartners.ed.gov/knowledge-center/fsa-handbook/2020-2021/vol2/ch1-institutional-eligibility

Webb, J. (2017, December 17). *How to manage and influence internal stakeholders.* Forbes. https://www.forbes.com/sites/jwebb/2017/12/27/how-to-manage-and-influence-internal-stakeholders/?sh=3fd688d271a7

PART IV

INFORMATION SPARKS

This section focuses on the importance of data-driven and information-driven decision-making during the accreditation process. Readers gain a deep understanding of how to collect, evaluate, and utilize data and information in accreditation reviews. The section offers practical tips on how institutions can use data and information to drive evidence-based improvements.

Chapter 9

Leading with Data and Collaborating with Academics on Assessment

**Terra Schehr and
Janet Simon Schreck**

*This chapter focuses on institutional research offices using data to
proactively partner with faculty and academic administrators to
improve student learning through deep assessment.*

Nearly every American institution of higher education routinely
engages in some type of accreditation activity. To cynics, assessment
and accreditation can be perceived as a game of "gotcha" looking only
for shortcomings, flaws, and problems or as top-down meaningless
mandates that waste precious resources. However, higher education
accreditation activities and milestones, such as self-study, provide
an opportunity to demonstrate and affirm the accomplishments

of the faculty and campus community in fulfilling the educational mission of their institutions. When executed authentically and rigorously, accreditation also provides an evaluative tool that colleges and universities can use to identify areas for improvement and gaps in capacity that, if filled, will enhance the student educational experience, and improve teaching and learning.

Most, if not all, of the data included in a self-study for accreditation should pre-exist the self-study process, and much of that data will reside in the office(s) of institutional research/effectiveness (IR/IE). This chapter focuses on IR/IE offices using data to proactively partner with faculty and academic administrators to advance the academic missions of their institutions.

At the end of each section is a set of considerations highlighting a few key factors for very small (or micro-) institutions and very large (often decentralized) institutions. While most colleges and universities fall between these two categories, the thoughts are provided to draw attention to the lack of a single solution, highlighting that approaches to using data and collaboration are most constructive when authentic to institutional contexts.

The Role of Institutional Research and Effectiveness Offices in Accreditation

Faculty and others outside of institutional research/effectiveness may not be aware that IR is a professional field that was formally recognized in 1965 by the establishment of the Association for Institutional Research. The functions of IR vary across institutions but generally include collecting and managing data about the college or university, fulfilling reporting requests both mandatory (e.g., federal IPEDS reporting) and non-mandatory (e.g., guidebook surveys), and conducting business analytics to develop and disseminate information used by campus decision-makers. In the most recent survey of institutional research offices, nearly two-thirds of their efforts focused on these areas (Jones, Keller, & Raza, 2022).

Institutional effectiveness, which makes up much of the balance of the efforts in IR/IE offices, has grown in response to calls from accreditors and others to provide evidence of institutional quality and effectiveness in delivering on the educational mission and student outcomes that colleges and universities advertise and promise. At its most basic level, institutional effectiveness seeks to answer two important questions: (1) Is the institution fulfilling its mission? (2) How do we know? This work involves engagement in strategic planning, analysis of resource allocation, effectiveness studies, assessment of student learning, program review, and accreditation.

A survey of IR/IE leaders showed that most have significant involvement in accreditation. Most IR/IE leaders identified the following eight tasks related to accreditation as being part of their job responsibilities to a *high* or *very high* degree (Lillibridge, Swing, Jones & Ross, 2016)[4]

- Acts as an expert on regional accreditation activities

- Ensures annual reports are prepared for regional accreditor

- Manages documentation of regional accreditation efforts

- Provides data support for regional accreditation

- Provides information for various accreditation initiatives

- Reports data for regional accreditation

- Understands regional accreditation processes

- Understands specialized accreditation process

---

4   At the time of the study, the common terminology was "regional" and "specialized" accreditors/accreditation, with "regional" being the primary accreditation that reviews the entire institution and not for subunits within institutions (colleges, schools, programs, etc.). Currently, "regional" and "institutional" accreditation is often used interchangeably.

Because of their access to–and deep understanding of–their institution's data on operations and student success, as well as their expertise in institutional and specialized accreditation processes, IR/IE leaders should be included in self-study teams. Additionally, the IR/IE office(s) should be prepared to be "on call" during site visits to respond to data-related questions from peer reviewers that may not be addressed in the self-study or any supplemental materials that have been made available to the review team. Considerations for very small and very large institutions are shown in Exhibit 9.1.

Exhibit 9.1: Accreditation Involvement Considerations for IR/IE Offices at Small and Large Institutions

Considerations	
Very Small Institutions	**Very Large Institutions**
• May not have a formal IR/IE office; IR responsibilities may be distributed among staff who have other job responsibilities. • Clarity of who is responsible for IR/IE functions must be communicated regularly (e.g., who is responsible for reporting data to federal agencies on behalf of the college, who is responsible for making decisions about survey participation). • Coordination to ensure the use of common data sources, definitions, and data analytics is important.	• May have central IR/IE as well as IR/IE offices located in colleges/schools; sometimes the data stewards in colleges/schools are not called IR/IE. • Relationship-building between the Accreditation Liaison Officer (ALO) and the college-/school-based data stewards is critical. • Clarity of central IR/IE roles and functions vs. those of the college-/school-based data stewards must be communicated regularly (e.g., only central IR/IE reports data to federal agencies on behalf of the university). • Coordination to ensure the use of common data sources, definitions, and data analytics is important.

Expected Use of Data in Accreditation

The data expectations for accreditation self-studies, supplemental materials, and other required reports will vary based on the accrediting organization and its standards. For institutional accreditation, the metrics found on the IPEDS Data Feedback Report are a good baseline. Those include data on admissions, student enrollment, retention, graduation rates, and completions; tuition/ fees, financial aid, and average net price; core revenues, expenses, and endowment assets; staffing and student-to-faculty ratio; and library collections.

These IR data, which are direct and indirect indicators of an institution's and/or unit's health and capacity to deliver on its educational mission, should be shown as a trend of at least the most recent five years. As much as possible, the data included in institutional self-studies should be the same as those reported to IPEDS, which are publicly available. Discrepancies between what a peer reviewer sees in the self-study and what they find in IPEDS data may raise questions about the integrity of the self-study.

Specialized accreditations generally require similar metrics for disciplinary units but often seek additional data supporting the various accreditation standards, such as specific faculty-to-student ratios, student performance on standardized summative exams, as well as faculty credentials and research. Those self-studies should also include carefully curated institutional data so that the accreditor and, if applicable, peer reviewers can understand the larger context in which the disciplinary unit exists.

Since IPEDS data are primarily at the level of the institution and not the unit, most data for a specialized self-study cannot be sourced from IPEDS. To maintain comparability, however, the data sources and definitions used for producing disciplinary self-studies should, as much as possible, be the same as those used for an institution's externally mandated reporting. Thus, the IR/IE office plays a critical role in producing and reviewing data utilized in both institutional and specialized accreditation, particularly in instances where data are maintained at the department/school/discipline level.

It is best practice for institutional leadership, including the provost and deans, to review these metrics and associated trends annually so that quick course corrections can be made and resources reallocated as needed. However, the self-study for accreditation provides a cyclical opportunity for reflection on the 8- to 10-year trajectory of the university/college/unit and may reveal areas of concern that should be addressed to maintain institutional health and meet accreditation standards. Further, since self-study documents are typically informed by and made available to the campus community, accreditation provides an opportunity for more perspectives to be invited into that reflective process.

Accreditation self-studies and associated supplemental materials will also require data trends related to institutional priorities (e.g., time-to-degree for PhD students or change in percentage of first-generation, Pell-eligible undergraduate students over time), assessment of institutional strategic planning, and student acquisition of learning outcomes. This is discussed further in the following section, and shown in Exhibit 9.2. The important thing to note here is that while the IR/IE office may have some data on these key activities, much of the related evidence is likely distributed across the institution; amassing that information and making meaning of it can be a time-consuming task that should be a high priority for the self-study steering committee.

Combining Data and Assessment

Data, assessment, review, evaluation . . . what are the differences? Data are facts, statistics, and/or evidence; they are the "what" of an inquiry. Data are used in accreditation to support or provide evidence of assertions made by the institution. Assessment, review, and

Exhibit 9.2: Data Considerations for IR/IE Offices at Small and Large Institutions

Considerations	
Very Small Institutions	Very Large Institutions
If trend data are displayed as %s, small changes in the numbers of students, staff, faculty, etc. may appear as large fluctuations; consideration should be given to providing data as counts instead of, or in addition to, %s.	• The amount of data available can be overwhelming. Data used in accreditation self-studies and reporting should be carefully curated and depicted to tell a meaningful story. • Determining which trends to depict and at what levels (institution/school/program/ • undergraduate vs. graduate) is essential. For example, it may be necessary to depict retention, admission, and completion rates for all graduate students at the institutional level followed by breakdowns by school at the master's and doctoral levels. • Multiple data sources across an institution increase the risk of data errors and inconsistencies. Data should be carefully checked by IR/IE to ensure accuracy and consistency.

evaluation are processes that incorporate an analysis of data that helps answer ensuing questions—"So what? What do these data call for us to do?"

Using data and systematic ongoing assessment enables an institution to maximize its efficiency and effectiveness in the development and implementation of strategic plan(s) and the renewal and delivery of academic and co-curricular programs.

Until recently, institutional accreditors were generally interested in determining whether colleges and universities demonstrated an ongoing and sustained engagement with the *process* of assessment of student learning outcomes and institutional goals. The only exception concerned the assessment of general education learning outcomes for undergraduate students. Since each of the regional accreditors requires a coherent general education program for undergraduate students, and most require specific general education outcomes, they expected self-studies to include evidence of student achievement relative to those outcomes as well as improvement plans, if applicable.

Disciplinary accreditors, on the other hand, have typically been interested in both the process for ongoing assessment and the *product*—that is, seeing evidence that students are achieving program-level outcomes/standards for learning that the accrediting organization defines. It is important to note that in the past several years, many institutional accreditors have raised the stakes and begun to focus on both process *and* product, requiring institutions to provide evidence not only of student learning assessment at the course, program, school, and institutional levels across all student populations but also of how results of those assessments were used to improve the quality of education (also known as "closing the loop").

Assessment of Student Learning

Assessment of student learning takes place across multiple levels. Most faculty members are very familiar with the assessment of individual student learning in their courses. Not to be confused with grading (although the terms are often mistakenly used interchangeably), assessment of learning at the student level measures individual student attainment of knowledge, skills, and competencies. Formative assessment is an ongoing process as faculty identify student strengths and weaknesses and provide feedback to students to improve their learning. Summative assessment involves using evidence to demonstrate the attainment of key learning outcomes at the end of a course or program.

Frequently less familiar and more challenging to faculty is the assessment of student learning at the programmatic and institutional levels, which of course takes time, effort, and devoted resources. As seen in Exhibit 9.3, however, this process is as simple as answering three questions: (1) What are we trying to teach students? (2) How well are students learning? (3) How can we improve *(if needed)*?

Exhibit 9.3: Simple Learning Assessment Cycle

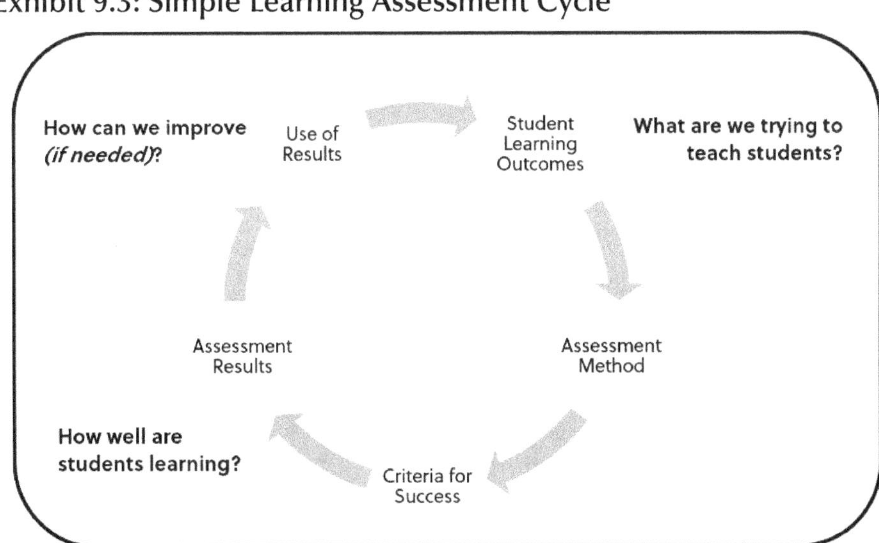

This model has the following advantages:

- It simplifies the language associated with learning assessment. Faculty spend years becoming expert in the terminology of their specific discipline(s); becoming "conversant" in another lexicon—or two, if one includes the language of accreditation—can be a barrier to faculty engagement in learning assessment outside of the context of their courses.

- The simplified language often elucidates for faculty that learning assessment is already happening—so the associated labor is not wholly new. What is required is an integration of what faculty are already doing with the institution's need to demonstrate that they consistently examine and improve the effectiveness of their programs and student learning.

- To the extent that assessment (although perhaps unnamed and unsystematic) is already happening based on faculties' lived experiences with their students, systematic assessment is likely to reveal that students are achieving outcomes at the expected level and no changes to andragogy/pedagogy and/or curriculum are warranted. This is made explicit in the final of the three questions in the simple assessment cycle. On the other hand, faculty have a keen interest in helping their students succeed and should welcome the opportunity to learn, through research, if their students as a group are falling short of expectations and improvements are needed.

To build a culture of learning assessment, the learning assessment process must be *meaningful* to faculty and their students; *feasible* given all the other elements of faculty and student labor; and *authentic* to the individual disciplines. For example, it is unlikely that authentic assessment in an art history program will look the same as authentic assessment in an engineering program. Following the model in Exhibit 9.4 empowers faculty to identify critical learning outcomes; work together to assess student performance; and collaborate on interpreting and using the results of the assessment. In doing so, faculty become more deeply engaged in the holistic creation, evaluation, and improvement of the curriculum instead of remaining solely focused on the individual courses they teach.

What are we trying to teach students? Faculty and others determine the extent to which students as a group achieve expected levels of knowledge; competency with the skills; and engagement with the dispositions identified as being critical to the institution (institutional learning outcomes), discipline (program learning outcomes), and courses (course learning outcomes). As shown in Exhibit 9.4, these outcomes should be rooted in an institution's mission/vision.

Exhibit 9.4: Relationship of Student Learning Outcomes at Various

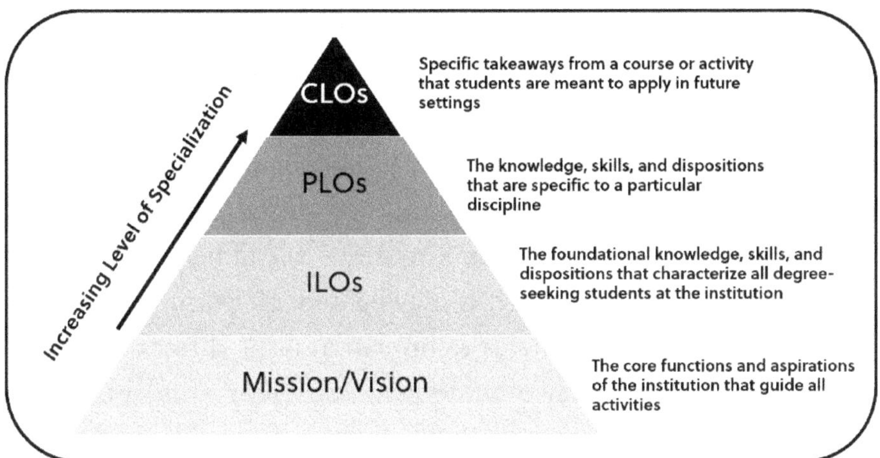

Levels

How well are students learning? Many methods can be used in learning assessment, ranging from surveys and standardized tests to observations or portfolio reviews. While it is not possible to give full treatment to all assessment methods in this chapter, some aspects of collecting evidence of student learning are important to note.

Evidence of learning can be direct or indirect. Direct evidence results from student work that produces observable behaviors or products. Faculty conduct direct assessments of student learning throughout a course by such means as exams, presentations, portfolios, and capstone projects. Direct assessments are often meaningful and feasible as they are typically created by faculty and embedded directly into coursework. However, not all learning can be measured directly; for example, dispositional outcomes can be difficult to observe using direct evidence.

Indirect evidence, commonly gathered on surveys of students and alumni, involves perceptions of personal abilities and/or whether learning has occurred. While very useful, indirect evidence alone is generally insufficient for summative assessment of cognitive or skills-based outcomes. Most robust learning assessment practices incorporate both direct and indirect assessment of student learning to offer a more comprehensive view of student achievement.

One commonly overlooked benefit of indirect evidence is that it can help prioritize future assessment efforts. Because of the labor involved in using direct evidence in learning assessment, it is typically not possible to assess all of a program's or institution's outcomes every year. Indirect evidence, such as student exit surveys or employer surveys, can serve an important role in helping faculty identify outcomes where students may be underperforming that should be prioritized for further examination using direct evidence. For example, if on a survey of undergraduate seniors, students report little growth in their intercultural competence, faculty may prioritize assessing that outcome using direct evidence in order to identify the specific criteria or aspects of that outcome that are in most need of improvement.

As shown in Exhibit 9.3, part of answering the question "How well are students learning?" is identifying the criteria for success before reviewing the results. In other words, what would the data look like if the course, program, and/or institutional outcomes were being met in substantial measure so that one could be assured that the curriculum was functioning as intended? For example, a business school's/program's criterion for success for one or more learning outcomes might be that at least 75% of students pass the uniform certified public accountant (CPA) exam. A music composition program, on the other hand, might establish its criterion for success for one or more learning outcomes as having 80% of senior students rated as "meeting" or "exceeding" expectations on elements of a rubric developed by faculty to be used during a juried performance.

How can we improve (if needed)? Often referred to as "closing the loop," this final step in the assessment process is the most important. If faculty and others involved in the delivery of education do not engage in conversations about assessment results and how they might inform decisions about changes to curriculum and/or andragogy/pedagogy, then all the labor invested in the prior steps of the assessment process was for naught. Examples of closing the loop might include reordering a curricular sequence to improve introductory/foundational knowledge and skills; introducing a new capstone or summative project to provide additional opportunity for application and synthesis; or increasing student support via additional teaching assistants, tutors, and/or online resources. Once a change is introduced for the purpose of improvement, the assessment cycle begins again to evaluate the effectiveness of that change.

To the extent that assessment of learning is viewed as top-down, prompted by external mandates, and lacking value to faculty and students (the proverbial "stick"), promoting meaningful, feasible, and authentic assessment (the proverbial "carrot") can build toward an institutional culture of assessment for the benefit of faculty and students that is more than episodic. Whether or not a college or university is successful in changing the narrative around assessment from being a "stick" to being a "carrot," the reality is that institutions need to be able to meaningfully demonstrate to their stakeholders and accrediting organizations that students are learning what is intended to be taught. The only way to accomplish this is through robust learning assessment. Considerations about student learning at small and large institutions are displayed in Exhibit 9.5.

Exhibit 9.5 Student Learning Considerations at Small and Large Institutions

Considerations	
Very Small Institutions	Very Large Institutions
• Some best practices of student learning assessment are impractical or impossible to follow at small institutions. For example, a best practice is that the faculty member(s) reviewing student work be "blind" to whose work they are assessing; this is not always possible at small institutions. • Faculty should be encouraged to focus on what would be feasible and provide meaningful information. In this case, they would be urged to follow rubrics and scoring guides closely to reduce any bias that may occur because of knowing the student(s) who produced the evidence.	• Central collection and analysis of learning assessment is often not feasible in very large institutions. Central functions should focus on providing policies, technology, and other resources that support best practices in learning assessment across the institution. • Some institutional assessment data, such as data associated with general education outcomes, are often collected, and analyzed centrally. • Even though disciplinary learning assessment practices may vary widely, it is often helpful to convene a university-wide learning assessment committee or advisory body. Such bodies promote collaboration, consistency, and sharing of best practices. • The inclusion of IR/IE leadership on university-wide learning assessment committees is highly encouraged as these individuals are frequently the stewards of indirect assessment data and evidence.

Collaboration Between Institutional Research and Academic Leaders

Although often separated by organizational structures, reporting lines, and delineations such as "staff" vs. "faculty," collaboration between the IR/IE and academic affairs areas of colleges and universities is key to demonstrating ongoing assessment of institutional mission, operations, and student learning. As mentioned previously, the IR/IE office likely collects and analyzes indirect evidence of student learning from surveys of students and alumni. It also routinely collects and reports indirect measures of educational quality such as retention and graduation rates, time to degree, average class size, student-to-faculty ratios, and student accomplishments. The collection and analysis of direct evidence of student learning is largely the responsibility of faculty and student affairs professionals who develop, oversee, and deliver the curriculum and co-curriculum.

On a survey of IR/IE leaders, 40 to 59% indicated that "Act[ing] as a campus resource in assessment and quality improvement processes" is part of their job responsibilities to a *high* or *very high* degree, and even more stated the same about their role in "Foster[ing] the value of the integration of institutional research and assessment" (Lillibridge, Swing, Jones & Ross, 2016). Additionally, over three-quarters of IR leaders report directly to the president/chief executive officer or provost/chief administrative officer (18% and 58%, respectively), and 35% serve as their institution's accreditation liaison officer (Jones, Keller & Raza, 2022). With these facts in mind, one would think that collaboration between IR and academic leadership and faculty would be easy to establish, but truly constructive collaboration on assessment requires proactivity and intentionality from both IR and academic leaders.

Depending on the maturity and role of the IR office and underlying data structures, institutions may find themselves data rich but information poor. This is often the case when data collected for external reporting and routine assessment are either not routinely communicated to academic affairs leadership and/or faculty or not shared in a format that meaningfully answers the questions "How well are we doing what we intended to do?" and "How can we improve?" All too frequently, assessment data and evidence remain siloed in IR/IE offices, academic departments, student affairs offices, etc.

IR/IE leaders can play a role in making a cultural shift in this area by synthesizing the data that they have and regularly presenting their findings to academic leaders in ways that are accurate, timely, and useful. For IR/IE leaders to be able to be proactive in this way, they need to know what issues are being considered by decision-makers (see Exhibit 9.6). Therefore, academic leaders need to regularly include their IR/IE leaders in key meetings and discussions. IR/IE leaders also need exposure to faculty so they can build social capital and be viewed as trusted partners when opportunities arise for the IR/IE functions to leverage their expertise in assessment to guide faculty in best practices. The following are concrete ways of establishing pathways for collaboration:

- IR/IE can develop a standard set of institutional strategic indicators in collaboration with campus leadership and then presents those data to key governance groups on an annual basis for discussion.

- IR/IE can regularly present results from surveys of students about their academic experiences and acquisition of institutional and general education learning outcomes to academic and faculty leadership.

- Academic affairs leaders can routinely require the incorporation of said data and outcomes in department and academic program evaluations that require recommendations that "close the loop."

Exhibit 9.6: Data Synthesis Considerations at Small and Large Institutions

Considerations	
Very Small Institutions	Very Large Institutions
• The number of requests for data/analysis that come from across all areas of a small institution may exceed the capacity of the IR/IE professionals (in terms of human resources, data systems, and skill sets). • Academic leadership should help their IR/IE staff prioritize requests, and common ad-hoc requests should be built into routine reporting.	• In most larger institutions, the IR/IE lead is a vice-president–/provost-level position. Ideally, the lead IR/IE should have at least a dotted reporting line to the provost to promote collaboration. • It is easy for data to become siloed in very large institutions. For that reason, both IR/IE and academic affairs leadership must intentionally seek to formally and informally connect functional areas. For example, the central IR/IE office can convene a monthly meeting of school-based data stewards so that information is shared and redundancies are reduced. • Faculty are often more familiar with their school-based IR/IE leads and data stewards than they are with central IR/IE leads. It is important for central IR/IE to proactively communicate with faculty regarding their role in assessment and the types of data they collect and analyze routinely as well as what sorts of data/analyses they can supply on demand.

- IR/IE leader can join an academic affairs or faculty member as co-chair of an institutional assessment committee.

- Academic affairs leaders can seek expertise of IR/IE leads to gather and analyze data regarding a new institutional initiative or area of inquiry.

Discussion Questions

1. Does your institution invest in the professional development of the IR/IE staff to expand their knowledge base and capability to work with faculty and academic leaders on deep assessment?

2. Does your institution have a standing assessment committee? Is an IR/IE leader a member or co-lead of that committee?

3. Are IR/IE leaders included in regular meetings with academic and faculty leaders so they are known and trusted colleagues when opportunities for collaboration arise?

4. Are faculty at your institution familiar with data routinely collected, analyzed, and reported by IR/IE? Do they utilize the data to assess the effectiveness of their courses, programs, and schools/colleges?

5. Does your institution have a culture of assessment, or do most people (faculty, staff, leaders) view assessment only as an accreditation requirement? If you do have a culture of assessment, what factors have contributed to its success? If you don't have a culture of assessment, what are three actions that might promote improvement in that area?

Discover and Propel

- Organizations

  - ◊ Association for the Assessment of Learning in Higher Education (AALHE) https://www.aalhe.org/

  - ◊ Association for Institutional Research (AIR) https://www.airweb.org/

- Conferences

  - ◊ Association for the Assessment of Learning in Higher Education (AALHE) Annual Conference https://www.aalhe.org/annual-conference (Typically in early June)

  - ◊ AAC&U Conference on General Education, Pedagogy, and Assessment https://www.aacu.org/event/conference-on-general-education-pedagogy-and-assessment (Typically in early April)

- Resources

  - ◊ AAC&U's Valid Assessment of Learning in Undergraduate Education (VALUE) Initiative https://www.aacu.org/initiatives-2/value

References

Jones, D., Keller, C., & Raza, Z. (2022). *2021 AIR national survey of IR offices: Executive leadership for the data and analytics function.* Association for Institutional Research. www.airweb.org/NationalSurvey

Lillibridge, F., Swing, R., Jones, D. & Ross, L. (2016). *Defining Institutional Research: Findings from a national study of IR work tasks. A focus on senior IR/IE leaders.* Association for Institutional Research. https://www.airweb.org/docs/default-source/documents-for-pages/reports-and-publications/defining-ir.pdf?sfvrsn=e98d04d8_2%22

Chapter 10

Delivering the Facts for Progress

Bethany L. Miller, Nancy D. Floyd and Marjorie A. Trueblood

Leadership roles require tough conversations to be had and difficult things that need to be said. Many times the data show decisions that can no longer be avoided. This chapter discusses and provides examples of delivering hard-to-hear and overlooked information so that resources are not wasted. Developing the skillset of having difficult but constructive conversations is critical for accreditation success.

In higher education, particularly in a C-suite supportive function such as institutional effectiveness or decision support, we often find ourselves in the unenviable position of having to deliver bad news, or a complex story that can be read as bad news, to high-level decision-makers and leaders. But by using the techniques of cognitive and social psychology and effective messaging, we can do a lot to ensure that the news comes with appropriate context and accompanying resources to set the stage for necessary conversation and planning for next steps. To do this, we need to fully assess the situation for the group dynamics of the individuals (hereafter "the team") receiving the news, the tenor of the atmosphere in which it will be released, and the amount of risk to the organization that the new information poses

In ideal circumstances, you are delivering such a message in a mature, professional setting, with all the necessary contextualizing information and sufficient time to control both how and to whom the news will be disseminated, the team working alongside the communications professionals of your organization, as well as the uppermost administrative functions. These conditions rarely occur even in the somewhat slow-moving world of higher education. In this chapter, we will note some of the more important aspects of these situations, help you prioritize the parts of the problem over which you have some control, and give some best practices for navigation.

Having Tough Conversations for Progress

When a difficult conversation is happening in a professional setting, particularly in one where the culture is collectivist in nature as in higher education, the team to whom it is assigned must function as a machine with individual parts that can only work in tandem with the others. If Person A is bringing structure to the table, and Person B is bringing good communication practice, and Person C is reminding the group of the external forces and context, and Person D is working to keep emotions from fraying, and Person E is laying out the logical path forward, then each of those people must feel free to perform their roles with a minimum level of shared trust and common understanding of the problem.

Without shared trust or some carefully agreed-upon ground rules, this conversation cannot go forward. At the very minimum, a period of establishing that trust may be required before the real conversation can proceed productively and the team can go to work. Tasks may be shared by multiple people or may be…but they all must be commonly understood to be necessary to move the conversation itself forward, independent of, and to some extent protected from, the needs or interests of the individuals team members. The makeup of those necessary tasks will of course vary from situation to situation, but the absence of one needed piece will prevent the process from ever even getting started.

That environment of shared trust can be ruptured very quickly, so each team member must do their share to sustain it, even if just for the short period of time required to move the conversation forward and reach a decision or a consensus. That often means giving each other a cover of privacy——an assurance that details of the conversation will not be repeated outside the process until it is over. It almost certainly means taking a beat before you speak up abruptly for "your side" of the issue. It may mean allowing for points of view within the conversation that the individual team members do not agree with outside of it, and understanding that everyone is putting the needs of the team ahead of the needs of each individual. It may also mean suspending the need to have a clear picture of the decision or consensus before you have the conversation, and having faith that the team will arrive at the best decision, even if it's not the one each person would have arrived at by themselves. As these are all difficult communication tactics for even well-trained, seasoned communicators, it helps to talk about laying this foundation deliberately before the actual conversation takes place.

According to Kezar (2018), people within higher education may be resistant to change for three reasons: (1) perceived lack of effort, (2) lack of trust in the decision-maker/leader, and (3) encounters with previous failed attempts at change. While resistance may be one reaction to receiving bad news, deliverers of bad news often misread questions asked for clarification or deeper understanding as resistance. These very questions may be a team's first attempt at establishing the environment in which to most effectively marshal the needed response.

Bad News as Grief

Applying the conceptual framework developed by Elisabeth Kubler-Ross and David Kessler (2005), Exhibit 10.1 below posits a decision-making environment that blends several of the five stages of grief (anger, resistance (denial), individual acceptance) with other reactions that a team engaged in decision-making might experience (fear, fatigue, curiosity). The team responds to the initial shock of receiving bad news much as an individual might (resource gathering, attempts to assign blame, identifying allies).

Although bad news can trigger something like a grieving process, the recipient doesn't need to go through all five stages of grief, which is why only some of them are represented in the model. Within higher education contexts, it is important to remember that different people will have different reactions. To keep everyone moving toward the desired outcomes, the team member responsible for shared communication should be aware of the myriad reactions they could encounter.

Possible reactions include:

- **Anger** According to *Harvard Business Review* (2019), people will want to shoot the messenger regardless of who is to blame for the bad news. Expect anger, and prepare to defuse the communication environment.

- **Grief** We often take for granted the grief that people experience in the face of change good or bad. Some within higher education are still grieving processes, projects, and people from years ago.

- **Fear** Upon learning bad news, some people will question what it means for them in particular.

Exhibit 10.1: Team/News Processing Cycle

- **Fatigue** Many people who have been in higher education for some time have encountered bad news and crises before, and so additional bad news can induce fatigue. Sometimes this is read as apathy, but it is more likely self-protection.

- **Curiosity** Some people hear bad news and want to know more. They ask questions to gain a deeper understanding, but their curiosity could be interpreted as resistance or undermining what is shared. It is important for the communicator not to become defensive.

- **Individual Understanding** There will be some on your campus who will understand the what, the why, and the how of your bad news, but it is essential not to conflate their understanding with everyone else's. Repeating key points and maintaining ongoing dialogue will help promote more widespread and shared understanding, the community.

- **Opportunism** There may be a few who see the bad news or the change that it brings as an opportunity to elevate themselves or their own agendas. Ensure that these individuals are promoting efforts that support the direction and vision that you are heading toward as a group and community

In the outermost level of the model are the desired outcomes—shared understanding, trust, resilience, clarity of the path forward—that have to be arrived at, really earned, through what comes next for the team. In order to reach those desired outcomes, team members must go through a middle stage together, working in tandem. This involves discussing everyone's understanding of the problem and the challenges in both the close and the longer range environments that affect it, identifying the key pieces of information that must be marshaled to respond, engaging in productive communication that keeps all the team members and important external constituencies involved in the work, and above all else clearly staking out the direction in which everyone will be moving together.

Key to this process is the use of data and information. But people—the people who make up teams can be notoriously bad at using data to move from indecision to decision, and the reasons they may navigate this path less than optimally have to do with their psychology. It is helpful to review the potential pitfalls that people may encounter while doing this work.

When People Avoid the Facts

Humans consume information in many ways, conscious and unconscious, but they do so in a constantly evolving environment. Logical reasoning is only one of a wide set of tools they muster to make decisions about what information to follow, trust, discard, or actively combat. We understand many of the phenomena at work but are just beginning to learn how to predict and plan for the way individuals use information in decision-making.

People avoid facts because facts don't correspond to their

understanding of a situation. We know that high-temperature records have been broken for several successive years now, and yet when we go outside and experience a temperate or lovely day, we forget the similar but slightly less temperate days of years past. Sometimes the variations are so slight or far from our recent memories that we don't have the cognitive capacity to correct any assumptions or differences in the current experience from past experiences that may vary slightly, nor the ability to walk the tiny change forward to finish the logical outcome. It is crucially important in the team response model described above to ensure that the entire team has access to the same information, that that information is all as clear as possible, and that team members have the opportunity to safely discuss misconceptions about the data in front of them.

People avoid facts that directly contradict the beliefs they hold dear. George Lakoff (Climate One, 2015) describes the process whereby people being presented with new information must decide in a split second which "frame" to store it in. If a person does not have a frame for a given piece of information because it does not fit with their overall worldview, they do not even acknowledge the new information as a fact; it just leaves their perception altogether. This is why attempting to persuade people by "delivering the facts" is often unsuccessful; if the audience is not prepared to receive certain facts, it is as if there was no effort made at all. Team members need an atmosphere of shared trust to have active conversations about how new information and data fit with their preconceived notions, and if necessary to have those schemas challenged with the space to reconfigure their own schemas (Bormanaki & Khoshal, 2017).

People avoid facts that may predispose them to actions they find objectionable. The team must know from the outset whether the handling of the particular piece of bad news they are managing absolutely must or must not include certain courses of action so that they do not expend team time or resources on those solutions. However, in order to fully create an environment of shared trust, higher education leaders must understand and allow for consideration of solutions that sound impossible at first. Otherwise team members will feel, understandably, that they are just carrying out a preconceived plan of action.

People will naturally prioritize facts that meet with their existing self-perceptions or identities (Rathje, 2018) and must be actively trained not to do so. But this can be altered by the community in which they receive the information. When people have more positive interactions than negative and are allowed to build an atmosphere of goodwill, they are more receptive to factual information that does not meet with their preconceived notions.

In the Difficult Conversations Lab at Columbia University (Ripley, 2019), researchers found that pairs of people previously selected for being on opposite sides of a highly contentious subject, when asked to reach even minimal consensus, were more successful than already exists or may be developed between potential team members negative emotions returned. The key to these interactions was complexity—not reducing the topic to a pat, simplistic either/or. The researchers went on to design an array of prompts for these conversations—some simplified and binary, others laying out all the factors at play. They found that pairs who were prepared for the conversation with more complex information functioned better at productive communication about the issue, even if they could not reach a consensus.

This can be mirrored in the team communication environment. It is important that the information being received or used by team members be clear and available to everyone, but if it is complex and does not meet with team members' preconceived notions or self-perceptions, both time and an atmosphere of shared trust can allow for cycling between emotions while team members attempt to make sense of bad news. The situation can be explored in all its complexity in an open environment where communicators trust each other, with trusted leadership guiding them in building consensus. Aspects of potential action plans can be laid out, discussed, and included or excluded.

How to Assess the Environment for Promoting Positive Communication

Performing this assessment should involve a multi-pronged approach; the team members' individual communication styles as well as the context of the situation and the quality of the resources and materials available should be examined. Here are a few models of both personal communication assessment and project material assessment to consider:

Emerson (2022) describes communication styles that are adopted by individuals. It is important to know which style each team member favors to optimize the way information is presented to them and discussed within the team. Direct communicators like hard facts and avoid ambiguous or emotional expression; they will be most receptive to a factual argument but can be intolerant of the environment needed to produce consensus.

Functional communicators are similar to direct communicators in that they like facts and dislike ambiguity. However, they are as focused on the process of the team as they are on the content of the work. These people are often considering multiple paths to an outcome simultaneously and appreciate the enjoy working independently. They will ask a lot of questions to help form their process and will need room to do so; these people may struggle if they feel that the leader's concept of the larger picture is not fully thought out.

Harmonizers or collaborative communicators prioritize finding a solution that meets the needs of other team members over the content or process of the task at hand. They will need guidance to stay on track and will not "buy into" the task until they feel that their perspective has been fully heard. Because they prioritize the needs of people, harmonizers can help to create the environment in which complex information can be processed in a consensus-making exercise. However, they will need leaders to provide structure and goals.

Influencers combine this focus on interpersonal communication with a broad ability to envision possibilities and an almost magnetic capacity for leadership. These people can be equally effective in logical and emotional processing but lack the ability to keep up with small details and so may need help managing more practical aspects of team activities. Influencers can make great team consensus leaders when paired with more practical types.

Communication is an often overlooked aspect of project management and one of the most difficult tools to wield well Moreover, in a high pressure situation, there frequently is not adequate time to fully vet data and resources. Engaging in these evaluations as a key part of project management can help ensure that the attention to communication across all aspects of the process are more than adequate to keep team members, leaders, and the community in the loop.

Strategies and Skills for Delivering Difficult Information Productively

This depends somewhat on the nature of the impact of the information; if it is an individual, personal impact such as someone losing a job or not being considered for a promotion, the way to deliver that information is understandably different than telling a group that they didn't meet their quarterly goals or a hoped-for benchmark. The approach must thus be tailored to the situation and the individuals impacted, as shown in Exhibit 10.2.

Exhibit 10.2: Strategies for Delivering Difficult Information
Productively

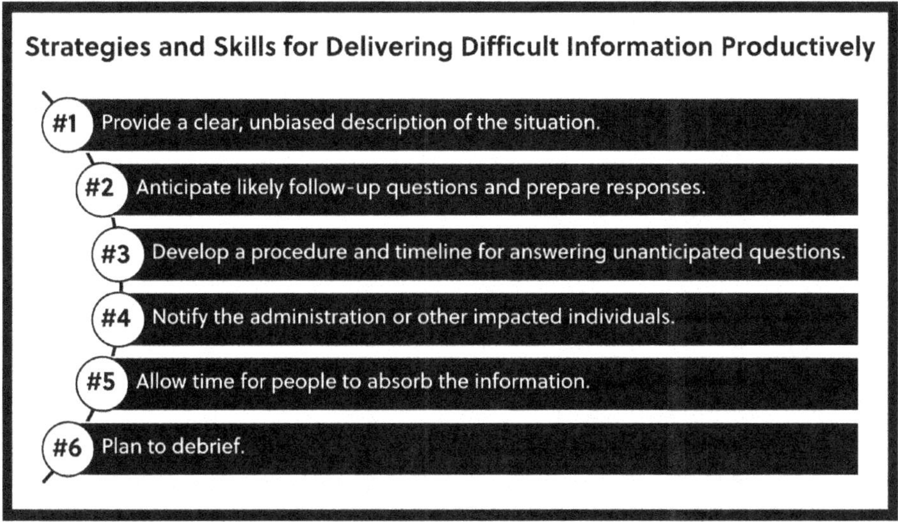

That said, the following are helpful when delivering almost any bad news: (1) a clear, unbiased description of the situation and what happened; (2) anticipation of likely follow-up questions and preparation of responses ; (3) a procedure for gathering answers to unanticipated follow-up questions and a timeframe for getting those answered; (4) notification of the administration or other impacted individuals so that they are aware the news is being delivered and can be briefed on the outcome in as timely a manner as possible; (5) a period of time allow people to absorb the information and clarity as to what actions if any should come next; and (6) structured plans for the team to reassemble and engage in debriefing, conversation. and comparison for consensus.

It is also useful to think about the communication styles of the persons receiving the news to develop responses to follow-up questions accordingly. If a person prefers factual information, have a table and accompanying graph ready. If someone needs to filter and slice the data to understand fully, design a quick dashboard or make a dataset available to that person (securely, using good practice) to conduct their own investigation. If a person prefers a story, have a narrative available (accompanied by data, ideally) so that they can start to meaning-make in their own way. If a person needs to process information via emotions, have a safe environment in which to do this without judgment or prioritization of one style over another. Follow good practice for knowing your audience and speaking to them in the most effective way both as individuals and as a group.

Part of the establishment of shared trust is to build an environment in which to deliver both good and bad news and to react to both in an appropriate and communally productive manner. For this to happen, participants need to understand that the person who coordinated the team and the establishment of this environment is prioritizing not only their needs and the psychological safety of each individual but also that of the group itself as a separate entity. They should be prepared to help sustain the environment of shared trust and extend that safe space to each other as well as to the person who set it up.

Concluding Thoughts

When a higher education institution must respond to less-than-ideal news to further its goals, a quick high-level triage must be done. First, identify the team to formulate a plan of action and respond to the situation. In so doing, pay careful attention to the level of trust that already exists or may be developed between potential team members.

Next, carefully establish the intended goal, being sure to allow team members to contribute They may be more aware than upper leadership of the situation on the ground, and their expertise must be acknowledged and put to the task.

As the team gathers additional information to respond to the news, keep their cognitive and communication styles front of mind. Pay attention to individual members' preferred roles and the way they will coordinate these roles to respond as a team.

Identify areas where team members may fall into the patterns that prevent humans from responding effectively to facts, and do what is possible to counteract those tendencies. Do not allow biased behaviors to derail the team's work.

Discussion Questions

1. Have there been previous situations where I have had to deliver bad news? What did I learn from that experience? How is this situation similar or different? Can what I learned from that experience be applied to this new situation? If so, in what ways?

2. What is the most important information to share, and what details will my audience care about? How will I frame the information in a way that can be received? Do I have the necessary resources (e.g., graphs, data, external correspondence) to help me share this information?

3. What is my communication approach? Do I enlist others with different communication styles to assist me in delivering the message to the most stakeholders possible? Recognizing that communication is a multidirectional process, do I create space for my audience to respond, comment, or question?

4. Recognizing that the receipt of bad news can be emotional and illogical, have I considered what the emotional fallout of delivering this information may be? Have I prepared myself emotionally to engage in this conversation?

5. Have I considered a follow-up communication to reassert what was shared and create space for emerging information and ideas from the collective?

6. Am I proactively building a culture of positive morale and trust so that in the future when bad news is delivered it will

be received in a better way? In what ways do I do this?

7. How can I quickly assess the communication styles of the people who are receiving the information? What can I use to quickly gauge the degree of trust among them?

References

Alavi, M., & Leidner, D. E. (2001). Knowledge management and knowledge management systems: Conceptual foundations and research issues. *MIS Quarterly, 25*(1), 107–136.https://doi.org/10.2307/3250961

Bormanaki, H. B. and Khoshal, Y. (2017) The role of equilibration in Piaget's theory of cognitive development and its implication for receptive skills: A theoretical study. *Journal of Language Teaching and Research 8*(5)http://dx.doi.org/10.17507/jltr.0805.22

Buckman, R. (1984). Breaking bad news: Why is it still so difficult? *British Medical Journal 288,*https://www.ncbi.nlm.nih.gov/pmc/articles/PMC1441225/pdf/bmjcred00502-0041.pdf

Climate One (2015, May 12). *Why don't facts move people?* [Video]. YouTube.https://youtu.be/w2u06oCxfv8?si=KLyoL0sA8aA-u1Kj

Emerson, M. S. (2022, February). Is your workplace communication style as effective as it could be? *Harvard Division of Continuing Education* Feb 04, 2022.https://professional.dce.harvard.edu/blog/is-your-workplace-communication-style-as-effective-as-it-could-be/

Kübler-Ross, E., Kessler, D. (2005). On grief and grieving: Finding the meaning of grief through the five stages of loss. United Kingdom: Scribner.

Rathje, S. (2018, October). Why people ignore facts. *Psychology Today.*https://www.psychologytoday.com/us/blog/words-matter/201810/why-people-ignore-facts

Ripley, A. (2019, January). Complicating the narratives. *Solutions Journalism*.https://thewholestory.solutionsjournalism.org/complicating-the-narratives-b91ea06ddf63

Holzmann, V. & Globerson, S. (2003). Evaluating communication effectiveness in a project environment. Paper presented at PMI® Global Congress 2003—EMEA, The Hague, South Holland, The Netherlands. Newtown Square, PA: Project Management Institute.

Chapter 11

Trusted Data Sources to Demonstrate Accreditation Compliance

Jessica M. Shedd

This chapter focuses on using existing national and state data to help institutions better understand their own placement and achievements within higher education and then share the results in the accreditation report. Overlooked and underutilized datasets will be shared along with institutional examples of using the data.

For both institutional and programmatic accreditation processes, the institution must successfully make its case for compliance with each of the agency's standards. Though each accrediting agency establishes its own standards of academic quality, these standards address similar facets of institutions and educational programs, including student achievement and outcomes, curriculum, program length and objectives, faculty size and qualifications, student and academic support services, facilities and environment, and financial capacity (CHEA, 2006). Further, a common goal of all accrediting agencies is to "create a culture of continuous improvement of academic quality at colleges and universities and stimulate a general raising of standards among educational institutions" (Hegji, 2020, p.2).

To commit to continuous improvement, an institution must understand its own strengths and weaknesses within higher education. To do so, it needs valid and reliable data. In some cases, a college or university may only be concerned with its own performance and changes in that performance over time; in other cases, putting those data in a broader context of similar institutions, or higher education as a whole, can be extremely informative. If an institution fully understands its strengths and weaknesses, where improvements have been made and where they have not, as well as its position within higher education, it already has a rich resource to draw from for an accreditation report.

One of the strongest means of demonstrating compliance with an accrediting standard is with data. However, not all data hold equal value or weight with reviewers. It is critical to rely on trusted and well-respected data sources, allowing reviewers to focus on the narrative communicated with the data as opposed to the quality of the data itself. This chapter reviews a number of trusted higher education data sources that address areas of focus for accreditors— government data collections, voluntary data collections often affiliated with professional and trade associations, and vendor-created sources. Given the varied missions of colleges and universities, not all data sources are applicable to all institutions; however, this chapter aims to provide potential data sources for the wide spectrum of higher education.

Publicly Available Data

Postsecondary education institutions dedicate a significant amount of human, intellectual, and financial resources to comply with federal data reporting requirements for participation in Title IV Federal Financial Aid programs. Completing the U.S. Department of Education's annual Integrated Postsecondary Education Data System (IPEDS) data collection is alone estimated to take, on average, between 4 and 5 weeks per year for 4-year institutions and approximately 3 ½ weeks for 2-year institutions, and this is only one of many annual data reporting requirements from the federal government (NCES, 2022). In addition, public institutions are required to report to their state agencies annually. However, one benefit of all this time and effort is that the government agencies then make those data available to the institutions for their own benchmarking and analysis, allowing them to better understand their strengths and weaknesses and progress being made.

Trusted, Complete Coverage, at No Cost

Federal datasets are widely trusted third-party data sources and thus carry a credibility that is especially valuable. One reason for this is that these data collections and administrative data systems share common, vetted, and agreed-upon definitions of key terms across the industry. In many cases, these definitions are long-standing over many decades. In fact, the definitions have been so widely adopted by the industry that they are relied upon by many other collectors of postsecondary education data beyond the federal government.

In the case of IPEDS, appropriate definitions for terms are discussed and debated in the industry through several processes. A peer review process, known as the IPEDS Technical Review Panel (TRP) process, brings together representatives from all sectors of the higher education community and is designed to promote the quality, comparability, and utility of postsecondary data and information. After a convening of the TRP, a summary is posted publicly, and stakeholders are given 60 days to provide comments. Further, in order to continue to collect data, all federal data collections must undergo the Office of Management and Budget's Paperwork Reduction Act cyclical clearance process for information collections. Typically involving two formal public comment periods that require response by the agency applying for clearance, this process provides ample opportunity for the vetting of any collection items and definitions of terms.

Federal datasets are also trusted sources because of the rigorous data quality checks that are built into the data collection and review process. For example, data may be flagged for being invalid or outside of an expected range and then reviewed by subject matter experts, after which the institution may be contacted for an explanation. The thorough quality-control processes involved in a statistical agency's release of final data make federal datasets widely accepted and trusted resources.

Perhaps the largest benefit of federal datasets is that colleges and universities are mandated to report in order to receive federal dollars, whether that be through federal financial aid programs or support for research. This highly motivates institutions to comply and results in near-perfect response rates. Though incredibly valuable for understanding higher education as a whole, for individual institutions this is uniquely advantageous for benchmarking against similar institutions, known as peers. Moreover, many federal datasets are long-standing and so can provide trend data on a wide variety of topics relevant to the accreditation process.

Lastly, the public availability of federal datasets is of enormous value to institutions. Having access to well-respected, complete, and trusted data resources at no cost is ideal for institutional researchers and accreditation professionals. Exhibit 11.1 details the higher education data sources provided by two federal agencies, the U.S.

Department of Education and the National Science Foundation. These data sources alone touch upon many of the areas evaluated for accreditation purposes.

Exhibit 11.1: Federal Government Data Sources

Source Office/Center	Data Collection or Resource	Accreditation Area
U.S. Department of Education		
National Center for Education Statistics	IPEDS Fall Enrollment Completions Graduation Rates, Graduation Rates 200% Outcome Measures	Student Achievement and Outcomes
	IPEDS Human Resources Fall Enrollment	Faculty Size
	IPEDS Academic Libraries	Academic Support
	IPEDS Finance	Financial Capacity Academic Support Student Services
Office of Postsecondary Education	Campus Safety and Security (as required by the Clery Act)	Facilities and Environment
Office of Federal Student Aid	Financial Responsibility Composite Score	Financial Capacity
Multiple Federal Offices/Centers	College Scorecard	Student Achievement and Outcomes
National Science Foundation		
National Center for Science and Engineering Statistics	Survey of Earned Doctorates	Student Achievement and Outcomes
	Higher Education Research & Development	Financial Capacity
	Survey of Science and Engineering Research Facilities	Facilities and Environment

Though not as ubiquitous as federal data collections such as IPEDS, state data collections go through similar processes and can also be of enormous value to institutions. In the past few decades, an increase in the number of states creating longitudinal data systems—following students from Pre-K to the workforce—has made these systems uniquely useful, particularly in the area of student achievement and outcomes across multiple institutions and even beyond graduation. Often relying on federal definitions where possible, state longitudinal data systems can also be of value to institutions that do not participate. For example, when appropriate, public institutions outside of the state may also find utility in a neighboring state's data system. As a result, there are several regional compacts that exist for exchanging data across neighboring states.

Two examples of long-standing regional compacts are the

Southern Regional Education Board (SREB) and the Western Interstate Commission for Higher Education (WICHE). Created to serve policymakers and institutions in their region, both organizations are well known and respected for producing national research as well as regular regional reports. For example, WICHE "Benchmarks" is a resource for student achievement data, and the factbook "Policy Indicators for Higher Education: WICHE States" provides data on both student achievement metrics and financial capacity. Colleges and universities can thus compare their performance to that of an aggregate of regional institutions.

However, every four years WICHE also produces "Knocking on the College Door," a detailed report on projections of the number of high-school graduates across the U.S., regions, and each state. These data can put institutional changes in enrollment in context. For example, an institution experiencing enrollment declines over the next decade may, in part, be explained by the declining birth rates following the Great Recession. Making a connection between an institution's unintentional enrollment decline and the decline in the number of eligible high school graduates tells a much fuller picture for a reviewer.

Similarly, the Southern Regional Education Board produces the "SREB Fact Book on Higher Education," which provides decades of national data on enrollment, degrees, faculty, and revenues and expenditures that are useful for context in student achievement, faculty, and financial capacity narratives. National data come from U.S. Department of Education's National Center for Education Statistics (NCES) and the U.S. Bureau of Labor Statistics, among other sources, while some sections rely on the SREB Data Exchange. As extracting raw data and conducting original analysis can be laborious, this factbook provides excellent ready-made metrics for use by institutions, including during accreditation.

Beyond Federal and State Agency Data Collections

Federal and state data collections hold a wealth of information, but they do not come close to covering all the areas that an institution should be evaluating for internal decision-making and improvement purposes and that will be necessary as part of the accreditation process. Because there is much written and much focus on student achievement data, this chapter and the examples presented herein are not directly related to student achievement but instead highlight other factors typically evaluated by an accrediting agency.

Trusted, No-Cost, but Incomplete Coverage

One of the most well-known of these nongovernmental sources is the Common Data Set (CDS), which is "a collection of standardized questions," often relying on established federal definitions. The template is created annually by the College Board in partnership with U.S. News & World Report and Peterson's and includes several measures of student achievement and outcomes also available in the resources discussed above, as well as others pertaining to academic and student support services and faculty. Unlike other data sources discussed in this chapter, though, the CDS is not a survey that institutions submit; it is a form that they voluntarily complete and make publicly available on their website. Therefore, the CDS can be more laborious to use than other data sources; analysts must go collect the forms for their peer institutions' websites, and since not all institutions participate, data may not be available for a particular peer. [5] However, there are pieces of data in the CDS that are not otherwise available and that can be of particular use for narratives related to size and quality of faculty.

---

5   The Institute for College Access's College Insight Tool displays IPEDS and
    CDS data for institutions that allows for easy viewing of select data from these
    two sources and beyond.

For example, on the CDS, institutions detail the number and percentage of instructional faculty with a terminal degree, which for some institution types may be one proxy for demonstrating faculty qualifications. In addition, institutions report class sizes for undergraduates, which for institution types that pride themselves on small classes may be a proxy for the appropriateness of the size of the faculty. A related measure, the student-to-faculty ratio, that is reported to IPEDS is also included on the CDS. An example, Exhibit 11.2 below, shows data for a small, liberal arts college being evaluated, 6 peer institutions, and an average across the peer institutions to demonstrate that the college is "in-line" with its peers on these measures. As shown, the institution has a relatively high percentage of class sizes below 20 students, a relatively low percentage of class sizes of 50 or more students, an about average student-to-faculty ratio, and an about average percentage of full-time faculty with a terminal degree in comparison to its peer institutions—all facts in support of a claim that the size of the faculty is appropriate in that it allows for class sizes that are, on average, smaller than its peers' and that its faculty are similarly academically qualified/credentialed as those at its peers. This is far more informative for a reviewer than comparisons of straight counts of faculty.

Notable Professional and Trade Association Surveys

Several higher education professional associations have a long history of conducting well-respected data collection processes and providing related benchmarking services to the institutions that submitted data. In many cases, these data offer an opportunity to demonstrate institutional progress and achievements in the particular areas of focus for accrediting agencies.

For example, the College and University Professional Association for Human Resources (CUPA-HR) conducts annual surveys of institutions' full-time faculty, including tenure status, rank, discipline,

Exhibit 11.2: Example Table on Appropriateness of Faculty Size and Qualifications

	% of Classes with Less Than 20 Students	% of Classes with 50 or More Students	Student-to-Faculty Ratio	% of Full-Time Faculty with a Terminal Degree
Peer Institution #1	59	11	10:1	93
Peer Institution #2	71	7	6:1	95
Peer Institution #3	69	8	6:1	97
Peer Institution #4	69	11	5:1	96
Peer Institution #5	63	8	8:1	96
Peer Institution #6	67	8	7:1	94
Peer Institution Average	67	9	7:1	95
Institution Under Review	65	5	8:1	96

salary, highest degree earned, and demographics, and then makes that data available to participating institutions. For an additional fee, these institutions can access a custom analysis tool that allows for more fine-tuned benchmarking reports. CUPA-HR's "signature" surveys are a "go-to" source for data on the higher education workforce and can be used for benchmarking related to size and composition of an institution's faculty and its appropriateness for the number of students served.

For those institutions that have an endowment, the National Association of College and University Business Officers (NACUBO) conducts an annual survey, the NACUBO-Commonfund Survey of Endowments. Each year, NACUBO makes several summary tables from the study publicly available. Most notably for accreditation purposes, the data detailing colleges' and universities' endowment market values per FTE student can be helpful when discussing financial resources available to the institution. For some metrics colleges and universities use in accreditation reports, it may be appropriate to consider a peer group of institutions with similar endowments per FTE as opposed to the institution's typical peer or aspirant institutions used.

Trusted, Incomplete Coverage, at a Cost

There are many examples of trusted and well-respected higher education datasets that only include member or participating institutions and that come at a price. These may be provided by vendors, service providers, and organizations specific to a survey administration.

Some financial management organizations, such as Moody's, offer benchmarking services. Moody's Municipal Financial Ratio Analysis (MFRA) is a tool that allows customers to evaluate their financial health through a variety of ratios and peer comparison data. Operating cash flow margin, monthly days cash on hand, and debt-to-cash-flow ratio are some indicators of an institution's financial health and capacity that are available through this tool. In addition, the capital-expenditures-to-operating-expenses ratio is an indicator of investment in capital projects that could be useful in discussions of facilities and environment. For example, an institution that is challenged by a lot of deferred maintenance may raise concerns with reviewers. However, these concerns could potentially be tempered by a capital-expenditures-to-operating-expenses ratio that has been increasing over the past several years, indicating that the institution is already working to address the problem.

Satisfaction and Experience Surveys

Though indirect measures of quality, satisfaction and experience surveys can be informative and actionable. Examples of surveys that can address aspects of student services, faculty, facilities and environment are shown in Exhibit 11.3; certain of these are discussed in more detail below. Though surveys can be cost prohibitive, it is important to note that they do not have to be administered on an annual basis to provide meaningful information. In fact, in many cases, institutions are unlikely to see any significant change in responses in just one year. If possible, colleges and universities should consider conducting a survey every other year, or even every third year, to measure progress.

Benchworks, as a partner of the Association of College and University Housing Officers – International (ACUHO-I), offers an annual survey of student experience and satisfaction with housing and residence life. The survey is mapped to ACUCO-I professional standards and the Council for the Advancement of Standards in Higher Education's (CAS) general learning outcomes, allowing institutions to identify areas of strength and weakness with ease. Through its interactive tool, participating colleges and universities can benchmark against other institutions regarding residence hall satisfaction, programming within residence halls, residence staff, and dining, among other measures. For residential institutions, these data can be tied directly to student services as well as facilities-and-environment–related narratives. For example, a university may have had low student satisfaction with interactions with residence hall staff in the past, overall, and compared to peer institutions participating in the survey. As a result, over the course of several years, the student affairs team provided additional training to residence hall staff to increase their knowledge of academic and student support services available and to improve capacity to interact with many different student personalities. Showing Benchworks data on this topic will demonstrate that the university noted a weakness, acted on that weakness by providing additional training, and continues to assess the area to see if improvements are being made. Even if the student satisfaction scores haven't increased over time, it is critical to be able to demonstrate that the institution is tracking its progress and reacting appropriately.

The Collaborative on Academic Careers in Higher Education's (COACHE) Faculty Job Satisfaction Survey—administered by Harvard's Graduate School of Education—provides detailed data on full-time faculty members' satisfaction with almost all aspects of the institution. For accreditation purposes, this can be valuable to address issues such as appropriate faculty size or facilities and environment. For example, the survey addresses satisfaction with teaching responsibilities as well as service and research responsibilities, if applicable. High satisfaction scores, on their own or comparatively, may be an indirect indicator that the size of the faculty is appropriate for the institution. Similarly, the survey asks about satisfaction with a variety of facilities, including the faculty member's office space, classrooms, and lab/research space (if applicable), which can be used to support narratives related to sufficient facilities. Though the Faculty Survey of Student Engagement (FSSE) and the Community College Faculty Survey of Student Engagement (CCFSSE) are designed to measure instructional staff expectations of, and actual experience with, undergraduate student engagement, they contain a handful of similar questions that can indirectly inform about classroom facilities and environment.

Concluding Thoughts

As demonstrated in this chapter, there are many data resources that focus on areas of evaluation by accreditors beyond student achievement and outcomes. Colleges and universities have a wealth of information available to them free of cost, as part of their institutional memberships to organizations and associations, and as part of large-scale satisfaction and experience survey administration.

Exhibit 11.3: Participation and Fee-for-Service Datasets

Source	Data Collection or Resource	Accreditation Area
National Community College Benchmark Project (NCCBP)	Enrollment Tracking Module	Student Achievement and Outcomes
	Workforce Training & Continuing Education	Student Achievement and Outcomes
	Student Services/Affairs	Academic Support
		Student Services
	Costs & Productivity	Financial Capacity
Benchworks	Housing & Residence Life Survey	Student Services
		Facilities and Environment
CUPA-HR	Faculty in Higher Education Survey	Faculty
COACHE	Faculty Job Satisfaction Survey	Faculty
		Facilities and Environment
University of Texas at Austin, College of Education	Community College Faculty Survey of Student Engagement (CCFSSE)	Faculty
Indiana University Center for Postsecondary Research	Faculty Survey of Student Engagement (FSSE)	Faculty
Moody's	Municipal Financial Ratio Analysis	Financial Capacity
		Facilities and Environment
NACUBO	NACUBO-Commonfund Endowment Survey	Financial Capacity

Discussion Questions

1. In what ways can trusted data sources support your institution in demonstrating compliance with accreditation standards and meeting accountability requirements?

2. What are some key indicators or metrics that you can track using trusted data sources to evaluate the institution's overall performance and progress?

3. How can the use of trusted data sources help senior leaders effectively communicate their institution's strengths and achievements to internal and external stakeholders?

4. How can trusted data sources assist senior leaders in assessing the effectiveness of various institutional programs and initiatives and identify areas for improvement?

5. How can benchmarking and regular analysis of data from trusted sources help inform strategic decision-making, planning, and resource allocation within your institution?

6. What are some challenges or considerations that senior leaders should keep in mind when utilizing data from trusted sources to inform decision-making processes?

7. How can faculty and student satisfaction data obtained from trusted sources guide your efforts in improving teaching and learning environments?

8. How can data on student outcomes and success rates, obtained from trusted sources, enable you to identify areas for improvement and implement evidence-based interventions?

9. Though incredibly valuable, an institution should not be held back by considering only external data collection metrics for

evaluating its performance. Creating its own metrics that are specifically meaningful to its unique goals is critical; the institution can then measure its progress by looking at its own performance over time. What metrics should institutions consider tracking internally?

Discover and Propel

Given the wide spectrum of areas covered by accreditation processes and the fact that institutions and academic programs are not all accredited by the same organization, there is one-stop resource for keeping up to date on potential changes and new data sources. However, it is critical to at least skim the headlines of both The Chronicle for Higher Education and Inside Higher Ed on a daily basis. This ensures familiarity with the broader higher education landscape, including emerging areas of interest or concern that may impact future data collections and/or accreditation standards.

Many higher education organizations provide email alerts or regular newsletters to ensure institutions are aware of happenings (e.g., proposed federal or state policy) that may impact them in the future. For example, newsletters from the American Association of Community Colleges (AACC), the American Association of State Colleges and Universities (AASCU), the Association of Public and Land-Grant Universities (APLU), the American Association of Universities (AAU), and the National Association of Independent Colleges and Universities (NAICU) can be incredibly valuable. These associations carefully follow proposed legislation and provide helpful, condensed explanations of what the legislation is and how it may impact their member institutions. Regional associations offer similar services; WICHE email alerts provide helpful news summaries that are valuable to those both in and outside of the region.

Participating in particular institutional consortium listservs and/

or discussion boards is extremely helpful as well. Though regionally focused, the Accreditation in Southern Higher Education (ACCSHE) listserv is one example, and much of the discussion is applicable to the other regions as well.

Beyond Federal and State Government Resources Discussed

- Benchworks: https://www.skyfactor.com/student/housing-residence-life/

- Campus Safety and Security: https://ope.ed.gov/campussafety/#/

- COACHE Faculty Job Satisfaction Survey: https://coache.gse.harvard.edu/faculty-job-satisfaction-survey

- College Insight: https://college-insight.org/

- Common Data Set (CDS): https://commondataset.org/

- Community College Faculty Survey of Student Engagement: https://www.ccsse.org/

- CUPA-HR Surveys: https://www.cupahr.org/surveys/cupa-hr-signature-surveys/

- Faculty Survey of Student Engagement: https://nsse.indiana.edu/fsse/

- Knocking at the College Door: https://knocking.wiche.edu/

- Moody's MFRA: https://www.moodysanalytics.com/product-list/mfra-municipal-financial-ratio-analysis

- NACUBO-Commonfund Study of Endowments: https://www.nacubo.org/Research/2020/Research-at-NACUBO

- SREB Factbook: https://www.sreb.org/fact-book-higher-education-0

- WICHE: https://www.wiche.edu/policy-research/data-resources/

References

Council for Higher Education Accreditation (CHEA) (2006). *Accrediting organizations in the United States: How do they operate to assure quality? [Fact sheet #5]*.https://www.chea.org/accrediting-organizations-us-how-do-they-operate-assure-quality

Hegji, Alexandra. (2020). An overview of accreditation of higher education in the United States (R43826). *Congressional Research Service*.https://crsreports.congress.gov/product/pdf/R/R43826/10

National Center for Education Statistics, U.S. Department of Education (2022). *Integrated Postsecondary Education Data System (IPEDS) 2022-23 through 2024-25*. OMB Control No: 1850-0582. Information Collection Request (ICR) Reference No: 202202-1850-008.https://surveys.nces.ed.gov/ipeds/public/institutional-burden

Chapter 12

Dashboards as Catalysts for Enrollment Success

Angela E. Henderson & Resche D. Hines

This chapter explores the strategic value of dashboards in enrollment management, highlighting the key features and benefits of a well-designed dashboard that can support leaders in identifying and addressing challenges, tracking progress, and making informed decisions to optimize enrollment outcomes while effectively communicating the results to accreditors.

This chapter begins with a general discussion of the expanding demand for accountability in enrollment management before moving on to explore specific accreditation requirements related to student achievement. With a focus on student outcome metrics commonly required by institutional accreditors, the chapter then examines how a college or university might develop and leverage a single dashboard for multiple purposes. The general benefits of dashboards, as well as tips for intentional design, are discussed as well.

Why Accreditors are Focusing More on Enrollment Management

As colleges and universities struggle with one-size-fits-all federal outcome metrics that often fail to reflect institutional nuances, expectations for extended transparency and data visibility continue to grow. These increased expectations, coupled with the enrollment decreases and diminished resources many institutions have experienced in recent years, present a widespread challenge in higher education.

As further proof of the increasing desire for greater institutional accountability and transparency, in 2023 Congress proposed the College Transparency Act to make more information available to stakeholders. This proposal centers on the development of a student-level data system designed to facilitate reporting of institutional metrics and to "accurately evaluate student enrollment patterns, progression, completion, and post collegiate outcomes, and higher education costs and financial aid" (H.R.2957, 2023). Although the idea of a student-level data system was initially proposed in 2004 and subsequently banned as part of the Higher Education Act reauthorization bill in 2005, its reemergence highlights the increasing pressure on institutions to demonstrate outcomes and financial responsibility (Laitinen & McCann, 2014, pp.7-9).

As Gardner (2023) noted in the article The ROI Riddle, "attempts to determine the value of a college degree or credential have led to a recent surge of legislative efforts at both the federal and state levels to improve the data available to students on postgraduation earnings" (para. 2). To ensure institutions are actively monitoring student outcomes, institutional accreditors are placing greater emphasis on evidence of student achievement and outcomes. In addition, many have specifically articulated an expectation that colleges and universities not only provide achievement data but also demonstrate that they are using those data in institutional planning and decision-making and disseminating them to wide audiences.

Perhaps unsurprisingly, a 2019 survey report by the Council for Higher Education Accreditors (CHEA) found that "most accrediting organizations reported making significant changes in their approaches to examining student achievement in the last five years" (p. 8). Institutional accreditors cited fostering transparency and responding to related changes in federal policy as reasons for making changes to standards and policies specifically related to student achievement (CHEA, 2019, p. 9).

Respondents indicated that the primary metrics used to demonstrate student achievement for institutional accreditors included graduation/completion rates (83%), retention rates (50%), certification/licensure rates (50%), and job placement rates (42%) (CHEA, 2019, p. 10). Retention and completion rates are well-established outcome metrics, and most colleges and universities have well-worn systems of reporting such as spreadsheets and local databases that provide high-level outcome information. Although such reports have been sufficient in addressing accreditation requirements, they have not allowed institutions to adequately and effectively support, monitor, and track the progress of all key student groups. Often student achievement metrics have been based on a narrow population such as first-time full-time undergraduate students. Institutions may have very limited systems, if any, to track other key groups such as transfers or readmitted, returning, non-traditional adult, work force, or graduate students. What institutions may not be considering is that as demand for data changes, so too must the scope and methods in which those data are presented and communicated.

Value of Dashboards Over Spreadsheets in Enrollment Management/ Accreditation

With the demand for student achievement and outcomes data rising, it is crucial for institutions to develop effective and efficient ways of providing that data to stakeholders. We've all heard the arguments for sticking with the tried-and-true static forms of reporting such as spreadsheets and pdf factbooks: lack of resources, stakeholders wedded to specific reports, users unwilling to learn a new system, etc. While these challenges may exist, a refusal to embrace new technologies and data sharing techniques can be detrimental to institutional decision-making, transparency, resource allocation, and growth.

Let's consider the amount of data required for demonstrating student achievement from an accreditation perspective. Colleges and universities may be asked to provide student completion rates by academic program for the last 10 years. Depending on the number of academic programs an institution has, this could result in a substantial spreadsheet. Now let's say an accreditor would like the data further disaggregated by student race/ethnicity and gender. Not only will the report grow even longer, but in all likelihood, additional resources will be required to include the new variables. Depending on resource availability, adding the additional variables may take some time. Once they are added to the report, they will need to be validated to ensure accuracy. Additional parameters may be needed, or definitions revised, resulting in the final report being further delayed. As this example illustrates, the time investment/resource cost of manual piecemeal updates can be significant.

Relying on static forms of reporting that may appear outdated can influence perception. Consider that the primary purpose of accreditation is to demonstrate that a college or university is meeting the needs of stakeholders effectively. Providing an 80-page downloadable report does not convey that the institution has prioritized the allocation of resources to innovation in planning and evaluation processes. Further, technological advances have created certain expectations in data users and reviewers. Few of us want to review an 80-page report when we are trying to locate a specific piece of information.

While many institutions have limited resources to devote to reconstructing reports and may not relish the idea of developing new systems with current resources, investing in automated reporting systems up front can only be beneficial in the long run. Given the data trends we've seen in the last few years, it seems unlikely that institutions will ever be asked to provide *less* data, so developing more efficient and effective automated means of communicating data will ultimately be advantageous.

Benefits of Dashboards

While interactive dashboards are not magic bullets, they do provide significant benefits over static reporting. They allow institutions to communicate key priorities clearly, make informed decisions, plan strategically, and use resources more efficiently. Further, dashboards are designed to be *shared*—their very purpose is to efficiently convey information to a shared audience to facilitate a shared understanding of their content. This makes them an ideal vehicle for responding to increased demands for institutional transparency.

Whereas static reports are too often designed for a specific topic or user, well-designed dashboards are created to reach a wider audience and facilitate the ability of users to address multiple and complex questions with a single interactive solution. This approach ensures multiple users can leverage the same information, have clarity on the question being addressed, and have a shared understanding of how the data are being defined to make decisions. Well-designed data systems such as dashboards facilitate data exploration and discussion; they do not aim to answer a single question. A well-designed dashboard allows multiple data points to be included without the need for additional resources and follow-up reports. This facilitates deeper exploration of data and allows institutions to respond to requests for additional information quickly.

The inherently interactive nature of dashboards fosters

engagement at a deeper level than static reports, encouraging exploration of data. Data come to life and are more digestible to a broad audience when presented in a clean, simple, visually appealing manner. Dataphobes who cringe at spreadsheets are often willing to engage with interactive data tools simply because they are less daunting than static pages of data, empowering end users . Such engagement fosters a shared understanding of key data metrics across the campus and promotes a sense of institutional transparency.

Intentional design and development of dashboards provides clarity and contextualization of key institutional data priorities. Dashboards allow colleges and universities to highlight what is important to them and to provide contextual information that is critical to understanding their unique data story. Such context is often missing from static reports and spreadsheets and even from federal data websites such as College Scorecard. Interactive solutions also allow institutions to have a comprehensive and holistic understanding of all their data. Specifically, such systems provide every stakeholder, from students to the board of trustees, with a key understanding of the patterns and shapes of the data—how data are aligned, the gaps in existing data, and how to pinpoint the exact data that are needed to broadly and narrowly support every key stakeholder an institution serves and engages.

When incorporated into an institution's website, dashboards make data accessible to a wider scope of potential students. Although information about schools is available on the College Scorecard and a number of other sites, Gardner (2023) found that "students who were most likely to act on Scorecard data were white and relatively affluent." He further noted that "students who could most benefit from newly available data on college outcomes often have the least access to it" (Gardner, 2023). Providing public access to dashboards that clearly demonstrate student outcomes not only facilitates accreditation but also allows prospective students access to information they likely may not find otherwise. Simply stated, this process facilitates greater data access and understanding of data.

Democratizing data through the development of interactive solutions such as dashboards in support of accreditation offers a unique opportunity for colleges and universities to integrate data structures and destroy data silos. Ordinary sticking points and ownership issues that tend to derail data development processes can often be forced aside during accreditation preparation, allowing institutions to leverage this opportunity to implement much-needed changes. Not only does this approach yield more accessible data, but it also enables colleges and universities to identify and resolve roadblocks that are preventing them from making informed decisions efficiently.

Student Achievement Accreditation Standards that Can be Supported by Dashboards

A single dashboard can be leveraged to meet multiple needs, reducing the production of duplicative reports or spreadsheets that contain similar data for different stakeholders. Exhibit 12.1 provides a summary of select student achievement standards of institutional accreditors. Also included are the federal Higher Education Opportunity Act (HEOA) requirements pertaining to disclosures of student achievement.

Exhibit 12.1: Summary of Select Student Achievement Standards by Accreditor & HEOA Requirements

	Requirement				
Accreditor	Retention Rate	Completion/ Graduation Rate	Employment/ Placement Rate	Demonstrate use of data for improvement	Publish outcomes data
HEOA	X	X	X		X
HLC	X	X		X	X
MSCHE	X	X	X	X	X
NECHE	X	X	X	X	X
NWCCU	X	X		X	X
SACS-COC	X	X	X	X	X
WASC-ACCJC		X	X	X	X
WASC-WSCUC	X	X		X	X

These standards might be addressed through development of a dashboard showcasing student enrollment, retention, graduation, and employment outcomes (Exhibit 12.2). Exhibit 12.2 and 12.3 show two separate views contained within a single dashboard. Exhibit 12.2 focuses on persistence and retention rates, while Exhibit 12.3 shows persistence, retention, and four- and six-year graduation rates. Note that the filters across the top of each page allow for disaggregation of the data by cohort term, race/ethnicity, gender, home region and state, housing status, first-term residence hall, and first-term college and major. With the click of a button, users can view outcomes data for any of the desired groups. This flexibility allows users not only to view outcomes data for the traditional disaggregation groups but also to select multiple characteristics (i.e., Hispanic females from Florida who majored in economics in their first term). In addition, such dashboards can be customized to track these metrics for all student groups and programs, including those that are not traditionally reported for accreditation, such as transfer, stop-out/readmitted, and graduate students. This empowers institutions to own and deeply know their data.

Exhibit 12.2: Example Persistence and Retention dashboard

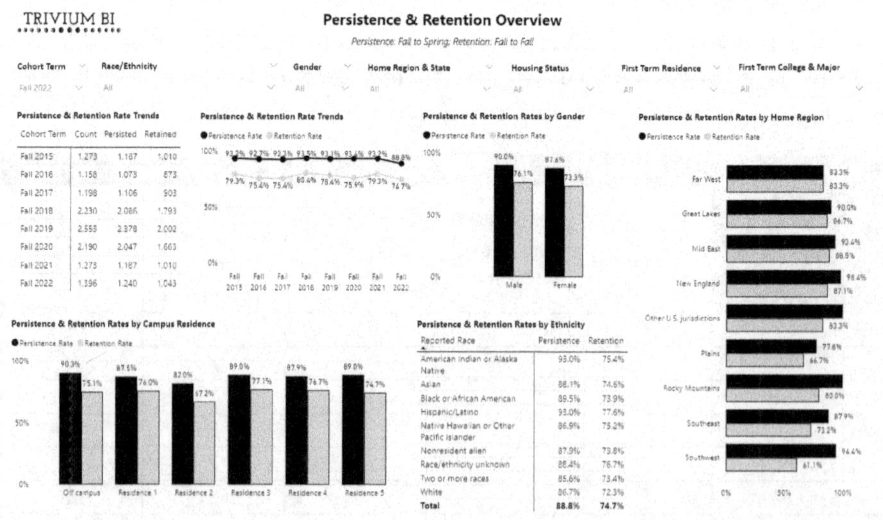

Exhibit 12.3 Example Persistence through Graduation dashboard

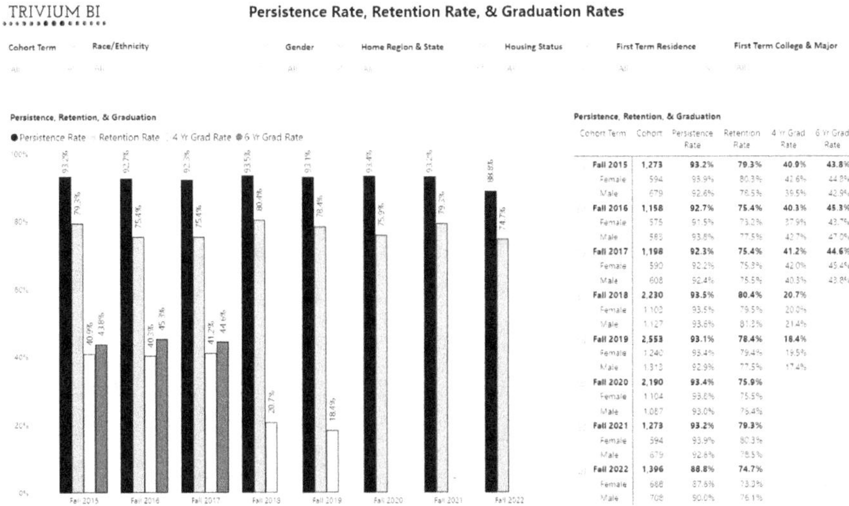

Cohort Term	Cohort	Persistence Rate	Retention Rate	4 Yr Grad Rate	6 Yr Grad Rate
Fall 2015	**1,273**	**93.2%**	**79.3%**	**40.9%**	**43.8%**
Female	594	93.9%	80.3%	42.6%	44.8%
Male	679	92.6%	78.5%	39.5%	42.9%
Fall 2016	**1,158**	**92.7%**	**75.4%**	**40.3%**	**45.3%**
Female	575	91.5%	73.2%	37.9%	43.7%
Male	583	93.8%	77.5%	42.7%	47.0%
Fall 2017	**1,198**	**92.3%**	**75.4%**	**41.2%**	**44.6%**
Female	590	92.2%	75.3%	42.0%	45.4%
Male	608	92.4%	75.5%	40.3%	43.8%
Fall 2018	**2,230**	**93.5%**	**80.4%**	**20.7%**	
Female	1,102	93.5%	79.5%	20.0%	
Male	1,127	93.6%	81.3%	21.4%	
Fall 2019	**2,553**	**93.1%**	**78.4%**	**18.4%**	
Female	1,240	93.4%	79.4%	19.5%	
Male	1,313	92.9%	77.5%	17.4%	
Fall 2020	**2,190**	**93.4%**	**75.9%**		
Female	1,104	93.8%	75.5%		
Male	1,087	93.0%	75.4%		
Fall 2021	**1,273**	**93.2%**	**79.3%**		
Female	594	93.9%	80.3%		
Male	679	92.6%	78.5%		
Fall 2022	**1,396**	**88.8%**	**74.7%**		
Female	688	87.6%	73.3%		
Male	708	90.0%	76.1%		

Given the commonality of expectations related to student achievement across accreditors, a well-designed dashboard could not only meet the needs of the current institutional accreditor but also be leveraged effectively if the institution were to change accreditors. As colleges and universities may now seek accreditation from institutional accreditors outside their historical region, intentionally developing dashboards that can be leveraged to meet requirements of multiple accreditors is advantageous.

As shown in Exhibit 12.1, many accreditor expect colleges and universities not only to provide student achievement data but also to analyze that data and use findings for targeted improvement. Dashboards provide a simple means of demonstrating data use by institutional decision-makers. Many dashboard software programs provide access reports, which can help demonstrate which areas across campus are using the information. To further encourage demonstrable data usage, an institution might require each academic program to interpret data from the dashboard as part of the program review process.

While some accreditors require colleges and universities to publish outcomes data, which could be interpreted in a variety of ways, some specify that the data must be published on the institution's website. Here, again, dashboards present an effective way to satisfy the requirements of accreditors. Not only are dashboards inherently more engaging, but they are more accessible to audiences outside of higher education. As one of the primary reasons for making outcomes data public is to enable prospective students to make informed decisions, it is essential to provide the information in a way that is understandable and engaging to that audience. If data reports are merely posted on a website without any context or definitions, they are essentially useless to the intended audience, resulting in wasted institutional resources and potentially lost enrollments.

The impact on potential students is further shown in the findings from EAB's 2023 Student Communication Preferences Survey, which collected data from over 20,000 high school students. Eighty-one percent of respondents agreed that "a poorly designed website will negatively affect my opinion of a college" and 67% indicated that they would "abandon college websites that are not user-friendly" (Donaher et al., 2023, p. 15). Respondents also indicated that the best representation of an institution's value is successful job placement upon graduation (Donaher et al., 2023, p. 20). All of these findings underscore the need for institutions to provide easily accessible outcomes data for prospective students.

Strategically Utilizing Accreditation Enrollment Standards and Policies

Well-designed interactive solutions such as dashboards help institutions not only to meet the needs of accreditors but also to create a data culture nested in data-driven and data-informed decision-making. Enrollment dashboards can be used for multiple purposes, from identifying high- and low-performing programs over time to facilitating intentional and strategic implementation of new programs in high-interest areas to understanding the timing and enrollment patterns of targeted groups of students. Incorporating data from external sources such as the National Student Clearinghouse and the Bureau of Labor Statistics (BLS) can further strengthen a college's or university's strategic enrollment and program planning. Data from the National Student Clearinghouse provides a greater understanding of enrollment patterns of graduates, non-returning students, and non-enrolled applicants. .

Integrating BLS data with enrollment data enables institutions not only to demonstrate that they are aligning programs to employment needs but also to strategically consider how best to prepare students for potential employment opportunities. Adjusting learning outcomes curriculum, and other elements to meet demands of growing occupations demonstrates intentional program development and timeliness. Similarly, job outlook data can be used to inform the need to create new programs in high-demand fields and restructure programs in low-demand fields. Specifically, leveraging these data empowers colleges, universities, students, and employers to make informed decisions. Understanding this broader data context is key to unlocking the full potential of education and employment in a rapidly changing world.

Retention and attrition dashboards can uncover roadblocks for specific populations or programs that may contribute to student loss. These dashboards facilitate an institution's journey of discovery, providing data needed to inform pivotal insights and to develop a culture grounded in clear data visibility. These interactive solutions help educational institutions see their enrollment, retention, and graduation data like never before, bringing clarity and alignment to the most complex datasets. Through the leveraging of interactive solutions, institutions can ensure that every data point related to student success is accessible and understandable. In addition, institutions gain the ability to uncover realities formerly obscured by the sheer amount of data in static reports. Understanding student

Exhibit 12.4: Key considerations for development of well-designed dashboards

Consideration	Guidance	Questions to ask	Tips
Audience	"Customize the visual portion of dashboard presentations to the needs of different audiences" (Shacklett, 2022).	Who is the primary audience?	Consider developing multiple views within a single dashboard to address different audience needs.
Focus	"When using a dashboard, it's important to ask the questions that will produce actionable results" (Shacklett, 2022).	What are the 3 questions the dashboard should answer?	Do not attempt to answer every question within a single dashboard.
Clarity	"We have a spouse rule—most of our partners do not work in higher ed, and if they can't look at the dashboard visualization and, within 30 seconds, have a general idea of what it tells us, we need to revamp it," Gold says (Mowreader, 2023).	Is the dashboard understandable to a wide range of users?	Label *everything*; avoid abbreviations. Do not make users guess. Use common visuals (bar and column charts, tables, etc.).

Simplicity	"Whatever the main storyline is, a well-designed dashboard with widgets that can access information on each story element helps to orchestrate the story of a problem and what will solve it. Storytelling is further enhanced by wise choices of visual artifacts (graphs, pie charts, etc.) that can visually summarize the issue for viewers" (Shacklett, 2022).	What is the best way to address your key focus with simple visuals?	Limit the number of visuals on the dashboard. Maintain white space.
Terminology	If developing a dashboard that will be made available to the general public, minimize use of higher ed terminology.	Do users share an understanding of the terms used in the dashboard? Would a prospective student or parent know what a term means?	Provide a glossary of definitions within the dashboard. Consider using more descriptive terms (e.g., "number of students enrolled in second fall" instead of "retained").
Data source		How will users know when the dashboard was last updated?	Provide the date of the last data update. Indicate the data sources used to populate the dashboard.

data aren't just about seeing it; it's about recognizing the patterns and structures that lie beneath the surface. Dashboards empower colleges and universities to uncover these insights, turning raw data into actionable knowledge that can improve student outcomes.

Finally, institutions gain the ability to effectively communicate data findings. It's not enough for an institution to have insights; these findings must be shared with key stakeholders, including academic leaders, faculty, students, administrators, and accreditors. Effective retention and attrition dashboards give educational entities the skills and tools to articulate their data findings persuasively, enabling them to guide and influence decision-makers and improve enrollment, retention, and graduation rates.

Indeed, a key benefit of student achievement dashboards is their ability to facilitate strategic communication. These dashboards allow institutions to develop expertise that ensures that messages related to enrollment, retention, and graduation strategies are clear, persuasive, impactful, and nested in data-informed decision-making. An additional benefit is institutional leadership development for leaders at all levels and specifically senior academic leaders. Such dashboards, when nested in a culture of data, can break down data silos and provide leaders at all levels of the institution with a lens to understand what questions are being asked and what data from across the campus can be leveraged for support in navigating the challenges of today's educational landscape. Dashboards help leaders to harness data for informed decision-making and strategic planning, ultimately contributing to improved student outcomes.

In summary, dashboards facilitate organizational learning within the realm of enrollment, retention, and graduation. They assist colleges and universities in answering their most critical questions by harnessing the power of data. Well-designed dashboards are not simply interactive tools; they provide a transformative experience that empowers educational institutions to thrive in a data-rich world and enhance enrollment, retention, and graduation success.

Concluding Thoughts

You may have noticed that throughout this chapter we have specified that institutional planning and decision-making can benefit from *well-designed* dashboards. It cannot be overstated that the key to leveraging dashboards for institutional gain is for the dashboards to be designed, developed, and disseminated with great intentionality. Poorly designed dashboards can result in user frustration and data distrust. If an institution is going to develop a dashboard, it must do so thoughtfully to avoid wasting resources. Exhibit 12.4 provides a quick list of key considerations and tips for developing an effective dashboard.

Discussion Questions

1. How is your institution currently collecting student achievement data? How might the current process be improved?

2. Does your institution make student achievement data available to the public?

3. Ask someone from outside of higher education to look at an institution's student outcome report and tell you what they see. Are you surprised by their interpretation? What does their reaction tell you?

4. Can you identify existing data gaps at your institution (e.g., no information available for achievement of specific student groups)? How might student outcomes be improved if such data were available?

Discover and Propel

- Power BI - https://powerbi.microsoft.com/en-us/learning/

  ◊ SQLBI - https://www.sqlbi.com/training/data-visualization/

  ◊ Visuals Reference - https://www.sqlbi.com/ref/power-bi-visuals-reference/

  ◊ Guy in a Cube - https://guyinacube.com/

- Tableau - https://www.tableau.com/learn

  ◊ Learning Center Resources - https://community.tableau.com/s/elearning

  ◊ DataCamp - https://www.datacamp.com/tutorial/tableau-tutorial-for-beginners

- Stephanie Evergreen - https://stephanieevergreen.com/

  ◊ https://stephanieevergreen.com/rate-your-visualization/

- The Big Book of Dashboards - https://bigbookofdashboards.com/index.html

- Storytelling with Data - https://www.storytellingwithdata.com/

References

Council for Higher Education Accreditation (CHEA). (2019, June 24). *Accreditation and student learning outcomes: Perspectives from accrediting organizations.* https://www.chea.org/accreditation-and-student-learning-outcomes-perspectives-accrediting-organizations

Donaher, L., Dodson, A., Koppenheffer, M. & Royall, P. (2023). *Recruiting 'Gen P' 6 insights into how the pandemic has altered college search behavior from EAB's survey of 20,000+ students.* https://pages.eab.com/Recruiting-Gen-P-InsightPaper.html

Gardner, L. (2023, May 17). The ROI riddle - the Chronicle of Higher Education. *The Chronicle of Higher Education.* https://www.chronicle.com/article/better-data-on-graduates-earnings-is-coming-soon-to-a-dashboard-near-you-will-it-make-a-difference

Higher Learning Commission (HLC). (2023, November). *Policy book.* https://download.hlcommission.org/policy/HLCPolicyBook_POL.pdf

H.R.2957 - 118th Congress (2023-2024): College transparency Act. (2023, April 27). https://www.congress.gov/bill/118th-congress/house-bill/2957/text

Laitinen, A., & McCann, C. (2014, March 11). College blackout. *New America.* https://www.newamerica.org/education-policy/policy-papers/college-blackout/

Middle States Commission on Higher Education (MSCHE). (2023). *Standards for accreditation and requirements of affiliation. 14th ed.* https://www.msche.org/standards/fourteenth-edition/

Mowreader, A. (2023, April 19). CSU success dashboard gives data visibility. *Inside Higher Education.* https://www.insidehighered.com/news/student-success/college-experience/2023/04/19/building-systemwide-data-dashboard

National Postsecondary Education Cooperative (NPEC). (2009). Information required to be disclosed under the higher education act of 1965: Suggestions for dissemination (Updated) (NPEC 2010831v2), prepared by Carol Fuller and Carlo Salerno, Coffey Consulting. Washington, DC. https://nces.ed.gov/pubs2010/2010831rev.pdf

New England Commission of Higher Education (NECHE). (2021). *Standards for accreditation.* https://www.neche.org/standards-for-accreditation/

Northwest Commission on Colleges and Universities (NWCCU). (2020). *NWCCU 2020 Standards for accreditation.* https://nwccu.org/accreditation/standards-policies/standards/

Shacklett, M. (2023, June 26). How to build a better data dashboard in higher education. *Technology Solutions That Drive Education.* https://edtechmagazine.com/higher/article/2022/03/how-build-better-data-dashboard-higher-education

Southern Association of Colleges and Schools Commission on Colleges (SACS-COC). (2020). *Resource manual for the principles of accreditation: Foundations for quality enhancement.* 3rd ed. https://sacscoc.org/app/uploads/2019/08/2018-POA-Resource-Manual.pdf

Western Association of Schools and Colleges Accrediting Commission for Community and Junior Colleges (WASC-ACCJC). (2023, September). *Accreditation handbook.* https://accjc.org/wp-content/uploads/Accreditation-Handbook.pdf

Western Association of Schools and Colleges Senior College & University Commission (WASC-WSCUC). (2023). *2023 handbook of accreditation.* https://www.wscuc.org/handbook2023/

Appendix: Select Student Achievement Standards

Accreditor	Standard
HEOA Disclosures	The disclosures include the information that **institutions are required to provide to the general public**, current students, current employees, prospective students, prospective employees, families of current or prospective students, or prospective student athletes and their parents, high school counselors, and coaches. Retention Rate Institutions must make available to current and prospective students the retention rate of certificate- or degree-seeking, first-time, undergraduate students as reported to IPEDS. Completion/ Graduation and Transfer-out Rates Each institution must annually make available to prospective and enrolled students the completion or graduation rate of certificate- or degree-seeking, first-time, fulltime, undergraduate students. The data are to be available by July 1 each year for the most recent cohort that has had 150 percent of normal time for completion by August 31 of the prior year. The HEOA (Sec. 488(a)(3)) added a provision requiring that the completion or graduation rates must be disaggregated by gender; major racial and ethnic subgroup (as defined in IPEDS); recipients of a Federal Pell Grant; recipients of a subsidized Stafford Loan who did not receive a Pell Grant; and students who did not receive either a Pell Grant or a subsidized Stafford Loan. Completion/ Graduation and Transfer-out Rates for Students Receiving Athletically Related Student Aid Placement in Employment Institutions must make available to current and prospective students' information regarding the placement in employment of, and types of employment obtained by, graduates of the institution's degree or certificate programs. Job Placement Rates An institution that advertises job placement rates as a means of recruiting students to enroll must make available to prospective students, at or before the time the prospective student applies for enrollment the most recent available data concerning employment statistics and graduation statistics; any other information necessary to substantiate the truthfulness of the advertisements; and relevant state licensing requirements of the state in which the institution is located for any job for which the course of instruction is designed to prepare students. (NPEC 2009 • A.23-A26)

HLC	4.C. The institution pursues educational improvement through goals and strategies that **improve retention, persistence and completion rates** in its degree and certificate programs. 4.C.1. The institution has **defined goals for student retention, persistence and completion** that are ambitious, attainable and appropriate to its mission, student populations and educational offerings. 4.C.2. The institution collects and analyzes information on **student retention, persistence and completion of its programs**. 4.C.3. The institution **uses information on student retention, persistence and completion of programs** to make improvements as warranted by the data. 4.C.4. The institution's **processes and methodologies for collecting and analyzing information on student retention, persistence and completion of programs reflect good practice**. (HLC, 2023, p.15) **FDCR.A.10.070** An institution's website for students and the public shall include a webpage containing (or linking to) accurate information regarding student achievement. The institution must disclose data that address the broad variety of its student populations and programs, including at the undergraduate and graduate levels as applicable. This information must include, at a minimum, retention, completion, required state licensure exam pass data, and data about the institution's students after transfer or graduation (such as continuing education, job placement and earnings). The institution must also accurately disclose which student populations are excluded from the data. (HLC, 2023, p.38)

MSCHE	Standard I.3. outcomes and student achievement that: a. include **retention, graduation, transfer, and placement rates** (MSCHE, 2023, p.7) Standard IV.1.e. processes to **disaggregate and analyze student achievement data to inform and implement strategies that improve outcomes for all student populations** (MSCHE, 2023, p.11) Standard II.8.c c. full disclosure of information on institution-wide assessments, graduation, retention, certification and licensure or licensing board pass rates (MSCHE, 2023, p.8)
NECHE	8.6 The institution defines measures of student success and levels of achievement appropriate to its mission, modalities and locations of instruction, and student body, including any specifically recruited populations. These measures include **rates of progression, retention, transfer, and graduation; default and loan repayment rates; licensure passage rates; and employment. The institution ensures that information about student success is <u>easily accessible on its website</u>**. 8.10 The institution integrates the findings of its assessment process and measures of student success into its institutional and program evaluation activities and **uses the findings to inform its planning and resource allocation and to establish claims the institution makes to students and prospective students.** 9.22 The institution publishes statements of its goals for students' education and **<u>makes available to the public timely, readily accessible, accurate, and consistent aggregate information about student achievement and institutional performance</u>**. Information on student success includes rates of retention and graduation and other measures of student success appropriate to institutional mission. If applicable, recent information on passage rates for licensure examinations is also published. (NECHE, 2021, p. 24-25, 28)

NWCCU	1.D.2 Consistent with its mission and in the context of and in comparison, with regional and national peer institutions, the institution **establishes and <u>shares widely</u> a set of indicators for student achievement including, but not limited to, persistence, completion, retention, and postgraduation success**. Such indicators of student achievement should be disaggregated by race, ethnicity, age, gender, socioeconomic status, first generation college student, and any other institutionally meaningful categories that may help promote student achievement and close barriers to academic excellence and success (equity gaps). 1.D.3 The institution's **disaggregated indicators of student achievement should be <u>widely published and available on the institution's website</u>**. Such disaggregated indicators should be aligned with meaningful, institutionally identified indicators benchmarked against indicators for peer institutions at the regional and national levels and be used for continuous improvement to inform planning, decision-making, and allocation of resources. (NWCCU, 2020, Student Achievement)
SACS-COC	8.1 Student Achievement An institution needs to be able to document its success with respect to student achievement. In doing so, it may use a broad range of criteria to include, as appropriate: **enrollment data; retention, graduation, or course completion; job placement rates; state licensing examinations**; student portfolios; or other means of demonstrating achievement of goals. Note the three related obligations of the institution in order to meet this standard: student achievement goals (target levels of performance) must be identified; data for student achievement must be presented and evaluated (outcomes); and both the goals and the outcomes must be **published**. The institution identifies, evaluates, and **publishes** goals and outcomes for student achievement appropriate to the institution's mission, the nature of the students it serves, and the kinds of programs offered. The institution uses multiple measures to document student success. (SACS-COC, 2020, p. 65)

WASC-ACCJC	1.3 The institution holds itself accountable for achieving its mission and goals and regularly reviews relevant, **meaningfully disaggregated data to evaluate its progress and inform plans for continued improvement and innovation.** 1.5 The institution regularly **<u>communicates</u> progress toward achieving its mission and goals with internal and external stakeholders** in order to promote understanding of institutional strengths, priorities, and areas for continued improvement. (WASC-ACCJC, 2023, p. 54-55)
WASC-WSCUC	CFR 3.10 Data are regularly and systematically **<u>disseminated internally and externally</u>**, and analyzed, interpreted, and applied in institutional decision-making. (WASC-WSCUC, 2023, Standard 3) CFR 4.2 The institution collects, analyzes and acts on **disaggregated student outcomes data including retention and graduation rates**. (WASC-WSCUC, 2023, Standard 4)

PART V

POST-GRADUATE SUCCESS SHAPING

This section demonstrates how institutions can use accreditation to shape the success of their students beyond graduation. The section explores the role of institutions in preparing students for the job market, equipping them with valuable skills that they can use in their careers, and measuring their success once they leave the institution.

Chapter 13

Career Services as an Integral Component to Institutional Success

Angela Schmiede and Lashonda Kennedy

This chapter examines the role of career services in promoting student success and institutional outcomes, offering insights on how to create effective career services programs that meet the needs of diverse student populations, align with industry trends and workforce demands, and contribute to overall institutional success.

As institutions of higher education and their accreditors are increasingly called on to demonstrate the quality and value of a college degree, career education has emerged as both a strategy for and a measure of a degree with a positive return on investment. Even as higher education budgets are squeezed, many institutions are allocating more resources than ever into career services and elevating career education structurally and strategically.

Whether in response to or in concert with these shifts, accreditors are refining their standards and offering new tools that enhance the transparency of educational outcomes. Institutional and programmatic accreditation uses standards to assess and benchmark in order to communicate to stakeholders the quality of a college or university and its offerings. Stakeholders are increasingly seeking assurance not only of the quality of the student experience while students are enrolled but also that a degree is a pathway to quality career and educational opportunities for which its holders are effectively prepared (Finley, 2023).

Calls for Accountability

Both the federal government and accreditors are responding to the demands of stakeholders, ranging from students' families to employers, by increasing transparency of post-graduate outcomes. In place since 2015, the U.S. Department of Education's College Scorecard has been modified several times in an attempt to increase transparency around the value of attending a higher education institution.

Taking transparency and accountability one step further, the U.S. Department of Education's new financial value transparency and gainful employment rule goes into effect on July 1, 2024. The regulation applies to all sectors—public, private, not-for-profit, and for-profit—as well as all degree programs, certificate through doctorate, including professional programs. The rule is designed to demonstrate whether an academic program leads to higher wages than a non-college graduate would earn, and that a graduate can afford student debt payments based on their income. It has faced some opposition from higher education institutions based on the perception that the performance metrics are subjective. Higher education leaders have also voiced concerns that the federal government's accountability measures focus almost solely on financial metrics, which doesn't provide consumers with less tangible or qualitative information about the quality of the outcomes of an academic program (Knott, 2023).

Addressing Career Outcomes in Accreditation Standards

There are seven institutional (formerly called "regional") commissions in the United States that accredit higher education institutions ranging from for-profit career colleges to research universities (e.g., the WASC Senior College & University Commission, or WSCUC, and the Higher Learning Commission, or HLC). In addition, there are a number of accrediting bodies that focus on specific disciplines (e.g., the Accreditation Board for Engineering and Technology, or ABET, and the Association to Advance Collegiate Schools of Business, or AACSB), some of which are inherently more career focused and licensure-driven than others. Accreditors are paying closer attention to career outcomes as they update their accreditation standards. For example, WSCUC's new 2023 Standards encourage colleges and universities to reflect on the following in their compliance with *Standard 2: Student Learning and Performance* (WSCUC, 2023, p.5)*:*

> What does evidence show about what graduates do after they complete a degree and program? Measures of graduate success vary widely based on the nature and level of the program. For example, to what extent do undergraduates pursue further education? What proportion of graduates find employment in their chosen field, and what other measures of success and value does the institution consider? To what extent do graduates pass licensing or other milestones related to

the occupation or field they were studying? What is the longer-term impact of their education on graduates?

In 2021, WSCUC launched a transparency initiative called Key Indicator Dashboard (KID), which displays multi-year federal data including post-graduation outcomes, as well as more traditional metrics such as student completion and student finances. The KID benchmarks each institution against both WSCUC-accredited institutions and national averages. In an effort to help institutions better understand how they are serving the needs of diverse student populations, data are also disaggregated by demographics. Given that data are drawn from federal datasets, post-graduation outcomes are narrowly focused on financial metrics, including earnings, student debt, and debt default rates (WSCUC, 2021).

In September 2023, the Higher Learning Commission launched the HLC Credential Lab, which is an innovative response to supporting institutions and students who "....need high-quality credentials that build skills, stack toward degrees, support mobility and provide on-ramps and off-ramps to further education and employment" (Higher Learning Commission, 2023). The HLC Credential Lab is just one example of how quality assurance and accreditation standards and processes are evolving to meet the changing landscape of higher education and employer demands. The Lab aims to provide quality assurance to employers regarding content providers and programs that help address skill gaps in the workforce.

Career Services Trends and Innovation

Shift in Career Services as a Strategic Priority

Since the COVID-19 pandemic, a number of higher education institutions have restructured and rebranded their career services offerings in response both to the accountability pressures noted earlier in this chapter as well as concerns about declining enrollment. While a strategic focus on career education has been institutionalized in higher education sectors such as community colleges, it has largely been resisted in more elite and selective colleges and universities (Schmiede, 2003) until recently (Marcus, 2023). For example, Brown University revamped and renamed its career services operation as the Center for Career Exploration and doubled the number of career advisors. William & Mary integrated career education into its strategic planning, and Grinnell College restructured career services to report directly to the president (Marcus, 2023).

The following patterns are emerging from colleges and universities that are positioning career services more strategically:

- These strategic changes are often the result of changes in senior leadership (NACE, 2022).

- Fewer career centers are housed under student affairs, while more are reporting solely or jointly to academic affairs (NACE, 2023a), or even the president (Alonso, 2023; Marcus, 2023; NACE, 2022).

- A strategic change is typically accompanied by additional allocation of resources, particularly for staffing (Alonso, 2023; Marcus, 2023, NACE, 2023a).

- While engaging faculty in career education continues to be challenging, more and more institutions are integrating academics closely by translating career competencies from course syllabi and having career centers and employers engage directly with faculty (Marcus, 2023; Schrand & Tulante, 2021).

- Rebranding is often part of restructuring; career counselors are now "career catalysts," and "career communities" are more common, engaging stakeholders from across campus (Marcus, 2023, NACE, 2023a).

- Institutions are recognizing a stronger connection between career success and alumni engagement and fundraising (Hanover Research, 2022; NACE, 2022).

In general, the higher education field is moving away from career and education as dichotomies, allowing career services to move from the margins to the core of the institution. These shifts suggest an imperative that higher education leaders consider carefully how career education aligns with their institution's mission, strategic priorities, and commitments.

Changing Role of Employers

Prioritizing career education and outcomes has both influenced and been influenced by how colleges and universities engage with employers and other external partners. In response to an increasingly competitive market for new employees, large employers are shifting their recruiting timelines anywhere from one academic term to one year earlier (Smith & Green, 2021). Efforts to diversify their workforces have led larger employers especially to develop diversity-focused recruiting programs to engage students from historically marginalized backgrounds. Examples include the Google BOLD Immersion Program and the range of programs Deloitte offers as early as the first year of college through their Discovery Internships and on up to the Deloitte Consulting Immersion Program for master's students. Internships have continued to evolve into recruiting pipelines, where employers benefit from a low-risk trial period during which both employers and interns can assess and affirm the viability of longer-term employment, with the goal of employee retention.

In their quest to secure the strongest talent, employers are looking beyond the walls of career centers and going into classrooms and meeting with athletic teams, essentially expanding their role beyond recruitment into career education. For example, at Menlo College, Enterprise Mobility recruiters regularly offer workshops on interviewing and networking. Recognizing a niche with student-athletes, Enterprise recruiters also establish strong relationships with athletic coaches to partner on outreach and programming. Large employers such as EY look for opportunities to partner with faculty in the classroom.

Diverse Offerings for Enhanced Accessibility

The landscape of career services has witnessed a significant evolution marked by innovations aimed at meeting the diverse and evolving needs of students. One of the central themes reshaping career services is the diversification of offerings. Exhibit 13.1 summarizes examples of the trends, innovations, and sector-specific strategies that have redefined the essence of modern career services, from how centers engage with students to increasing the priority placed on special student populations.

Remote and Online Engagement. Adaptation to remote environments has led to the emergence of online career fairs and remote job and intern opportunities, facilitating access for a broader audience by eliminating geographical barriers. Virtual career fairs, which came into prominence during the COVID-19 pandemic, have remained an impactful way for students and recruiters to engage in the recruitment and hiring process. As Booth (2019) aptly suggests, the transition to digital platforms has transformed the recruitment landscape, offering companies access to a global pool of high-quality applicants.

Micro-internships. Gaining in popularity, micro-internships are project-based opportunities, typically completed within 10 to 40 hours, that aim to democratize experiential learning by providing short-term but potentially valuable skill-building experiences. Parker Dewey (2023), an early network creator of micro-internships, recently reported that over 80% of their micro-interns were from underrepresented populations. These short-term opportunities are

Exhibit 13.1: Diverse Offerings for Enhanced Accessibility

more accessible to those less likely to be able to participate in full-time or longer-term internships. Given the nascent stage of adoption for micro-internships, long-term outcomes research will be important for career centers in considering further adoption.

Micro-credentials and Stackable Credentials. In response to the need for more flexible, on-demand skill development, micro-credentials—primarily in the form of certificates and badges—have proliferated in recent years. Stackable credentials build on related skills and often serve as on-ramps to two- or four-year degrees, although few California community college students earning credentials complete four-year degrees (Bohn & McConville, 2018). The introduction of micro-credentials and stackable credentials has disrupted traditional education models, providing specialized, modular certifications that empower students to acquire targeted skills aligned with the demands of the ever-evolving workforce (Finley, 2023). As evidenced by the growing number of students earning and stacking credentials, these specialized certifications not only enhance employment prospects but also contribute to increased earnings, highlighting their significance in shaping a more competitive workforce (Daugherty, Bahr, Nguyen, May-Trifiletti, Columbus & Kushner, 2023).

While there is some evidence that stackable credentials for low-income workers can help bridge equity gaps (Daugherty et al., 2023), employers are often unsure about the credibility and effectiveness of micro-credentials (D'Agostino, 2023). Initiatives such as the HLC Credential Lab aim to address these challenges and provide information and greater transparency. Quality assurance will be a critical consideration for higher education institutions as these credentials proliferate.

Reverse Career Fairs. Reverse career fairs are a major departure from traditional recruitment settings, offering a unique platform that flips the dynamics of engagement between students and employers. Unlike conventional job fairs where employers showcase opportunities to job seekers, reverse career fairs empower students to exhibit their skills, talents, and accomplishments while allowing employers to actively seek out individuals possessing specific and sought-after skills and competencies (Mowreader, 2023). At a reverse career fair, students take center stage, setting up booths or presentations, which allows them to showcase their skills, projects, and achievements more actively than is typically possible during a traditional career fair.

Campus Partnerships. Institutions are reimagining career services as a hub for community building, not just a physical center on campus. From students and faculty to employers and alumni, career centers are addressing the unique needs of all stakeholders through more collaboration and partnership (Akmal, 2023). Strengthening on-campus partnerships is a departure from the conventional siloed approach to career services, shifting to a new era of collaboration and synergy. Partnerships between libraries, academic departments, academic advising, student affairs, and industry stakeholders foster an environment that supports students in multiple ways throughout their time at the institution.

Libraries, long revered as centers of knowledge and learning, have become instrumental in this collaborative model. At institutions such as Florida International University, they serve as spaces for resource access, offering career-related materials, workshops, and information sessions. These collaborations leverage the library's extensive resources, transforming them into dynamic centers for career exploration, skill-building, and professional development (Lafferty, 2018).

First-generation Students. A particularly important shift in focus that has occurred within career services is heightened attention to supporting underrepresented groups, including first-generation students, and addressing intersectionality in an increasingly diverse student population (Goldberger, McLaughlin & Snyder, 2021). Initiatives designed to build social capital among first-generation students have gained popularity, acknowledging the importance of tailored resources and support to promote inclusivity and equitable access to career development opportunities both during college and after graduation (Montoya, 2022).

First-generation students whose parents have not attained a four-year college degree often face a distinct set of obstacles as they navigate the unfamiliar terrain of higher education. The pursuit of academic success for these students can be filled with challenges related to acclimating to college life, understanding the complexities of academic culture, navigating the many resources available to college students, and building a professional network that can provide access to good internships and jobs. Recognizing these challenges, career centers have undertaken proactive measures to cater to the distinctive needs of first-gen students, equipping them with tailored support systems. Through mentorship programs, networking opportunities, workshops, and one-on-one counseling, career professionals can create a nurturing environment that fosters academic success, professional growth, and personal development. They can provide guidance on career exploration, resume building, interview preparation, and networking strategies tailored to the unique backgrounds and aspirations of first-gen students (Montoya, 2022). Moreover, career centers can actively promote access to internships and experiential learning opportunities, recognizing the significance of hands-on experiences in building a strong professional portfolio; they should begin this process when students arrive on campus, if not before (Delgado, 2021).

More importantly, the intersectionality of identities adds another layer of complexity to the experiences of first-gen students. Career centers have an opportunity to acknowledge and embrace these intersecting identities, recognizing that students may face compounded challenges due to such factors as race, gender, sexual orientation, accessibility needs, and socioeconomic status. This understanding drives the provision of holistic support that respects and honors the diverse experiences and needs of each individual. Increasingly, career centers serve as more than mere advisory teams; they become champions and allies of first-gen and other underrepresented students, amplifying their voices and advocating for their representation within the greater workforce ecosystem. By fostering connections with alumni, industry professionals, and various other networks, these offices can create pathways for students to build social capital and forge meaningful ties that can significantly impact their career trajectories.

Community Colleges as a Catalyst

The evolution of career services presents differently across higher education sectors, with each sector navigating its own challenges and opportunities based on its mission and the particular student population it serves. Community colleges are unique in their focus on linking education to specific vocational paths. At the same time, sector goals and missions are increasingly blurred, with two-year institutions pressured to create clearer transfer pathways to four-year institutions and in some cases, community colleges offering bachelor's degrees. Four-year institutions have taken a keen interest in partnerships with two-year institutions to increase their enrollments with transfer students. As a result, community colleges and their career services offerings have a powerful impact on the entire higher education and career system.

Given the diversity of the higher education sector, the blurring of boundaries across sectors, and the critical questions about educational ROI, it is helpful to take a brief look at the unique challenges, opportunities, and metrics for success within the community college sector with regard to career education and accreditation, and how those strategies for addressing challenges and opportunities might apply to best practices across all sectors. The examples below are drawn from the California Community Colleges system.

Strong Workforce. California's Strong Workforce Program focuses on identifying high-demand sectors within the regional job market and tailoring educational programs to develop students' skills, ensuring relevance and employability after graduation. This is an important initiative that forges connections between academia and industry to shape student success. Established because of the volatile and ever-changing job market, Strong Workforce offers a significant boost to community college students seeking to propel their educational journeys towards meaningful careers. The program influences community college curricula to better align with the demand of employers, all in an effort to ensure that students are equipped with the essential skills and knowledge needed to secure job opportunities within high-demand sectors of California's competitive job market.

A key reason the Strong Workforce program is effective is its emphasis on built-out career pathways and guided support for students. By providing clear roadmaps that define the needed courses, experiences, and skills required in various industries, students are empowered to navigate their educational pursuits with a much stronger career direction. This approach has the potential not only to shorten their time spent acquiring academic credentials but also to enhance their career readiness.

Guided Pathways. Guided Pathways is an initiative being adopted widely within the community college sector, including commitments from all California community colleges to adopt the framework (Fischer, 2018; California Community Colleges Chancellor's Office, 2023). Guided Pathways is premised on the belief that every student deserves a clear and comprehensive pathway towards their academic and career goals. It stands as an example of structured support and purposeful direction so that students have the opportunity to enjoy the college experience while remaining focused on the pathway to graduation and subsequent employment. Pathways are a direct attempt to increase community college degree completion, as only 40% of community college students nationwide and 36% of California Community College students complete their two-year degrees within six years (Weissman, 2021). The California Community Colleges system's goals to improve success include increasing completion rates by 20% and transfer rates by 35% (California Community Colleges Chancellor's Office, 2021). The Guided Pathways framework represents more than just an educational model; it is a holistic approach that prioritizes not only academic success but also the seamless transition into meaningful careers or further educational pursuits (McNair & Bonneville, 2021).

In an effort to improve graduation and transfer rates, the California Community Colleges system has adopted Guided Pathways to help students prepare for the next step in their careers or educational pursuits. Guided Pathways reflects a commitment to equity and inclusivity within higher education. By breaking down barriers and providing strategic resources and support, this framework is designed so that students, irrespective of background or circumstance, have equitable access to a structured and comprehensive educational experience and timely degree completion that prepares them for the demands of the modern workforce. As most California community colleges are still in the early stages of implementing Guided Pathways, future research will highlight the extent to which the initiative impacts transfer and completion rates. There are opportunities to continue to refine the model as community colleges institutionalize it.

Work Experience Programs. California cooperative work experience regulations were established in 1971. Since that time, the system has experienced significant changes that affect student experiences in education and work. As the state's economy continues to shift, systems need to adjust to ensure that students have access to experiential learning and are prepared for evolving workforce demands. In 1991, Economic and Workforce Development was adopted as the third primary mission of the California Community Colleges system.

Current changes reflected in California Title V amendments expand opportunities for work experience and career technical education (CTE). Most importantly, changes are geared towards enhancing accessibility and equity in work experiences by expanding credit opportunities for work experience, eliminating lifetime limitations on units, and standardizing credit hours awarded for work experience. These regulatory changes seek to create a more inclusive and flexible framework that allows students from diverse academic backgrounds to access and benefit from a greater range of work experience opportunities, better preparing them for their future careers (Curry & Roberson, 2023). Initiatives to remove barriers to gaining meaningful work experience can be adapted to all higher education sectors.

A Lens to the Future: Measuring What Matters and When

Measuring the outcomes of a college degree through the lens of the federal government has primarily involved degree completion and economic outcomes such as earnings and student loan debt. Traditional metrics such as employment rates and salaries, while important, are no longer the only indicators of success. There has been a noticeable shift within institutions towards recognizing competencies, skills, and more holistic measures encompassing both student satisfaction and skill attainment.

Though many institutions have long focused on using job placement as a key indicator of success, it has been difficult to obtain the necessary data. Often institutions can only access this information long after students have graduated, making it difficult to fully evaluate success. Many forward-thinking institutions have begun to measure what is happening during a student's time on campus to better assess progress, satisfaction, and overall outcomes. Satisfaction metrics encompass students' perceptions of their overall educational experience, the relevance of coursework to their career goals, and the effectiveness of career support services. These dimensions provide valuable insights into the overall impact of education on students' career pursuits (Chan & Cruzvergara, 2022).

First Destination Surveys (FDS), when following standards and protocols such as those institutionalized by the National Association of Colleges and Employers (NACE), collect data on outcomes six months after graduation, including type of employment (full-time, part-time, freelance), continuing education enrollment, and starting salary (NACE, 2023b). Following standards established within the field of career services allows colleges and universities to compare first destination outcomes over time and with peer institutions. When customized, First Destination Surveys also allow institutions to gather data on student usage of and satisfaction with their specific services, including evaluation of experiences and outcomes of required experiences such as internships versus voluntary use of career services.

The limitations of FDS data include difficulty obtaining survey responses once students leave the institution. In addition, FDS provides more of a rear-view rather than a real-time view into career outcomes, which highlights the importance of supplementing summative assessment data with formative assessment. With career education being integrated as early as first-year experience programs, campuses can gather both usage and satisfaction data early and often to inform programming needs and outreach methods and to identify the potential need for intrusive career advising.

Gathering demographic data are increasingly important to ensure equitable access to career education and equitable post-graduation outcomes. By disaggregating usage, satisfaction, and placement data by demographics, institutions can answer the following questions and formulate strategies for addressing potential issues of diversity and equity:

- Who is using career services voluntarily? Who is less likely to use these services, and why?

- Who is taking advantage of high-impact practices that build skills, such as internships, co-ops, undergraduate research, and service-learning? Who is less likely to participate, and why?

- What are potential barriers to access services, such as hours of operation or modality?

- Are graduates with accessibility issues able to secure quality employment or participate in graduate or professional education at equitable rates?

- Are there significant differences by race, ethnicity, gender, or first-generation or veteran status in terms of outcomes such as degree-related jobs, pursuing graduate education, or earnings?

Using Data and Trends to Inform Curriculum and Planning

Understanding the outcomes and needs of specific student populations within the context of current higher education and workforce trends is essential to designing and adapting curricula and programs that ensure equitable outcomes and communicate the value of a college degree. As shown in Exhibit 13.2, the evolving needs of both students and employers build a case for using data to inform curriculum and planning.

Exhibit 13.2: Using Data and Trends to Inform Curriculum and Planning

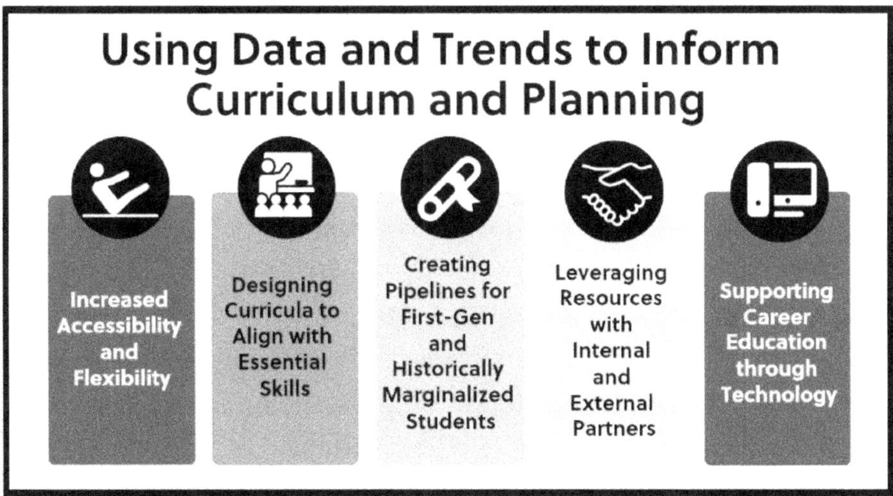

Increased accessibility and flexibility. Current trends indicate that colleges and universities need to continue to offer services and opportunities for gaining experience and skills in more accessible, flexible, and adaptive ways, often by optimizing technology. A single parent might not be able to participate in a full-time internship but could effectively build skills through micro-internships and online micro-credentials. Students might not be able to afford summer housing on campus but can benefit from completing required internships remotely while living at home or in more affordable areas. Having a staff member work evening hours remotely can support students with job or family obligations who are unable to access services on campus during the day. Understanding the specific needs of an institution's students is key to identifying the type of flexibility that would benefit them.

Designing curricula to align with essential skills. As employers evaluate candidates with an eye towards skills and away from degrees, career centers have an opportunity to partner more closely with faculty to ensure curricula are aligned with needs of employers. Likewise, faculty can benefit from partnering with employers to align and integrate theory with practice. Creating advisory boards with alumni and employers is another strategy for providing faculty with feedback on curricula and experiential opportunities. Initiatives such as Guided Pathways create greater alignment between curriculum and employment. Accrediting bodies have an opportunity to ensure that the core competencies they expect institutions to develop in students and assess are aligned with employer needs.

Creating pipelines for first-generation and historically marginalized students. Career center teams and faculty that build strong partnerships with employers committed to diversifying their workforces, with a special emphasis on those offering developmental immersion programs, help create visible and diverse talent pipelines for candidates that might otherwise be overlooked. Providing stipends or scholarships for travel or registration to participate in special programs can further support access to opportunities for low-income students.

Leveraging resources with internal and external partners.

Leveraging partnerships with student clubs, affinity alumni groups, and centers that support underrepresented students is another path to connecting students and employers. These partners can support outreach and mentorship efforts and co-host events. Other student services partners can support career education in a variety of ways, from mental health services educating students about work-life balance to tutoring centers providing support with ePortfolios and writing strong cover letters. Internal partners help provide more holistic and developmentally appropriate support.

While external partners are often limited to employers, career services can expand outreach to student access and success organizations such as Management Leadership for Tomorrow, College Track, Summer Search, TheDream.us, 10,000 Degrees, and others. Collaborating with external organizations is also a potential way to maximize resources through co-hosted events and shared initiatives.

Supporting career education through technology. As career centers look beyond career platforms such as Handshake and Symplicity to support student success, they can explore how artificial intelligence (AI) can be leveraged for career readiness. If a student can use an AI resume writer or interview prep tool, career center teams can use time with that student to have more substantive advising sessions that are not yet possible with AI. Although there are widespread concerns about AI, ranging from plagiarism to displacement of jobs, students and institutions should evaluate if and how they can utilize it for greater accessibility and efficiency.

Given that employers are increasingly looking for skills and achievements beyond just degrees, tools such as ePortfolios can help students showcase their achievements digitally, using multimedia formats to present projects they have completed in classes or during internships. The use of ePortfolios as an assessment tool for course, program, or institutional learning outcomes also supports accreditation activities.

Concluding Thoughts

Higher education institutions, educational accreditors, and employers share a common goal of ensuring that students have access to a quality education that prepares them for jobs that meet workforce needs. Applying an equity lens to both educational and accreditation standards and processes can have a positive impact on the economic mobility of students and graduates, especially those from historically marginalized backgrounds. Engaging employers and stakeholders such as faculty in these processes fosters a more holistic approach to career readiness to ensure that employers have access to a diverse and skilled workforce. By clarifying and measuring what matters, higher education leaders can create an effective cycle of continuous improvement to respond to the needs of students and a dynamic workforce.

Discussion Questions

1. What are best practices for career centers to ensure equitable access to services?

2. How can accreditation standards and practices evolve to expand career success definitions beyond just economic metrics?

3. What are the best mechanisms for identifying and closing the gap between employer assessments and new graduate assessments of career competencies? What are the most effective ways to engage employers in these discussions?

4. What is the optimal organizational reporting structure to enhance closer integration of career education into academics?

5. What data has your institution found to be most useful in leveraging change and additional resources for career services?

6. What are the outcomes of micro-internships? What impact do micro-internships have on addressing equity issues at your institution?

7. How will the value of micro-credentials evolve relative to the value of a college degree?

8. How will artificial intelligence impact the longer-term role of career services, and how will AI-based career development tools be evaluated?

9. Six strategies were discussed in the diverse offerings and accessibility section. Which of these strategies does your institution currently offer? What are one or two strategies you think your institution should initiate or expand upon?

Discover and Propel

Below are resources that can assist higher education leaders in leveraging career services to enhance student and institutional success.

Career Readiness and Career Services Trends

- National Association of Colleges and Employers https://www.naceweb.org/

- The National Career Development Association (NCDA) Career Convergence Web Magazine https://www.ncda.org/aws/NCDA/pt/sp/CC_home_page

DEI Best Practices for Career Services

- NACE DEI Best Practices https://www.naceweb.org/diversity-equity-and-inclusion/best-practices

- NASPA First Gen Resources https://firstgen.naspa.org/

Influencers

- Brandon Busteed, Author of *Busteed Bold: Bold Insights @ The Intersection Of Learning And Work* newsletterhttps://www.linkedin.com/newsletters/busteed-bold-7072880775750127616/

- Christine Cruzvergara, Contributor to *Handshake Blog* https://joinhandshake.com/blog/students/lessons-in-leadership-from-a-handshake-vp/

- Farouk Dey, Host of *#VisionChats* https://provost.jhu.edu/offices/integrative-learning-and-life-design/vision-chats/

- Eloy Oakley, Host of *The Rant with Eloy Oakley* https://www.youtube.com/@EloyOakley-eg2gm

References

Akmal, H. (2023) Designing the future of career services. *National Association of Colleges & Employers.* https://www.naceweb.org/career-development/trends-and-predictions/designing-the-future-of-career-services

Alonso, J. (2023, June 7). Career centers get a makeover. *Inside Higher Ed.* https://www.insidehighered.com/news/students/careers/2023/06/07/bigger-budgets-and-higher-profile-college-career-centers

Bohn, S. & McConville, S. (2018). Stackable credentials in career education at California community colleges. *Public Policy Institute of California.* https://www.ppic.org/publication/stackable-credentials-in-career-education-at-california-community-colleges/

Booth, B. (2019). Why virtual career fairs are one of the easiest ways to land a top tech job. *CNBC.* https://www.cnbc.com/2019/02/06/why-virtual-career-fairs-are-an-easy-way-to-land-a-top-tech-job.html

California Community Colleges Chancellor's Office. (2023). Guided pathways. https://www.cccco.edu/College-Professionals/Guided-Pathways#:~:text=Every%20college%20is%20implementing%20Guided,systemic%20obstacles%20to%20their%20success

California Community Colleges Chancellor's Office. (2021). 2021 State of the system report.

Chan, A. & Cruzvergara, C. (2022). Outcomes and metrics that matter: Embedding career services at higher education's core. *Handshake.* https://go.joinhandshake.com/FY21Q3-EDU-AMER-WC-Outcomes-that-MatterOutcomes-and-Metrics-that-Matter-Whitepaper.html

Curry, S. & Roberson, C. (2023, February). Work experience regulation changes: expanded opportunities for experiential learning. *Academic Senate for California Community Colleges.* https://www.asccc.org/content/work-experience-regulation-changes-expanded-opportunities-experiential-learning

D'Agostino, S. (2023, March 02). Microcredentials confuse employers, colleges and learners. *Inside Higher Ed.* https://www.insidehighered.com/news/2023/03/03/microcredentials-confuse-employers-colleges-and-learners

Daugherty, L., Bahr, P. R., Nguyen, P., May-Trifiletti, J., Columbus, R. & Kushner, J. (2023). Stackable credential pipelines and equity for low-income individuals: evidence from Colorado and Ohio. *RAND Corporation.* https://www.rand.org/pubs/research_reports/RRA2484-1.html

Delgado, J. (2021). Rise up for first-generation students through career development. *The Career Leadership Collective.* https://www.careerleadershipcollective.com/post/rise-up-for-first-generation-students-through-career-development

Finley, A. (2023). The career-ready graduate: what employers say about the difference college makes. *American Association of Colleges and Universities.* https://www.aacu.org/research/the-career-ready-graduate-what-employers-say-about-the-difference-college-makes

Fischer, K. (2018). Community colleges try new 'pathway' to student success. *Ed Source.* https://edsource.org/2018/community-colleges-try-new-pathway-to-student-success/601264

Hanover Research. (2022). The 2022 state of alumni giving report: understanding the factors that turn graduates into donors. https://www.hanoverresearch.com/reports-and-briefs/the-2022-state-of-alumni-giving-report/?org=higher-education

Goldberger, S., McLaughlin, J. & Snyder. (2021). Mobilizing for opportunity: connecting low-income college students to internships and good first jobs. *The Boston Foundation.* https://www.tbf.org/news-and-insights/reports?q&sortBy=date&sortOrder=desc&page=4

Higher Learning Commission. (2023). HLC's credential lab. https://www.hlcommission.org/News-Reports/credential-lab.html

Knott, K. (2023, September 27). Game on, again, for gainful employment. *Inside Higher Ed.* https://www.insidehighered.com/news/government/student-aid-policy/2023/09/27/education-department-finalizes-gainful-employment

Lafferty, A. (2018). You're hired! a library's collaboration with the career services department. Works of the Florida International University Libraries. https://digitalcommons.fiu.edu/glworks/87

Marcus, J. (2023, November 24). Colleges refocus on career services as students seek return on degrees. *The Washington Post.* https://www.washingtonpost.com/education/2023/11/24/colleges-career-counseling-programs/

McNair, T.B. & Bonneville, L. (Eds.) (2021). Paths to success: how community colleges are strengthening guided pathways to ensure students are learning. *American Association of Colleges & Universities.*

Montoya, D. (2022) Serving our first-generation university students. *National Career Development Association.* https://www.ncda.org/aws/NCDA/pt/sd/news_article/441488/_PARENT/CC_layout_details/false

Mowreader, A. (2023). Career prep tip: host a reverse career fair. *Inside Higher Ed.* https://www.insidehighered.com/news/student-success/life-after-college/2023/11/17/organizing-reverse-career-fair-college-students

National Association of Colleges & Employers (NACE). (2022). Positioning career services as an institutional strategic priority. https://www.naceweb.org/career-development/best-practices/d42d80eb-d3dc-4bcf-b599-9afb58c45acd

National Association of Colleges & Employers (NACE). (2023a). 2023 NACE career services benchmark report. https://www.naceweb.org/store/2023/2023-nace-career-services-benchmarks-report-and-dashboard

National Association of Colleges & Employers (NACE). (2023b). The NACE first destination survey. https://www.naceweb.org/job-market/graduate-outcomes/first-destination

Parker Dewey. (2023). Micro-internships by the numbers. https://www.parkerdewey.com/

Schmiede, A. (2003). The legitimacy of experiential learning in research universities. *Stanford University Dissertation.* https://www.academia.edu/64597481/The_legitimacy_of_experiential_learning_in_research_universities

Schrand, T. & Tulante, T. (2021). Power skills for work and life. *Liberal Education.* American Association of Colleges & Universities, 42-47. https://www.aacu.org/liberaleducation/articles/power-skills-for-work-and-life

Smith, K.N. & Green, D.K. (2021). Employer internship recruiting on college campuses: 'the right pipeline for our funnel', *Journal of Education and Work*, 34:4, 572-589.

Weissman, S. (2021). Lagging behind, *Inside Higher Ed.* https://www.insidehighered.com/news/2021/11/22/california-community-colleges-suffer-low-completion-rates

WSCUC. (2021). Key indicators dashboard. *WASC Senior College and University Commission.* https://www.wscuc.org/resources/kid/

WSCUC. (2023). Understanding the 2023 WSCUC standards. *WASC Senior College and University Commission.* https://www.wscuc.org/handbook2023/

Chapter 14

Enhancing Workforce Development through Cultural Responsiveness

Alana Olschwang

In this chapter, leaders discover the critical importance of cultural responsiveness in workforce development programs. Through an exploration of best practices and institutional examples, readers will gain valuable insights and practical strategies on how to create inclusive and culturally responsive workforce development initiatives that effectively serve diverse populations and foster equitable opportunities for all.

For decades, higher education has provided evidence that people with college degrees are more likely to be employed, to achieve social and economic mobility, and to contribute to their community, among other benefits. This is evidenced by economic impact studies, studies of the financial return on investment, and employer reports about what they seek in employees (Finley, 2021). Less is published, however, about the details of the roles and responsibilities of bachelor's degree–granting institutions in workforce development. How do colleges and universities prepare students for their first destination after graduation, advances across their careers, and continued learning over their lifetime?

Colleges and universities create pathways for students that align with the institution's vision, values, and goals. The link to workforce development extends the college pathway to meet the needs of employers to create, sustain, and retain a qualified workforce. This also includes the needs of the public sector, community-based organizations, and other entities in the ecosystem. Economic modeling and forecasting provided universities with insights into 5-to-10-year trajectories. Examining emerging markets and trends, universities can create plans for the curriculum and co-curriculum for students to develop associated knowledge, skills, and abilities to meet future demand. Universities that leverage these data can close skills gaps, position their alumni for strong workforce alignment, and strengthen a regional economy.

Community colleges have long been a part of the workforce development conversation, given the dual mission to meet vocational and associate degree goals. Community colleges are also likely to have relationships with local workforce investment boards to support and augment training. However, fewer bachelor's and graduate degree granting universities are working in this space. This chapter aims to highlight how this can change in the future, including references to research and practice to encourage communities to build out their ecosystem to include 4-year, public and private universities. Additionally, the evidence will point to ways that this supports the goals and purpose of accreditation. University administrators and practitioners will hopefully glean supportive or new ideas on how they can strive to meet standards, demonstrate quality and accountability, strengthen capacity and enhance effectiveness as a learning organization.

A closer look at the components of accreditation reveals several keys to building a workforce development program (WDP). Accreditation standards for student learning include language about classroom and community engagement, learning relevant content, and experiences in addressing pressing social issues. Community engagement is a central component of a WDP, especially for modern urban universities. In a review of four institutional accrediting agencies and how standards were applied, Paton, Fitgerald, Green, Raymond and Borchardt (2014) found that community engagement was central to scholarship, learning, and goals; albeit ill-defined and poorly measured. Accrediting bodies commonly ask institutions to center their context and values and define engagement for themselves. This chapter will provide examples of how conversations about workforce development can take root in key components of accreditation. These include program review, faculty development around equitable pedagogy and communities of practice, student engagement and internships, overcoming basic needs, and advancing transparency of outcomes and impact.

This chapter describes the way that workforce data can be used in program review and how conversation about skills can link curriculum to and through career. Applying workforce data to planning at a university can bring new insights to discussions about meaning, quality, integrity and return on investment for a degree. All of this feels formulaic without context; therefore, a section of this chapter will describe how the work connects faculty and students, in the classroom. The next section will review various approaches to enhancing equitable pedagogy and the links to an engaged classroom. This engagement can extend to high impact practices and into the workforce. Next, these ideas are presented as a conceptual framework and then in a more comprehensive model that includes partnerships outside the university. Finally, the chapter closes with a model to measure maturity of workforce development. The goal of this chapter is to present information about workforce development in a way that is adaptable for other universities and provides enough examples, references, and tools, to create several onramps to next steps, no matter where a university is, now.

Starting Small, at the Center, with Program Review

While each accredited college and university engages in program review, the specific requirements and depth of inquiry vary by program and institution. In my role of providing data, information, benchmarking, and analysis support, one of the most fruitful ways I can serve those involved in program review is by answering key questions on the minds of the program faculty. This often includes how meaningfully to show evidence that student achievement in the program across the curriculum adds up to what students need to succeed once they complete their degree programs and for lifelong learning. Faculty seek to understand where students are excelling, where gaps exist, and how to enhance quality of experience more equitably.

Learning about workforce development and the impact on accreditation began for me twelve years ago, by integrating student and market demand in program review. Later stages included mapping curriculum to the market with faculty and then entering the classroom with them to understand better how students learn. This led to links in learning across academic and co-curricular spaces and partnerships, in and outside the university. Each stage of development was coupled with new technology, assessment, and reflection. Academics who already are building a program may benefit from the tools cited and how they have been integrated. Others may find interest in expanding a pilot program, especially in support of a student body that reflects the changes projected across the United States toward an increase in Latino and Black students, more students who are foreign born, and more students who are the first in their family to attend college (Crown, 2024).

Student and Market Demand

Faculty often face a set of market-based questions such as: What is the student and market demand for a program? How large should it be? Who is most likely to enroll? What career destinations are most popular, for who, and how is this changing? Using an application called *Analyst* developed by Lightcast, faculty can explore the student and market demand based on region parameters and degree level. This will show that while there may be many other programs in a crowded marketplace, the enrollment across the top 10 institutions have been growing over the last few years and the market data project that more retirements and new positions will create openings for these new graduates.

This is the case for computer science, healthcare, and transportation in many cities. The tool is based on Classification of Instructional Programs (CIP) and Standard Occupational Classification (SOC) codes. This has been a useful frame of reference as some programs have seen shifts in what the curricula emphasize and what code is used. A few programs noted new job titles emerging and found areas of specialization (e.g., Title IX positions from a women's studies degree; biochemistry for new positions within green jobs; quality assurance within logistics for automation; or computer science with linguistics for natural language learning). When a business program sought accreditation, they realized that they were better positioned to create specialized master's degrees as opposed to an MBA, given the trends and landscape.

Translating Learning Outcomes into Skills

Measuring student learning outcomes and creating crosswalks and scaffolds are not new concepts in higher education. To date, there is no standard across institutions for creating learning outcomes and no accepted format for connecting learning outcomes with skills. How do learning outcomes translate into the world of work? The outcomes often leave room for interpretation dependent on faculty expertise and experience. When learning outcomes are translated into skills, they connect with skills in an established taxonomy and hierarchy. Skills are recognizable in the job descriptions that institutions create, and common language is used across disciplines and locations. Skills can be divided into four categories: cognitive, higher-order, discipline-specific, and transferable. This enables faculty to map onto their courses the skills that their students will be able to transfer to the workplace. This can help students understand the value of each course to the workplace and how courses build on each other. For some, this highlights the value of doing well in class as preparation for a successful career. The connection of course-career relevance can be highly motivating. Faculty have noted that students appreciate drawing direct attention to the connections and note that once a course is complete, students can add the skills to their job-seeking documents and LinkedIn profile.

There are a few tools for faculty to make the process of mapping skills onto a course as easy as possible. A tool developed by the economic modeling firm Lightcast provides a two-part system for academic programs. First, faculty submit their syllabi to be reviewed and prepared for analysis. This requires an interpretation of educational goals and pedagogy within a contextual framework as well as how the software reads these and codes as skills. The software extracts information based on predefined criteria. The software, "*Skillabi*", then recodes learning outcomes as skills. Analysts on campus can use this information along with other reports to create a map of what skills are taught and which are sought. These maps will look different by region, department, and area of specialization. From this map, faculty can see where there might be more demand than what is taught, or vice versa. Having this map has provided faculty with a common language to discuss skills inside each class, cluster, and major. Once mapped, the skills are loaded into an application for students called Skillsmatch. Students can select skills they have and plan to gain and then view industries and occupations that are a strong match. They also can reverse this and search by occupation for the skills required. This program can be matched with state economic development data for alumni to show students their likely earnings.

Workbay, another second tool for skills exploration, takes a more relationship-based and streamlined approach. Students can search for a job title and view in one space a video of someone who holds that position, the skills required, and other relevant data. Workbay was developed with career exploration and upskilling in mind. Therefore, pathways are easy to follow, and students can see what additional degrees or certifications they may need to obtain. Using O*NET, they then can explore more details such as associated tasks and whether the occupation has a "bright" outlook.

Labor market data also can help identify where occupations have a large position base, are growing, and pay a living wage for a family in that area, on average. While students who seek public-sector, service, and nonprofit positions may not be in college strictly to earn high wages, institutions owe it to students to create a realistic wage picture. Further, new legislation extending from the Obama College Scorecard is calling for greater transparency. By visiting collegescorecard.ed.gov and entering an institution name, anyone can view information about a college or university and compare graduation rates, average annual cost, and median earnings for alumni. Recent conversations about rankings have elevated the importance of social and economic mobility. In the most recent ranking by CollegeNet, our institution was number one in the country for economic mobility. This highlights that students who come from low-income backgrounds and complete their degree go on to earn significantly more earnings than their families. Interestingly, in 2024, the Carnegie Classification of Institutions of Higher Education announced a Social and Economic Mobility Classification to measure how universities are delivering on the promise of becoming a socioeconomic engine to empower students to reach their goals. This is a critical change, as the director at the Georgetown Center on Education and the Workforce noted that, "a small number of selective colleges are launchpads to positions of influence, but these institutions remain highly segregated by race, ethnicity, and class". As universities continue to define their equity and justice plans, and are held accountable for them, we can look forward to a future where closing equity gaps is more likely and more students will have opportunity.

Return on Investment and Value of the Degree

The value of a college degree has been called into question with increasing intensity, especially since the advent of online and open programs, short-term and stackable certificates, and alternative ways to learn skills. A recent report by the National Skills Coalition found that while the number of jobs posted included statements that no degree was required had grown by 240%, the actual percentage of new hires without a degree grew by less than 13% (National Skills Summit, 2024). To those familiar with workforce training, it may seem that offering such options at colleges and universities makes these institutions more like community colleges or community-based workforce training programs.

This tension in the conversation about whether students should pursue a degree or other skills training has taken on a relatively new format in the last two decades. Much of the funding for skills based training is provided by federal legislation. In a review of legislation that supports workforce development programs, Rojewski (2002) and Roumell (2020) provided important information about changes that happened between 2000 and 2020. In 2000, legislation expanded the workforce focus away from farms and factories to include skills related to technology and globalization; this was only twenty years ago. Further, the legislation recognized a change in the skills that were in demand to support a 21st century workforce, such as interpersonal skills for knowledge workers and the cultural responsiveness required in an increasingly global market. Perhaps the answer is both, a degree is of value, and the ability to perform specific technical tasks.

College completion rates have remained stagnant across the last ten years, despite considerable efforts to improve them. For those who began in 2017, the six-year completion rate was 62%, up eight percentage points since the 2006 cohort (Lee & Shapiro, 2023). The report included analyses for students by race, ethnicity, sex, and found that private nonprofit 4-year colleges had higher completion rates as compared to public 4-year colleges. At public 4-year colleges, almost 25% of students did not complete. These data are taking a new shape in the public eye alongside a growing and louder voice questioning the value of the degree, especially in an economic climate where short-term gains are more easily available in-service positions and other roles that offer recently increased salaries. According to the Education Data Initiative, the average starting salary of a degree-earner is $70,240 and offers lifetime earnings of $5.3million. On average, the lifetime return on investment for a bachelor's degree is 287%; however, the real payoff begins 10-15 years after degree completion. This evidence points to a need to change how institutions frame student success, thriving, and workforce development.

In 2016, Raj Chetty produced a series of maps that showed that where children grew up had a major impact on their opportunity to achieve the American Dream and how much they were likely to earn in a lifetime (Chetty, 2016). While 90% of children born in 1940 earned more than their parents, this has decreased to 50%. measuring earnings for children born in 1985 (Chetty, Hendren, Grusky, Hell, Manduca, & Narang, 2017). Chetty continued research through an organization called Opportunity Insights that showed deep inequities across race, ethnicity, and class (https://opportunityinsights. org/). Additional studies by the Georgetown University Center on Education and the Workforce ranked 4,500 universities and reported similar findings (https://cew.georgetown.edu/resources/reports/). Examining data from our state Economic Development Department, we found that women earned less than men and Latino and Black alumni earned less than White and Asian alumni (example: www.calstatepays.org). This information is vital for universities as organizations to consume and consider, as well as for faculty. What does this mean for programming designed to support all students or students in a specific group? How can faculty use this information to inform their teaching? What services and supports are needed?

The next section of this chapter discusses the role of faculty in addressing culturally sustaining practices. These have been found to increase student learning and positive outcomes, including higher completion rates (Paris, 2012). Further, workforce development that advances students' capital, agency, and experience can prepare them to enter their careers and can close these opportunity gaps.

The Role of Faculty and Systems in Supporting Engagement to Advance Equity

Any department chair who has completed a program review will attest that the process was more demanding than expected, even if the outcomes were beneficial. In her seminal work on outcomes-based program review, Bresciani (2006) notes the connections between curriculum design, pedagogical practices, and faculty development with the evaluation of student learning. To operate optimally and strategically, program review must also be connected to faculty reward systems.

Examining curricula through a workforce development lens can reveal strengths and weaknesses, opportunities, and threats. The campus climate and culture shapes much of the conversations and depth of exploration. How will the faculty in the department respond to calls to action for curricular revision or changes in pedagogical practices? How will the department or college find resources to provide faculty with the time to make changes? Will there be negative consequences when gaps are discovered? In learning communities, faculty have shared that they are uncomfortable making changes at times since they are unsure how well they will work with students. Changes that challenge students beyond their comfort zone can work well or can result in negative teaching evaluations. This can impact faculty professional progress and employability (especially for non-tenured faculty).

A recently revised version of the program review guidebook contains a new section on strategic planning for the future. This activity provided the change supported by the academic leadership and an opportunity to get on the same page. Adding market demand helped programs to create a clearer vision about what pathways the program led to. This was designed after integrating a review of data by multiple stakeholders and incorporating feedback. Conversations about challenges and opportunities encouraged new ideas about what was needed, who to include, and how to approach improvement efforts.

The magic in talking about workforce in curriculum is creating a language that connects educators, students, students' families, employers, and community organizations – skills. In many cases, universities refer to learning outcomes, employers refer to skills, and students talk about things that they know and can do. Program faculty can translate student learning outcomes into skills and then map these to the needs of their region. Colleges and universities can assess the skills students develop, whether enough students are completing degrees to meet the needs of the local market, and if students are pursuing the right degrees for the type of work they aim to do (Alic, 2019; Weise, Hanson & Saleh, 2019). Using taxonomies from the labor market, colleges and universities can include industry, occupation, job description, skills, and tasks; a common language.

The conversation moves from theoretical to practical using

skills-mapping tools and can engage stakeholders campus wide. When faculty participate in program review and improvement work and this work is connected to the faculty governance, development, and accountability systems, change is more likely to happen (Lee & Shapiro, 2023). The next section of this chapter will move from program to classroom, to highlight the kinds of faculty development activities that researchers and practitioners advance student engagement and learning.

Advancing Culturally Responsive and Sustaining Pedagogical Practices
National shortage of college-educated workforce

On the face of it, discussing culturally responsive and sustaining pedagogy may seem like a different chapter from workforce development. As the nation confronts a shortage of skilled workers, higher education faces scrutiny for not supporting more students to degree completion. A flat college completion rate of 62% moves from being an education and social issue to being an economic one (Lee & Shapiro, 2023). Economists estimated that by 2025 at least 60% of adults would need postsecondary credentials to meet the demands of the workforce, but only 40% did (Marisotis, 2015). Advancing completion rates will meet additional challenges as we approach a demographic cliff and face the continued issues of the COVID-19 pandemic in the form of college non-consumption rates (Gallup Foundation & Lumina Foundation, 2023; Grawe, 2018).

Ladson-Billing introduced the concept of culturally responsive teaching (1992). With training in critical theory and the four tenets of culturally responsive teaching, teachers can demonstrate that they care about their students, validate the heritage and learning style of students, and transform learning experiences (Gay, 2000). The tenets are high expectations, taking a critical view of structures and processes, honoring cultural connections, and viewing what students bring to class as valuable assets. Many faculty members did not experience culturally responsive pedagogy in their own classroom experiences as students. Having a space for different ideas and ways of knowing, or community cultural wealth and capital, can be challenging (Yosso, 2005). The faculty member is not the expert in these areas; the students will be. Culver and Kezar (2021), among others, provide examples of how to build this type of culture and what it looks like in the classroom. Faculty must take time to hear student counter-stories and learn about their experiences. Only then will faculty be able to understand where students come from and link learning to students and their cultures. Discussing the literature about culturally responsive pedagogy became a key for faculty to understand ways that they could strengthen student engagement in the classroom, with what students were learning, and relevance to their future.

Changes Faculty Made to Increase Transparency, Trust, and Capital

To bring about this space and opportunity for empowerment, faculty have participated in communities of practice. Small groups of faculty convened and discussed materials provided and then reviewed their own citations and examples present in their syllabi. Faculty noted that it was important to use primary sources and teach students to think like a scholar from their discipline rather than read only what other scholars have written. Other faculty have brought in journals for students to reflect on how course content relates to their own lived experience and how their knowledge informs how they learn. In another course, faculty have transformed their curriculum to replace one large, high-stakes assignment with multiple smaller practice opportunities with feedback. Faculty intentionally have linked assignments and student learning to directly transferable skills in the workplace. From these type of activities, faculty have reported that engagement, learning, and grades are improving.

In a recent survey of beginning college student expectations, students reported that they were more likely to go to a friend not at the university or family before asking for help from someone inside the university. Research has shown that many Black and Latino cultures are more collectivistic than individualistic and home communities are where they rely for support. This core value and related beliefs and behaviors run counter to the individualistic manner in most classrooms. With this information, faculty can think about what students have come to know in their lives and families and how the values of the campus do or do not align. Students learn better when culturally responsive and sustaining pedagogy pushes faculty to do less lecturing to make space for connection and community in classrooms This can shift a faculty member with a large power differential into a trusted mentor and begin to create a space where the students feel safe. If the faculty member demonstrates that they welcome student contributions and that wrong answers won't be punished, students can start to trust them.

What does the evidence show from these changes? Students are spending more time getting to know their peers and learning from them. Students report that the activities are fun and help to motivate them and contribute to their learning. Faculty members report greater interaction and student engagement. Faculty have shared that change only resulted from thinking differently about the approach, such as intentionally reducing the amount of time spent lecturing across multiple weeks of the semester while dedicating time for students to reflect and work together. An equity-driven approach is difficult to implement because it requires faculty to unlearn the ways that they have often experienced their own educational journey (Haas, 2006). Communities of practice provide faculty the time and space to learn together and share ideas, to ask questions and test out what they think might work, and why, with peers. However, creating effective plans and implementation takes time; time to try new things across a semester, for the faculty to reflect and receive feedback, and then to find ways to continuously improve. The questions in Exhibit 14.1 below are examples of ways faculty encouraged students to build their reflection and mega-cognitive skills for the classroom and how to apply the skills for the future of work.

Exhibit 14.1 Questions that Lead to Reflection and Metacognition

Questions that Lead to Reflection and Metacognition

- What is the main point of this reading?

- What information did you find surprising? Why?

- What did you find confusing? Why?

- How did you prepare for class? How well did that work?

- What do you plan to do next time to prepare even more effectively?

- How does the material connect to your culture?

- How does the material relate to what you are learning in other courses?

- What did you learn by taking a viewpoint different from your own?

Some faculty members who integrate career development in the classroom have found the process to be an effective engagement and retention strategy. For example, sharing with students how learning concepts across a semester begins with simple definitions and progresses to problem solving sounds basic. When this is translated to essential skills for the workforce and specific job roles, the conversations become much more engaging and exciting (Walker, Bair & Macdonald, 2022). This approach can help students understand how a general education course, whether in history or chemistry, can contribute to environmental studies, public health, or public policy.

Measuring Pedagogical Practices and Impact

When faculty create a sense of trust, students believe that the classroom is a safe space to ask questions, take risks, and try new things. Faculty can cultivate and measure the behaviors that engender strong relationships and trust. When faculty create an environment in which students are excited to learn and then identify needed skills for various careers, students can see how to learn within their discipline ("hard skills") and why common, or "soft" skills are so important. This has been labeled the "new vocationalism," a look at how education can work more closely with industry to understand the necessary habits of mind, as well as the ability to develop new knowledge, skills, and abilities (Hora, Benbow & Oleson, 2018). Some students may not look forward to group work, writing reflections, or presenting, but these activities become more relevant to students when they understand how the effort contributes to skill building in the problem-solving, decision-making, metacognitive, and communication skills that they will need in their careers. When faculty draw these connections and refer students to resources throughout the campus as essential in the skill development and career preparation network, students are more likely to take advantage of them. Hence, the most effective models integrate career exploration in the classroom, across academic and co-curricular programming, and in their institutional messaging.

Culturally Sustaining Pedagogy Framework: Unpacked

We developed a conceptual framework to bridge the space between research theory and examples of practice through communities of practice to increase transparency and test the theory of change. This framework focused on a specific project designed to advance digital equity for college students, first by ensuring that all students had access to a laptop and the internet. In addition, students were given three choices for upskilling (could choose from one of the following: marketing, data analytics, or project management). After a close analysis of the most popular skills across entry- and mid-level jobs, we found these across jobs that required a college degree and some digital literacy and competency (for example, visit https://www.cde.ca.gov/pd/ee/culturallysustainingped.asp). Faculty and staff taught these skills in the classroom and students applied them on site with their projects developed with partner institutions.

In the conceptual framework displayed in Exhibit 14.2 below, students are at the center. The grey, vertical modulation lines indicate communication between the faculty and student as the student enrolls in the capstone and internship courses. The student circle includes an arrow at the top indicating effort from the capstone to the community with descriptors such as "Try," "My Why," and "Connect with Career." These are the things that students are expected to do (with challenge and support from faculty) to achieve the objectives and outcomes of the project, including self-efficacy, critical thinking, and job-readiness. The students are more likely to achieve these outcomes when the capstone course includes autonomy and upskilling and the faculty work to empower the students. These assertions are backed by multiple studies and contexts that honor a culturally responsive and sustaining approach, where student knowledge and experience is viewed as an asset.

Exhibit 14.2 Conceptual Framework for Service Learning

Connecting Minority Communities
Conceptual Framework for Service Learning

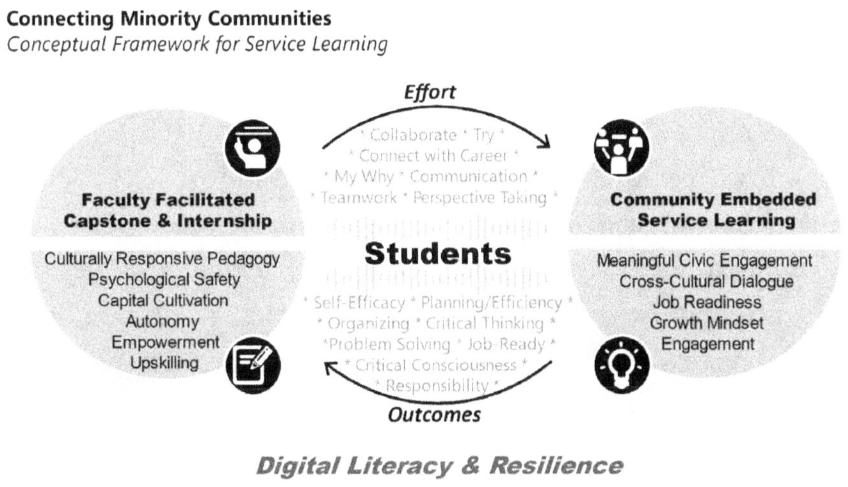

Psychological Safety

As we examined student and faculty feedback about what was happening in the classroom, we recognized that one reason students were more engaged, participative, and willing to take risks was psychological safety. This concept gained recognition in the 1990s and was amplified during the pandemic (Edmondson & Bransby, 2023). If college students come from classrooms that encouraged them to listen through lecture and studying for tests, the level of participation and preparation expected in college can be a difficult transition. Further, students may have come from classrooms that discouraged them from asking questions and resulted in less willingness to take risks. This can be extremely limiting for students who have experienced bias, stereotype threat, micro or macroaggressions, or who were threatened.

The transition to college can be difficult, and some students mention that this is partly due to a hidden curriculum. In this framework, we aim to make clear what faculty expect students to do, what they can expect others to do with and for them, and what outcomes they can expect. The trusted space facilitates conversations about important topics, such as : (1) we're building these behaviors in the classroom to promote learning and develop skills; (2) engagement in the class is critical to success; (3) the safe space and practice here is designed to prepare students for the workforce (Finley, 2021). We have created a through-thread in our design from the faculty development community readings and discussion to syllabi and classroom orientation to mid-point check-ins and student feedback surveys. If we seek to build culturally sustaining and safe classrooms for engagement, then we can examine the depth and breadth of impact of that intent. Further, these assertions are only perceived as authentic and received well by students when the faculty are skilled in creating an affirming and trusting classroom environment (Brooms, Clark, & Smith, 2018). Exhibit 14.3 below includes some of the questions asked of students to provide feedback to the faculty. This was compared to feedback the instructor provided to similar questions as the faculty reflected on their own behavior.

Exhibit 14.3 Questions that Lead to Culturally Sustaining Practices, Engagement, and Psychological Safety

> **Questions that Lead to Culturally Sustaining Practices, Engagement, and Psychological Safety**
>
> *How often has this instructor...*
>
> - focused classroom conversations on inequity?
> - asked me about my life outside of class?
> - helped me to develop relationships with your peers in the class?
> - used examples that people from different cultures can relate to?
> - asked for feedback on how the course is going?
> - talked about risks that they took?
> - encouraged students to take risks?
> - encouraged students to ask questions?
>
> *This instructor*
>
> - uses a mix of approaches to see what I'm learning.
> - has shown us what it looks like to change viewpoints.
> - has taken time to understand the struggles that I'm going through.
> - provides multiple opportunities to complete an assignment.

Impact of Racism on Student Discipline

Discussion with faculty about practicing equitable pedagogy can be a difficult topic. Asking faculty to change their classroom culture and teaching practices, often requires learning new things about the policies, practices, and systems in higher education. Faculty have called flexible deadlines and multiple attempts to complete work 'spoon feeding' students. Faculty have noted that reviewing syllabi and revising expectations is something students should be able to do for themselves. However, for students who are transitioning to college and have not felt safe in class before, or who have been marginalized and experienced micro and macroaggressions, these are changes that are necessary. The challenges of retention and degree completion begin before students even begin college.

The systems and structures in the United States, including education, benefitted from slavery (Wilder, 2013). The field of education has studied racial disparities in the context of policies, procedures, and systemic oppression and mistreatment, especially of Black and Latino students (Hooks, 2014; Patton, 2016). In the last decade, the Black Lives Matter movement and the impact of the legislative changes under the Trump presidency have given rise to more prominently, frequently, and deeply in conversations about the impact of racism (Lomotey & Smith, 2023). This has included an audit of language and the predominantly deficit framing associated with Black and Latino students (Davis & Museus, 2019). Specifically, labeling differences in test scores as achievement gaps puts the onus on the student. An alternative framing examines the role and responsibility of the university to be student ready (McNair, Albertine, McDonald, Major & Cooper, 2022). We have admitted the student, how do we now better understand what students need and how we can help them to transition successfully; especially students who are first in their family to attend college, and/or those who have come from under resourced schools. In addition to focusing on disaggregating retention and completion rates that flag that some groups of students who share certain characteristics are, overall, having a different experience as compared to others, equitable pedagogy creates a key to understanding why. Using the data and tools surrounding workforce development can support meaningful insights that lead to improvement efforts.

It is important that the institution take into consideration the years that a student may have spent in a neighborhood with less funding for resources, facilities maintenance, teacher training, and support staff.

Black students are four times more likely to be suspended than their White peers (Huang, 2018). Research shows that this is not correlated with the behavior of either group and that Black students are more likely to be suspended by a White teacher—and only 7% of public schoolteachers are Black (Peterson, 2021). These inequities in discipline have a significant effect on student outcomes in both the early and later years. Faculty report that students can be challenging to engage, don't participate if they aren't sure of the right answer, and are hesitant to offer ideas. Reading about experience and understanding the context that students experienced, if it was different from their own experience, has helped faculty reframe how they take in the information about practicing equitable pedagogy. Conversations about basic needs helped faculty to revisit what they may have learned about Blook's taxonomy, where students who are housing or food insecure are not able to focus on higher order tasks, like learning. According to the Institute for College Access and Succes (TICAS, 2023), college is not affordable for many Black, Indigenous, and Students of Color. Full acceptance of financial aid can cover only twenty-percent of the cost of attendance at a state university. This is hard to understand for some faculty, unless we also look at TICAS data showing in the 1970s, financial aid covered seventy-five percent of the cost of attendance. Our students today are facing a different reality. Faculty communities of practice help faculty discuss how their interventions can help students transition to a new kind of classroom and that this transition requires first acknowledging from where the student is coming from and their current needs. Expressing understanding, inviting student stories, and creating space for students to share can build strong relationships between faculty and students.

High-Impact Practices and a "Triple HIP"

A high-impact practice has been described as something that has significant benefits for students who participate in it because they invest time and effort, interact with faculty and peers, and have an opportunity to apply what they have learned in a real-world project. Students have a chance to practice their skills, receive feedback, and try again. Studies focused on first-generation college students and those historically underserved by higher education found that students from these marginalized groups have shown the greatest benefit from high-impact practices, including research, capstone courses, service learning, and study abroad. Interestingly, work experience is not formally recognized as a HIP, although it can advance those skills most sought after by employers, such as teamwork, digital fluency, leadership, and communication (Garib, 2020). These experiences also shape the habits of mind and behaviors of meaningful contributions for the public good and can contribute to lifelong habits that are rewarding, beyond earnings (Alonso, 2023).

Exhibit 14.4 High Impact Practice Example

> **Example: California State University Dominguez Hills' Workforce Development Impact Program**
>
> The Workforce Integration Network (WIN) developed a 3-part program that was funded $5.3M through an award by the National Telecommunications and Information Agency (NTIA). The project engaged faculty in a community of practice to help them create a course overlay that included digital upskilling and a project co-created with a community partner where students practice their skills and receive feedback. Students in the course dedicated fifteen hours to LinkedIn learning pathways and other supplemental instruction to learn data analytics, marketing, and project management. The faculty contextualized the learning to the discipline and the specific community project and provided guidance on using technology. Once the course was over, students enrolled in an internship for additional support and to complete the project through 120-240 hours of paid internship work. This program was labeled a Triple HIP because students completed a meaningful project, were paid to complete an internship, and then many partnered with faculty to conduct research on the outcomes.

This is an area of ongoing development as there have been mixed reviews on how well programs measure the consistency and quality of HIP (High Impact Practice) experiences (Kuh & O'Donnell, 2013). From an equity lens, students often lack flexibility to add

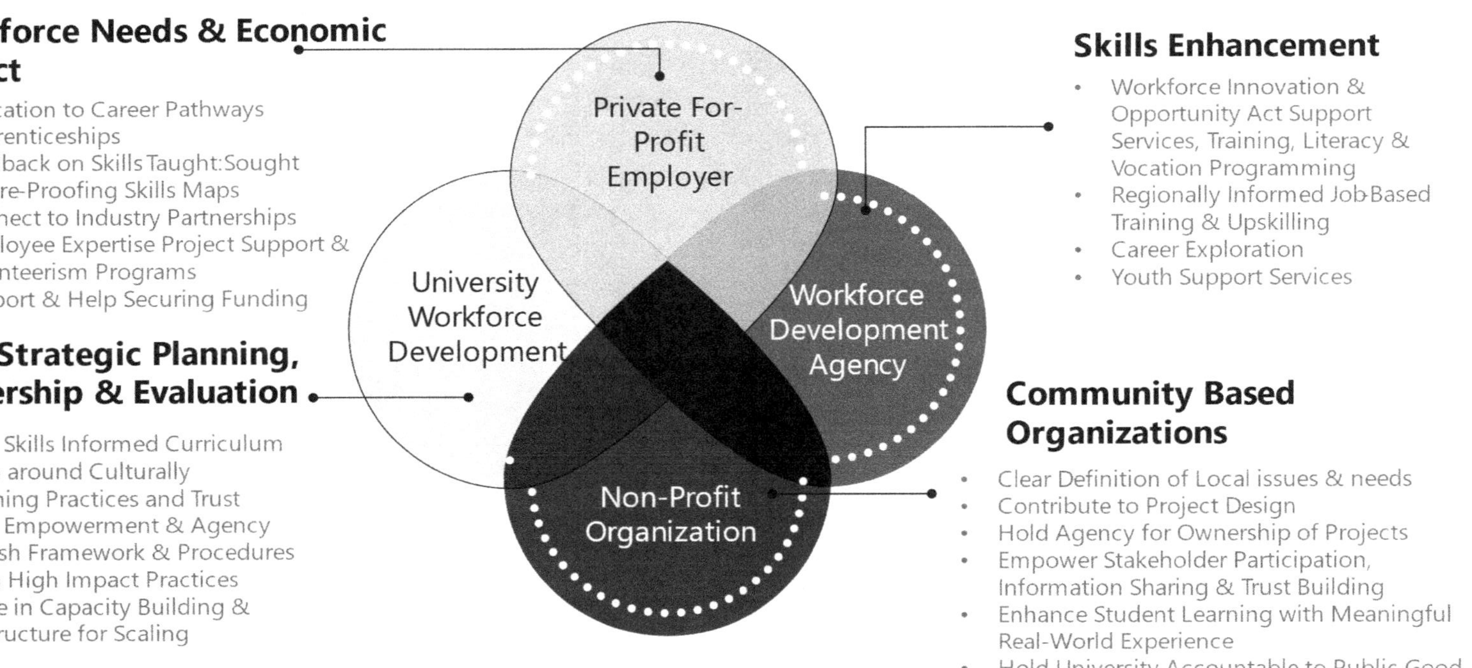

Workforce Development Design
Part I: Integrated Inter-Agency Model: Roles & Responsibilities

Workforce Needs & Economic Impact
Education to Career Pathways
Apprenticeships
Feedback on Skills Taught:Sought
Future-Proofing Skills Maps
Connect to Industry Partnerships
Employee Expertise Project Support & Volunteerism Programs
Support & Help Securing Funding

Strategic Planning, Leadership & Evaluation
Create Skills Informed Curriculum
Design around Culturally Sustaining Practices and Trust
Create Empowerment & Agency
Establish Framework & Procedures
Design High Impact Practices
Engage in Capacity Building & Infrastructure for Scaling

Skills Enhancement
Workforce Innovation & Opportunity Act Support
Services, Training, Literacy & Vocation Programming
Regionally Informed Job-Based Training & Upskilling
Career Exploration
Youth Support Services

Community Based Organizations
Clear Definition of Local issues & needs
Contribute to Project Design
Hold Agency for Ownership of Projects
Empower Stakeholder Participation,
Information Sharing & Trust Building
Enhance Student Learning with Meaningful Real-World Experience
Hold University Accountable to Public Good

Private For-Profit Employer
University Workforce Development
Workforce Development Agency
Non-Profit Organization

responsibilities outside of class, travel to alternative locations, and work without pay (Stewart & Nicolazzo, 2018). The research recommends how to define and measure quality and provides suggestions for advancing equitable experiences at scale. Exhibit 14.4 offers a high impact practice example.

Workforce Development Design

The workforce development design framework pictured below incorporates the theory, practice, and interconnected nature of the work. However, the full explanation requires a 2-part design. Exhibit 14.5 details the roles and responsibilities of the four entities involved: a university and its workforce development, the private for-profit organization(s), community based non-profit organization(s), and the workforce development agency (or workforce investment board). A first step to establishing an ecosystem is to clarify the distinct efforts of each entity. These are briefly discussed below before the second aspect of the model is reviewed; the work that happens at the intersection of each or multiple agencies through relationships and reciprocity.

Higher education has a long history of projects in the community. Some of these are community centered and embedded, and some are not. In some cases, the community partnerships serve instrumental purposes, where faculty aim to conduct research to publish and students seek to fulfill required service hours; these motivations are exploitative (Mitchell, 2006). Nyirenda (2018) recommends that universities keep in mind three "C's" for community engagement: collaboration, consultation, and communication. These are the key for building a trusting, reciprocal relationship. Another goal is to engage the community in social issues with a justice mindset, not a savior one. To increase the likelihood of this happening, training in community engagement is recommended at the institutional level. This parallels the work that was discussed inside the classroom, with culturally sustaining and relevant pedagogy. This work inside the classroom and across co-curricular programming, can set a tone for expectations to build a culturally engaging campus environment.

Another set of considerations comes into play when working with for-profit organizations. The workforce development and university pathways literature focus mostly on sectoral programs, where the high-growth sectors of the economy (e.g., computer science, healthcare, advanced manufacturing) look to upskill students and workers for greater efficiency and maximum profit. In these relationships, specific expectations, and checkpoints are very important. Employers can provide valuable information on what skills are needed at multiple advancement levels. Businesses can also detail how apprenticeships can be formed and what other industry partnerships will be important for the university to prepare students coming into the workforce. At times, business leaders may serve on advisory boards and their collective input can validate or stretch a curriculum and programming in new directions.

The relationship between the university and the workforce development agency is another interesting one. The agency may provide a program that enhances skills essential for starting a student journey, for building certificates that augment a bachelor's degree, or building a program that is housed in the university extended education curriculum (e.g., public service training requirements or certificates). Some workforce development agencies lead convenings for regional partners to discuss topics around upcoming opportunities, co-applications for funding, or networking. Additionally, this partner is a wealth of labor market information including unemployment, industry employment trends, occupational guidelines and profiles, and projected job openings. Workforce development boards are also eligible to disburse Workforce Innovation Opportunity Act funds for training and support services. The support services are a critical piece for recruitment, retention, and completion, including transportation, childcare, and funds to cover other basic needs.

The community-based organizations or non-profit organizations in the ecosystem serve an incredibly vital role. Once trusted partnerships are established, the organization can provide a clear definition of local needs and opportunities to advance existing projects to scale. The community-based organization can empower community members to participate in existing and new projects and provide a space for university stakeholders to engage in the broader community. For the campus that holds as part of its mission the ability to educate for economic and social mobility, for the common good, connections into the community across community-based organizations are key to the university's vitality. These organizations can become a site for service learning, internships, and a source of rich mentorship. The university can pour into these sites by offering support to catalyze efforts, enhance business practices, share resources and plan together.

Given funding and structures, there may be ways to leverage more continuity across these four entities between upskilling, networking, and collaboration to support students in their career exploration. In some cases, the Division of Apprenticeship standards can help to certify a pathway. In others, pipelines from K-12 may extend into the university. Pathway programs through community colleges have existed for over a decade with mixed results. However, many of these are about implementation. When programs focus on the quality of the intervention and implementation, results are more positive. One such effort has been in place since 2012 as a collaboration between Jobs For the Future (JFF) and the Harvard Graduate School of Education. This networked program brings educators alongside practitioners and policymakers across regions and states. The Pathways to Prosperity focuses on three pillars: (1) Every young person has clear goals for college and career and the support to achieve them, (2) Every employer has a talent pipeline of young professionals with the skills needed to contribute to and lead workforce, and (3) Every regional and state economy is thriving and provides its citizens with the opportunities for economic advancement. Exhibit 14.6 offers an example of a pathway program at Paul Quinn College.

Exhibit 14.6: Example of a Pathway Program

Example: Paul Quinn College

Paul Quinn College was recognized as the nation's first urban work college in 2017 and has received significant recognition for its 'learn and earn' model where students begin meaningful work to prepare them for life after college. They are mentored through each stage including campus experience, an internship, a career skills course, professional development, Microsoft Office certificate, and a corporate work program. The principles of exposure, engagement, and experience support development of the nationally recognized competencies endorsed by NACE (The National Association of Colleges and Employers such as problem solving, attendance, initiative, and accountability). The college has formalized thirty-five corporate partnerships with household names such as Southwest Airlines, Bank of America, and The Container Store. The college is among the few federally funded '*Work College Consortium*' located across eight states.

Part II: Relationships for powerful change and reciprocity

The next section will build on the first model by describing what happens at the intersection of the four organizations. In a study of how to build an equitable workforce development ecosystem in a city, Goldsmith and Coleman (2022) noted that students and community members face many challenges. They may not find resources that they need and may make decisions for training or education that do not provide a solid return on investment. Their model of equitable workforce development inspired some of the fundamentals of this model and confirmed the importance of other elements, such as the exponential value of authentic relationships that cascade across multi-institutional programs, see Exhibit 14.7.

In the planning and consideration of systems, the needs of students and their families are often not reflected. A primary goal of the workforce development program is to identify how the university may surface barriers to where students are and where they aim to be in their careers, and to consider the needs of other members of the larger ecosystem in the process. By centering values and bringing

Workforce Development Design

Part II: *People with Passion and Purpose Drive High-Impact Practices for Student Success*

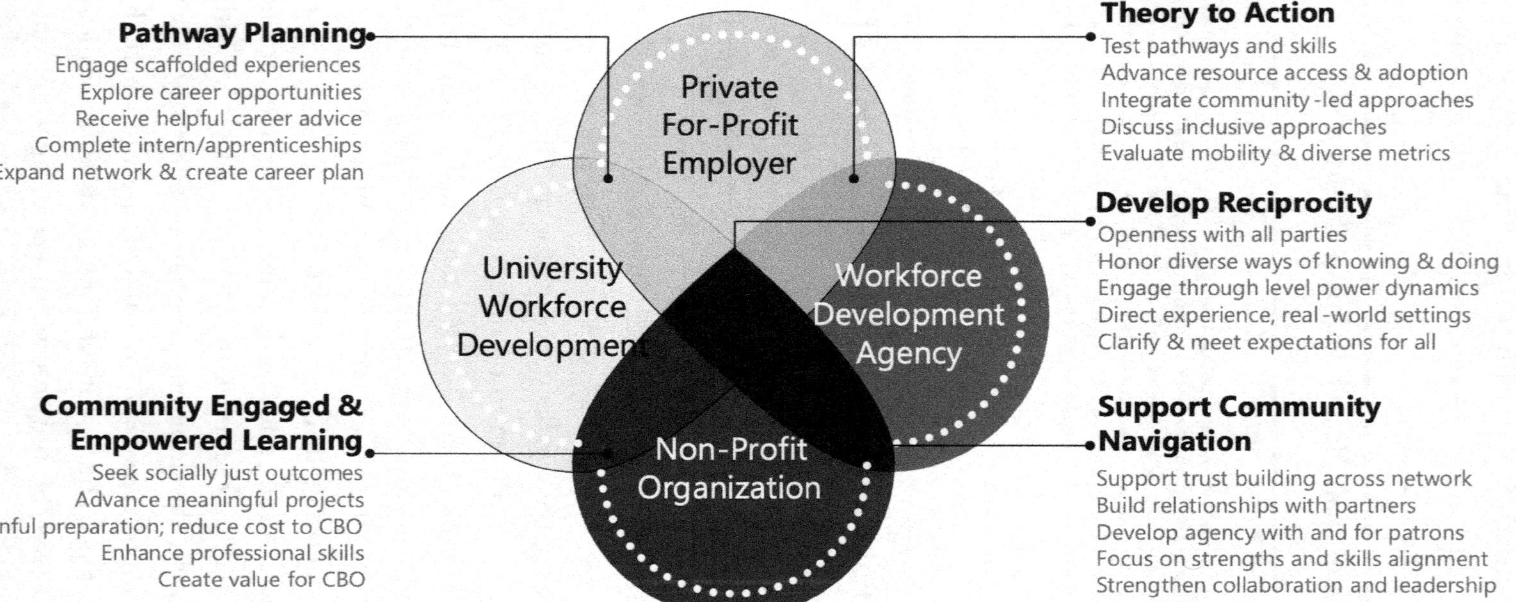

critical, culturally sustaining practices to workforce development programs, higher education can create partnerships that build skills for students while advancing the goals of community organizations with respect. In flattening hierarchies across organizations, students can learn skills from their experiences outside the classroom and contribute to how those organizations address and solve problems. Higher education can also use research and evaluation skills to streamline and simplify things for communities and build stronger connections.

While there are resources within and outside of the university for career support, faculty often find it difficult to answer questions such as: "What jobs are most likely with this degree?", "How much money will I earn in 5 or 10 years?" and "Will I need another degree?" They are also challenged to answer non-monetary return on investment such as the type of meaningful impact a career may have, what kinds of projects is someone in a certain position likely to complete, and how can students find mid-high wage positions in non-profit and public sector organizations? Once known, what's the bet way to share this information with students and their families? How early and often should the information be shared and who's best to deliver a trusted message? Exploring these type of pathway program communication plans are a natural way to open the door to multi-agency conversations. Through these conversations the organizations can grow projects and portfolios that help each understand the other's goals in new ways, identify innovations, and build truly reciprocal programming that enhances the experiences of all.

A recent survey of faculty was conducted through a partnership across three leading national organizations including the American Association of Colleges and Universities (AAC&U), National Association of Colleges and Employers (NACE), and the Society for Experiential Education (SEE). The researchers asked faculty about how they included career readiness in the curriculum (Gatta, Finley, & Green, 2024). The faculty (6,800 respondents) reported only sporadically using campus resources like the career or experiential learning center) and nearly half reported that they were not completely comfortable providing career advising. Fewer connected students to resources outside the university. The report recommended that administrators increase awareness about the importance of integrating competencies into the curriculum and provide development opportunities to do so, with incentives and learning community support, as well as data and information. The report recommended that faculty align learning outcomes with career readiness competencies and maintain connections with career and experiential learning centers to bring more opportunities into the course. Additionally, the report underscored the importance of strengthening institutional effectiveness from a relationship-based approach. These findings are in line with the workforce development ecosystem modeled in Exhibit 14.8.

Exhibit 14.8: Workforce Development Ecosystem Example

Example: The Onward First Year Forward Hamilton College Program

Before students begin their new student orientation, a cohort will be invited to participate in a special program designed to help students find their purpose, align what they need to prepare, and outline what active citizenship looks like on their path. The easy-to-navigate program provides a series of workshops across the first year to prepare students for an industry internship the next summer. Students learn skills like critical thinking and communication. Designed to build curiosity, students in the program are also mentored and supported through the program. The program works with employers to make posting positions and reviewing applications seamless.

Discussions across university, community based and workforce organizations have revealed similar challenges and barriers that undermine success and program completion. These challenges can hinder economic and social mobility. Each agency has noted the need for more resources to provide the following themed services, resources, and support (Exhibit 14.9):

Exhibit 14.9: Challenges that Undermine Student Success

*Time and stress management	*Disability support
*Goal setting	*Childcare and transportation
*Work-Life balance	* Food and housing insecurity

Through an ecosystem model, these challenges can be approached in a new way. For example, WIOA is under review and legislative staff are asking about how the program can be administered more innovatively to meet the needs of community members. With more coordinated assessment, research, and evaluation, a collaborative approach could identify a shared resources and support system to meet the needs across and within the four entities in the model. The evaluation project listed in Exhibit 14.10 below illustrates how a foundation can support an effort that leans in this direction.

Exhibit 14.10: Example of Evaluation Project

Example: The University of North Carolina at Chapel Hill

The Aspen Institute's Economic Opportunities Program awarded a grant to UNC in 2020 to evaluate and scale apprenticeships. The evaluation explored apprenticeship models across Chicago City College to identify the capacity needed for implementation. The project studied how the approach differed by location and partnership with business or community-based organization, including outcomes and impact. The $3.2M project reported benefits found in the short and longer term, including differences by the apprentices who were people of color.

In a recent article, others collated key factors necessary for colleges to contribute to workforce success in their division of the "future of work" (Deloitte, 2023). Specifically, they recognized that leaders should demonstrate collaboration, adopt culturally sustaining practices, center the community, and build relationships, growth mindset, and tolerance for ambiguity. Our models and ideas were developed through our Workforce Integration Network (WIN). The director frequently notes that advances forward are wins, and that we can win together when the network is strong.

Maturity Scale/Developmental Ladder

How can colleges and universities keep in sight where they are and where they aim to be, once matured? The lessons learned from experience and research are included in the five steps below. The maturity, like the workforce development design, considers organizational structures and systems, resources, and the people required to do the transactional and transformational work. Leadership is critical at multiple points in the development process from pilot to minimum viable product at scale. This chapter has included research across academic and student affairs, from multiple disciplines and authors in and outside of the academy.

Taking stock of the culture on campus is essential before analyzing strategy and a workforce development level of maturity. The assumptions included below were informed by the research and theory of change in the chapter. These helped to uncover the 'why' for the work before getting to the 'what' and 'how' to build a workforce development focus on campus and connect to an ecosystem, in practice.

- Faculty will be

    ◊ responsible for driving the scholarship, teaching, and reflective practice. Faculty will incorporate key principles of the theoretical model and provide feedback.

    ◊ willing to bring an open mindset as we build together our WDP, test new approaches, conduct boundary-expanding research, and support students in new ways.

- Students will be

    ◊ centered in all decisions made. Students will be seen, heard, and challenged. They will be supported and encouraged to rise to high expectations and ask for help.

◊ seen and met where they are. Each student arrives with a different set of experiences and goals. This is the essence of the diversity that we honor and support.

- We all will be

  ◊ cognizant of the history of higher education, rooted in racism and rife with systemic and structural inequities that are difficult to dismantle.

  ◊ applying a critical lens to all our activities and decisions,

  ◊ striving for more inclusion and access to resources.

  ◊ mindful of the taxation that often happens in higher education, especially for faculty of color.

  ◊ paying faculty, students, and community fair compensation.

The Workforce Development Maturity Model shown in Exhibit 14.11 advances from left to right. The first phase, fighting fires, is a beginning to early stage. Universities often take a reactive approach to a new venture with little infrastructure and many resources dedicated to laying foundations. Once some systems are in place, the program builds for the future (but the program is still largely in "start-up" mode). The program staff receive and integrate feedback. Once the program reaches stage three, leaders establish a common understanding of what the program is and where it's going. The university will have strong connections with partners. The last two stages are more difficult to move into, largely because they require both sustained focus on the work and significant funding along with campus support. The workforce development moves out of being seen as an idea shared by few, or a specific program. Instead, it may be visible in the vision, institutional learning outcomes, and s embedded into planning across the student lifecycle. In the final phase, the leaders of workforce development are regularly invited to tables where problem solving and strategizing happens.

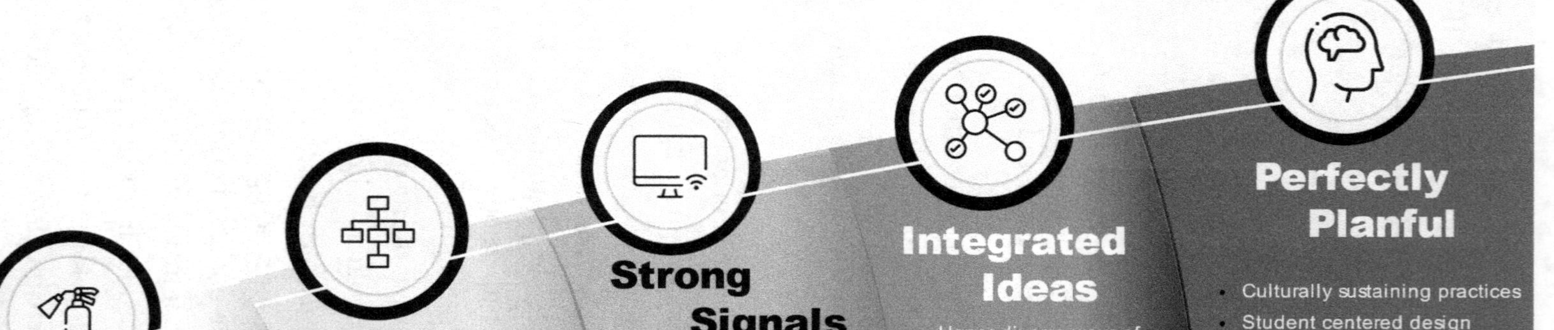
Workforce Development Maturity Model
Tracking progress, people, passion, and performance

Fighting Fires
Limited staff
Incomplete infrastructure
Gaps in procedures result in ad hoc case management
Unmet need by staff, faculty, students and community
Unclear leadership

Real Roles
Staff in place
Partnerships underway
Capturing SWOT
Building for the future
Integrate feedback for improvement
Capturing data about students served and impact

Strong Signals
Regular, robust partner communications
Tolerance for ambiguity
Dedication to collaboration
Shared vision and goals
Established procedures
Untapped campus and community potential
Unclear funding for growth and sustainability

Integrated Ideas
Honor diverse ways of knowing and doing
Form a theory-driven, evidencebased model
Student experiences contiguous across years
Student learning outcomes build/scaffold over time
Connected to leading practices and network
Invested partners resolve issues, are proactive

Perfectly Planful
Culturally sustaining practices
Student centered design
Community embedded with realized reciprocity
Exposure early and often
Experiences scaffold
Partnerships inplace
Seek new opportunities
Issues easily resolved
Measured outcomes &impact
Inspire and uplift others
Passion for project & mission

Concluding Thoughts

Strategies for getting started at your institution.

The Workforce Development Project and ideas discussed in this chapter grew into and out of a unit (University Effectiveness, Planning and Analytics) and in partnership with many offices across and outside of campus. While there are now many components and moving parts, these were developed and integrated over the course of five years. Each component was developed by the individual owner for a longer period than that, in some cases moving from a project to a proof of concept to prototype and then pilot. Below is a short list that might be useful in thinking about how to get started.

- Talk to people on campus across departments and spaces. Identify who has an interest, who has ideas about what might work, and who has done the work.

- Connect with key individuals on campus, including those responsible and accountable for university and specialty accreditation, program review, and institutional research. Connect with the career center, center for service learning, faculty development center, faculty with research grants on the scholarship of teaching and learning, and others involved in high-impact practice. Identify cross-cutting themes about workforce in recent reports, surveys, and assessments.

- If not already integrated, find ways to bring workforce and economic data into review spaces. Gauge campus readiness, level of understanding, resources, and leadership support.

- Support existing communities of practice, committees, and task forces that touch student success, student outcomes, alumni, engagement, culturally responsive and sustaining pedagogy, and modeling what works, where, how, for whom, and under what circumstances.

- Identify individuals who may combine into a coalition of the willing to test new ideas together.

- Find ways to integrate what you have found to build out a model and test ideas. Seek exposure and feedback by presenting in campus forums, including student and faculty research days, academic senate, and disciplinary conferences.

- Make connections with people and forums on LinkedIn. Find regional and national associations with leading practices. Review white papers and cases.

- Identify the regional leadership for convening community members to discuss workforce. Examine where you fit now and where you could fit into a future ecosystem.

Discussion Questions

1. What skills are needed in today's expanding fields in your region?

2. How can universities overcome the threat of boot camps and short-term credentials?

3. How can you effectively interpret job-market data to support program review?

4. How do relationships with employers and communities make the value of your students' degrees more evident?

5. What tools might be useful in forging deeper connections between academic departments and career services?

6. How can programs help traditionally underserved students get past barriers in the job market?

7. Where should future investments be placed to advance workforce development on your campus?

This chapter provided frameworks, tools, research, and examples for universities to consider ways to increase their focus on workforce development. The examples cited efforts at public and private, undergraduate and graduate institutions and included initiatives with themes of social, environmental, and educational justice. This may be especially useful for universities that seek ways to thread relevance and return on investment for the student, their families, the community and the regional economy. For first generation students, the programs described can make it easier to imagine possible futures. For students from diverse backgrounds, the programs provided examples of how to advance community cultural wealth. The goal for the chapter was to highlight the ways an ecosystem can uncover synergies by honoring the strengths of the different parties within. This can include the university's ability to amplify the value of the degree, highlight the importance of reciprocal relationships, and meet the need for more theory and practice in this area.

Discover and Propel

Influencers

Higher Education		Policy
Dr. Raj Chetty	Michael Sorrell	Secretary Miguel Cardona
Dr. Michelle Weiss	Dr. Stephen Goldsmith	Dr. Jamie Marisotis
Dr. Tia McNair	Dr. Anne Kress	Amy Ellen Duke-Benfield
Dr. Gina Ann Garcia	Dr. J. Luke Wood	Heather McKay
Dr. Sam Museus	Jeff Selingo	Amy Lloyd

Tools to Support Workforce Development

Labor Market Analytics, Economic Trends, and Skills Modeling for Student Success

1. Employment Development Department - Dashboard Example https://calstatepays.org/

2. Department of Labor: O*Net Online Occupation Exploration https://www.onetonline.org/

3. Jobs For the Future https://www.jff.org/work/education/

4. Lightcast https://lightcast.io/solutions/education/

5. National Skills Coalition https://nationalskillscoalition.org/creating-an-equitable-resilient-workforce-system/

6. Postsecondary to Prosperity Dashboard Example https://p2p.californiacompetes.org/

7. Regional statistics for social change Dashboard Example https://la.myneighborhooddata.org

Career development and Assessment

1. Cradle to Career Transparent Data System https://c2c.ca.gov/

2. Workbay https://www.workbay.net/what-is-workbay

3. CliftonStrengths based assessment https://www.gallup.com/cliftonstrengths/en/507263/cliftonstrengths-on-campus.aspx

4. National Survey of Student Engagement (NSSE) Career and Workforce Preparation https://nsse.indiana.edu/nsse/survey-instruments/topical-modules/work-career-prep.html

5. Common (Soft) Skills (National Association of Colleges and Employers, Self-Assessment) https://www.naceweb.org/career-readiness/competencies/career-readiness-defined

6. Skills Alignment to Career Goals (Lightcast, SkillsMatch Self-Assessment) https://lightcast.io/solutions/education/skillsmatch

7. Career Readiness (National Survey of Student Engagement, Career Readiness Module) https://nsse.indiana.edu/nsse/survey-instruments/topical-modules/work-career-prep.html

8. Guide to Writing a Workforce Program Design and Evaluation https://www.nrel.gov/docs/fy23osti/86302.pdf

Planning, Strategy, Funding, and Research

1. American Association of Colleges & Universities (AAC&U) https://www.aacu.org/research/how-college-contributes-to-workforce-success

2. Aspen Institute: College Excellence Programs https://highered.aspeninstitute.org/workforce-research-tools/

3. Society for College and University Planning (SCUP) https://www.scup.org/

4. Education Advisory Board (EAB) https://eab.com/resources/topics/student-success-and-experience/

5. Deloitte Future of Work https://www2.deloitte.com/us/en/pages/human-capital/topics/future-of-work.html

6. Georgetown University Center on Education and the Workforce https://cew.georgetown.edu/resources/reports/

7. Childhood roots of social and economic mobility https://opportunityinsights.org/paper/the-opportunity-atlas/

8. National Student Clearinghouse Research Center https://www.studentclearinghouse.org

9. Higher Education Equity network https://www.higheredequitynetwork.org/

10. ECMC Foundation https://www.ecmcfoundation.org/what-we-do/strategic-framework

11. Pew Research Center https://www.pewresearch.org/

12. Brookings https://www.brookings.edu/topics/workforce-development/

13. Gates Foundation: Equitable economic outcomes https://usprogram.gatesfoundation.org/who-we-are/education-to-workforce-framework

14. Strada Education Foundation https://stradaeducation.org/report/state-opportunity-index/?utm_source=InsideHigh%20erEd&utm_medium=Newsletter&utm_campaign=SOI&utm_content=DailyWeeklyNewsU%20pdates_Apr.2024

15. The Institute for College Access & Success https://ticas.org/

Note of appreciation

The work described in this space would not have been possible without the support of the leadership at my current and past institutions. The leaders saw the need to lean into economic data to bring relevant demand information to programs and to support risk taking in the changes that they made. Support from Vice President Manriquez to fund our start up Workforce Integration Network at the request of the President was instrumental. I am grateful for our Director, Dr. Krystal Rawls, who co-designed the program and grant with me. The passion that she brings to the work, alongside her expertise, creativity, and unrelenting energy to serve students and the community, is inspiring. I have also learned from the leaders in faculty development spaces, Dr. Kim Costino and Dr. Marisela Chavez, and the faculty in the communities, who invited me in as a participant observer and colleague.

References

Alic, J. A. (2018). What we mean when we talk about workforce skills. *Issues in Science and Technology, 34*(3), 30-36.

Alonso, J. (2023). Measuring Higher Ed's Benefits Beyond Earnings. *Inside HigherEd.* https://www.insidehighered.com/news/students/careers/2023/08/30/study-shows-higher-ed-linked-kinder-healthier-citizens

Beer, F., Samuel, G., Rawls, K. & Sirotnik, B. (2023) Are we moving the needle? An empirical evaluation of business faculty members' perceptions of DEI efforts. *Journal of Education for Business, 98*(5), 251-261, DOI: https://doi.org/10.1080/08832323.2022.2144987

Bresciani, M. J. (2006). *Outcomes-based academic and co-curricular program review: A compilation of institutional good practices.* Stylus Publishing, LLC..

Brooms, D. R., Clark, J., & Smith, M. (2018). *Empowering men of color on campus: Building student community in higher education.* Rutgers University Press.

Carnevale, A. P., Fasules, M. L., Quinn, M. C., & Peltier Campbell, K. (2019). *Born to win, schooled to lose.* https://cew. georgetown.edu/cew-reports/schooled2lose/

Chetty, R. (2016). Improving Opportunities for Economic Mobility. *Federal Reserve Bank of St. Louis* https://www.stlouisfed.org/ publications/bridges/fall-2016/improving-opportunities-for-economic-mobility

Chetty, R., Grusky, D., Hell, M., Hendren, N., Manduca, R., & Narang, J. (2017). The fading American dream: Trends in absolute income mobility since 1940. *Science, 356*(6336), 398-406.

Clayton, P., Bringle, R., Senor, B., Huq, J., & Morrison, M. (2010) Differentiating and assessing relationships in service-learning and civic engagement: Exploitative, transactional, or transformational. *Michigan Journal of Community Service Learning,* (16) 2, pp. 5-22.

Crown, D. (2024). The demographic outlook: 2024 to 2054. *Congressional Budget Office.* www.cbo.gov/publication/59697

Culver, K. C., & Kezar, A. (2021). Designing accessible and inclusive professional development for NTTF.

Davis, L. P., & Museus, S. D. (2019). What is deficit thinking? An analysis of conceptualizations of deficit thinking and implications for scholarly research. *NCID Currents, 1*(1).

Edmondson, A. C., & Bransby, D. P. (2023). Psychological safety comes of age: Observed themes in an established literature. *Annual Review of Organizational Psychology and Organizational Behavior, 10,* 55-78.

Finley, A. (2021). How college contributes to workforce success: Employer views on what matters most. *Association of American Colleges and Universities.*

Gallup and Lumina Foundation. (2023). *The state of higher education 2022 report.* Gallup, Inc. https://www.luminafoundation.org/resource/the-state-of-higher-education-2023-report/

Garib, V. (2020). Using high impact practice characteristics and career readiness competencies to examine a college work experience program. https://stars.library.ucf.edu/etd2020/47/

Garza, A. (2021). *Identifying transformational and transactional leaders in the public sector (DPSS) and their influence on employees* (Doctoral dissertation, California State University, Northridge).

Gatta, M., Finley, A., & Green, P. (2024). Faculty attitudes and behaviors: The Integration of career readiness into the curriculum. Produced in Partnership with National Association of Colleges and Employers (NACE), American Association of Colleges and Universities (AAC&U), and Society for Experiential Education (SEE). https://naceweb.org/research/reports/faculty-attitudes-and-behaviors-the-integration-of-career-readiness-into-the-curriculum

Goldsmith, S., & Coleman, K. M. (2022). *Growing fairly: How to build opportunity and equity in workforce development.* Brookings Institution Press.

Gooding, K., Makwinja, R., Nyirenda, D., Vincent, R., & Sambakunsi, R. (2018). Using theories of change to design monitoring and evaluation of community engagement in research: experiences from a research institute in Malawi. *Wellcome open research, 3.*

Grawe, N. D. (2018). *Demographics and the demand for higher education*. JHU Press.

Grilo S.A., Semler M.R., Rameau S. (2023). The sum of all parts: A multi-level exploration of racial and ethnic identity formation during emerging adulthood. *PLoS One, 8*(4):e0284275. doi: 10.1371/journal.pone.0284275. PMID: 37027386; PMCID: PMC10081756.

Hooks, B. (2014). *Teaching to transgress*. Routledge.

Hora, M. T., Benbow, R. J., Oleson, A. K., & Wang, Y. (2015). A different take on the "skills gap": Why cultivating diverse competencies is essential for success in the 21st century economy. *WISCAPE Policy Brief*, 1-14.

Huang, F. L. (2018). Do Black students misbehave more? Investigating the differential involvement hypothesis and out-of-school suspensions. *The Journal of Educational Research, 111*(3), 284-294.

Ladson-Billings, B. (1992). Reading between the lines and beyond the pages: A culturally relevant approach to literacy teaching. *Theory Into Practice, 31*(4), 312-320.

Kuh, G. D., & O'Donnell, K. (2013). Ensuring quality and taking high-impact practices to scale. *Peer Review, 15*(2), 32-33.

Ladson-Billings, G. (2021, July). Three decades of culturally relevant, responsive, & sustaining pedagogy: What lies ahead? *The Educational Forum 85*(4), pp. 351-354). Routledge.

Lareau, A. (2017). Concerted cultivation and the accomplishment of natural growth. *Childhood socialization*, pp. 335-344. Routledge.

Lee, S. & Shapiro, D. (November 2023), Completing college: National and state report with longitudinal data dashboard on six- and eight-year completion rates. *Signature Report 22*, Herndon, VA: National Student Clearinghouse Research Center

Lomotey, K., & Smith, W. A. (Eds.). (2023). *The racial crisis in American higher education.* State University of New York Press.

McNair, T. B., Albertine, S., McDonald, N., Major Jr, T., & Cooper, M. A. (2022). *Becoming a student-ready college: A new culture of leadership for student success.* John Wiley & Sons.

Merisotis, J. (2015). *America needs talent: Attracting, educating & deploying the 21st-century workforce.* Rosetta Books.

Mitchell, T. D. (2008). Traditional vs. critical service-learning: Engaging the literature to differentiate two models. *Michigan Journal of Community Service Learning, 14*(2), 50-65.

Mitchell, W. Bede. Higher Education for the Public Good: Emerging Voices from a National Movement. (2006.) *College & Research Libraries, 67*(2), pp. 192–94, https://doi.org/10.5860/crl.67.2.192.

Museus, S. D., Yi, V., & Saelua, N. (2018). How culturally engaging campus environments influence sense of belonging in college: An examination of differences between White students and students of color. *Journal of Diversity in Higher Education, 11*(4), 467.

Paris, D. (2012). Culturally sustaining pedagogy: A needed change in stance, terminology, and practice. *Educational researcher, 41*(3), 93-97.

Paton, V. O., Fitzgerald, H. E., Green, B. L., Raymond, M., & Borchardt, M. P. (2014). US higher education regional accreditation commission standards and the centrality of engagement. *Journal of Higher Education Outreach and Engagement, 18*(4), 41-70.

Patton, L. D. (2016). Disrupting Postsecondary Prose: Toward a Critical Race Theory of Higher Education. *Urban Education, 51*(3), 315-342. https://doi.org/10.1177/0042085915602542

Peterson. E. (2021). Racial inequality in public school discipline for Black students in the United States. www.ballardbrief.org.

Rios, C. (2015). *You call it professionalism; I call it oppression in a three-piece suit.* https://everydayfeminism.com/2015/02/professionalism-and-oppression/

Rojewski, J. (2002). Preparing the workforce of tomorrow: A conceptual framework for career and technical education. *Journal of Vocational Education Research, 27*(1), 7-35.

Roumell, E. A., Todoran, C., & Salajan, F. D. (2020). A framework for capacity building in adult and workforce education programming. *Adult Literacy Education, 2*(2), 16-32.

Siwatu, K. O. (2007). Preservice teachers' culturally responsive teaching self-efficacy and outcome expectancy beliefs. *Teaching and teacher education, 23*(7), 1086-1101.

Stewart, D. & Nicolazzo, Z. (2018) High Impact of [Whiteness] on trans* students in postsecondary education. *Equity & Excellence in Education, 51*(2), 132-145, DOI: 10.1080/10665684.2018.1496046

Walker, B., Bair, A. R., & Macdonald, R. H. (2022). Supporting students' career development: A call to action. *New Directions for Community Colleges, 199*, 93-106. https://onlinelibrary.wiley.com/doi/epdf/10.1002/cc.20526

Washington, M. L. (2019). *Towards a culturally critical andragogy: An exploratory study of the Black male experience in higher education* (Doctoral dissertation, The Claremont Graduate University).

Weise, M. R., Hanson, A. R., & Saleh, Y. (2019). The new geography of skills: Regional skill shapes for the new learning ecosystem. *Strada Institute for the Future of Work.*

Wilder, C. S. (2013). *Ebony and ivy: Race, slavery, and the troubled history of America's universities*. Bloomsbury Publishing USA.

Yosso, T. J. (2005). Whose culture has capital? A critical race theory discussion of community cultural wealth. *Race ethnicity and education, 8*(1), 69-91.

PART VI

THE AHA ADVANTAGE

This section concludes the book by reinforcing the importance of a strategic approach to accreditation. Readers gain important insights from the vantage point of key roles in the accreditation process as they share their perspectives so others can gain the "Aha" advantage, that is, the ability to see accreditation as a transformative tool that can drive institutional growth and excellence.

Chapter 15

What Commissioners Want You to Know

J. Joseph Hoey and Richard Mahon[6]

Accreditation agencies go to great lengths to ensure that information needed by institutions (or programs) they accredit have a clear understanding of the agencies' standards, criteria, policies, procedures and protocol. Among other things, many agencies require an appearance before the accreditation agency as one step in the process prior to the commission rendering a decision on accreditation or a substantial institutional change. Not infrequently, institutional presidents and other representatives are not sufficiently informed of what they should be ready to discuss during a commission hearing. The intent of this chapter is therefore to serve as a practical

---

6   Disclaimer: The views expressed in this chapter are those of the authors, and not of the commissions on which they have served.

> *guide for institutions appearing before an accreditation commission, to inform readers of the most salient areas commissioners would like institutions to be prepared to discuss with the commission or commission panel reviewing their case.*

This chapter begins with an overview of the purpose and roles of commissioners in comprehensive U.S. (a better phrase than "formerly regional") accreditation agencies. Written from the perspective of two seasoned commissioners, the chapter dwells at length on how a college or university can align its accreditation efforts with other structural, ongoing institutional processes as a singularly viable method to move forward on an improvement trajectory while simultaneously demonstrating alignment with the standards, criteria, and policies of the accreditor. Based on our experience as commissioners, such purposeful alignment saves precious financial resources and countless person hours, is easily communicated to campus constituencies, and produces positive results for the institution. Accreditation commissioners can see and appreciate the purposeful alignment, understand the magnitude of the undertaking, and more effectively render appropriate decisions regarding institutional accreditation.

Who Are Accreditation Agency Commissioners, and What Roles Do They Play?

The deeply held value of peer review in higher education finds powerful expression in the structure and processes of institutional accreditation. Comprehensive accreditation agencies in the United States include a CEO and professional staff to carry out ongoing processes, advising, consulting, and executive roles. For onsite review of individual colleges and universities, volunteer peer review teams undertake the responsibility of conducting in-depth standards-based reviews describing their findings, crafting recommendations aimed at advancing an institution's ability to be the best it can be, and ensuring alignment with accreditation standards.

It is critical to recognize that peer reviewers are almost always chosen because they have already been through this process at their own institutions. They have struggled with the challenge of articulating institutional strengths—and weaknesses—against the evaluative grid provided by the standards. They know the struggles of too many aspirations and too little budget and the need to identify the means most likely to benefit the students served by their institutions. On top of their experience, they are trained to apply accreditation standards to institutions not their own, and often not even *like* their own; they are trained to see the institution they will visit both sympathetically and critically. Once the team report and potential recommendations have been drafted and the errors and omissions review completed by the institution, the next step is for the commissioners to review the report and any potential recommendations.

For the vital standards- and evidence-based peer review and decision-making functions they conduct, accreditation agencies rely on a body of volunteer institutional administrators, staff, faculty members, and unaffiliated public members collectively referred to as commissioners (or when enacting decisions a body, as the commission). Actions routinely undertaken by commissioners include consideration of and decisions on periodic institutional reviews, approval or disapproval of major institutional changes, and consideration of changes or updates to commission policy and to the agency's accreditation standards themselves. In the two largest comprehensive accreditors, SACS-COC and the Higher Learning Commission, similar roles are played by a board of trustees. The Higher Learning Commission also includes the sizable Institutional Actions Council, appointed by the board of trustees as a decision-making body for recurring institutional reviews. Most comprehensive accreditors also have a separate appeals committee that hears institutional appeals to adverse commission decisions.

Drawn from institutions accredited by the agency, commissioners may include presidents, senior administrators, senior staff members, and faculty with previous accreditation experience. Together with members of the public at large, they form the commission roster. Most commissioners from member institutions have extensive previous experience serving on institutional accreditation teams, in some cases with multiple accreditors. Commissioners go through a nomination and vetting process and are elected to serve terms of varying length. Many, including the authors, consider their service on an accreditation commission as among the best professional development experiences they have had.

What Commissioners Want You to Know: It's a Lot of Work, so Make Everything Count Double!

Rhetorical question: Do college and university administrators really spend time thinking of how to get more busy work out of faculty? Succinct answer: No, administrators don't have the time! The authors' primary thesis in this chapter is that the more institutions can align efforts and expenditures to serve multiple purposes, the more apparent it becomes that doing so makes good sense all around. Exhibit 15.1 summarized how this can be done effectively.

What do commissioners want you to know? *They feel your pain!* Accreditation is a lot of work for *everyone* involved. Much time is spent organizing—finding documents, structuring meetings, leading workgroups, wrangling evidence, setting up webpages, and preparing for the site visit. All the elements of accreditation take a toll on already busy faculty, staff, and administrators. Commissioners

Exhibit 15.1 It's a Lot of Work, so Make Everything Count Double!

It's a Lot of Work, so Make Everything Count Double!

Intentionally Aligning Institutional Processes and Timelines With Accreditation Cycles

The standards of all the comprehensive accreditors include consistent structural elements, regardless of their sequence or how they are phrased. Aligning your own institutional processes to your accreditation cycle will save time and effort.

Challenges in Leadership and Governance

The flux and instability resulting from a change in senior leadership can be detrimental to the accreditation process if new leadership doesn't embrace it. A healthy institution should have clear procedures in place that do not grind to a halt because there is an interim or a new leader.

It's About Teaching and Learning Writ Large

Virtually all accreditation processes are what we do in every classroom on our campus or online, simply executed at a larger scale.

are aware of this because, more often than not, they have been involved in accreditation on their home campuses. Moreover, most commissioners have served on a variety of peer review visiting teams, and they have noted the contrast in stress and uncertainty between their colleagues at colleges where the many elements of accreditation are integrated into the ongoing processes of the institution (and they are grateful, if it's true, that their own campus works this way). But commissioners have also served on teams sent to colleges where the pending reality of an accreditation visit only came on the radar 18 months prior, distracting many members of the campus community from their core duties as they quickly assembled the institution's self-evaluation report, crossed their fingers, and prayed the team didn't notice that many of the documents were date-stamped within the last year and a half and often much more recently.

Finally, commissioners know how challenging accreditation can be if it is not integrated into the institution's ongoing core efforts to establish policies and procedures that do everything possible to ensure that students learn what the institution is committed to teaching. They know this because they read dozens of self-evaluation reports, meet with campus representatives during the institutional review process, and hear from commission staff members who report on the efforts the institutions make to comply with the guidance commissions provide and help them become the colleges and universities they aspire to be.

At heart, the entire enterprise of accreditation rests on the assumption that an endeavor as vast as higher education must be based in bureaucratic institutions that can take pride in their accomplishments, learn from their weaknesses, and improve so that students are better served over time. The further assumption is that society itself is enriched by the contributions of students who are also consumers, voters, and citizens who support a social order of astonishing complexity that aspires to meet the needs of all its members.

Intentionally Aligning Institutional Processes and Timelines With Accreditation Cycles

It is not an accident that the standards of *all* the comprehensive accreditors include consistent structural elements, regardless of their sequence or how they are phrased. Accreditors, and therefore commissioners, are interested in an institution's mission and the efforts undertaken to fulfill it. Accreditation standards ask colleges and universities to reflect and report on their curriculum, from the course to the program to the institutional level. They ask institutions to describe the student support services that, if designed effectively and utilized widely, should make it possible for *all* students to meet the curricular requirements of their school and to earn the appropriate recognition for their learning, whether that be a degree or professional certification. To be effective, all institutions need resources—human beings, facilities, technology, and the budget to sustain them—in spite of fluctuations in the larger economy. And institutions need leaders, at all levels, who are attuned to data and know that they must reset their course if the data indicate that the aspirations they have for their students are not being met. The structures to meet these needs are present on virtually every college and university campus, however formal or informal they might be.

Faculty can't teach classes individually without putting thought into creating the syllabus, and faculty can't create programs collectively without coming to some agreement about the goals (accreditors might say *outcomes*) of the program and how to know whether they are meeting those goals. Virtually every academic unit wishes its budget were larger, but money, as they say, does not grow on trees. This means that virtually every campus unit goes through an annual process of reflecting on its priorities (those things it *must* fund) and its aspirations (those things it wishes it could fund but may not be able to) in order to establish its budget for the subsequent year. These are structural, ongoing sequences of actions; they should not be divorced from the self-study/accreditation process. Rather, college and university leaders— from the facilities and IT departments to the offices of instruction and student services— should seek ways to align how the institution operates within the context of accreditation standards.

All institutional processes should be thoughtful and reflective— who wouldn't want that for their own campus? But there is no one-size-fits-all approach, and accreditors are certainly aware that processes that work at one institution won't necessarily work elsewhere. One of the Accrediting Commission for Community and Junior Colleges' (ACCJC's) member institutions has a *maximum* enrollment of 26 students and a curriculum committee that is primarily student run. The processes that fit that college well would not work at all at any other college in the ACCJC's portfolio. Commissioners are only interested in whether each college's processes work for the students it serves.

There are many processes at colleges and universities that must be performed annually—budgeting is probably the most obvious. Other processes are only meaningful if they are repeated at intervals of several years, since longitudinal data tell a different story than term-specific data. The ACCJC is in the process of lengthening its comprehensive review cycle to eight years. The Western Association of Schools and Colleges, Senior College and University Commission (WSCUC) grants reaccreditation for 6, 8, or 10 years. Both commissions ask member institutions to submit interim reports between those more distant goalposts. How difficult would it be for a school to take an inventory of its various institutional processes and, informed by a careful reading of the standards, create a timeline that ensures both that meaningful short- *and* long-term (*strategic*) planning are accomplished *and* that especially demanding cycles of effort are distributed in such a way that no one is ever frantically trying to beat the calendar?

Challenges in Leadership and Governance

One of the problems facing colleges and universities is the flux and instability that result from a change in senior leadership. It is natural and desirable that new leaders bring new ideas and new methods to maintain and improve the quality of an institution. But—and this is a big but—a healthy institution should have clear procedures in place that do not grind to a halt because there is an interim or a new leader. Indeed, a promising new leader will respect established procedures and seek to evaluate and improve them, not to abandon them and start over from scratch. One of the authors recalls serving on a visiting team that inquired why so few program reviews were completed; the answer came back that the president spent money as he saw fit, generally without regard for the program review and planning process. No wonder faculty and staff didn't want to invest much time in a process everyone believed to be a charade.

One regular question of accreditors is whether the governing board is doing its job. Trustees (governors, regents, etc.) have the challenge of setting meaningful policy and priorities for the institutions they oversee without micromanaging the CEO they have chosen and to whom they have delegated responsibility for day-to-day management. Asking institutional leaders to establish the kind of integrated institutional and accreditation timeline described above would be a stellar responsibility for trustees to embrace.

It's About Teaching and Learning Writ Large

Here's a claim that might be helpful to some of our colleagues who have struggled to make sense of what accreditation asks of them and also clarify why alignment is so important: Virtually all accreditation processes are what we do in every classroom on our campus or online, simply executed at a larger scale. Faculty decide what they want students to learn and craft a syllabus to articulate those goals and expectations. Accreditors do the same thing, crafting accreditation standards and revising them periodically (since even the best syllabus needs periodic refreshing).

Faculty make assignments and review student work; accreditors ask institutions to reflect on the syllabus (the standards) and how well they have met expectations, being candid about where they could improve. Faculty want even very high-performing students to strive to improve even when it's clear the expectations of the syllabus have been met; commissioners seek a similar drive for excellence in institutions. Faculty spend disproportionate time working with students who are struggling, whatever the reason might be; the same is true of commissioners and underperforming institutions.

Some students miss class because their off-campus jobs (which they need to pay their tuition and living expenses) demand more hours than are compatible with the hours they need to study; similarly, some institutions have made more fiscal commitments than they can fulfill given the income stream they can reliably project. Good faculty don't just grade student work but provide feedback to students on how they can improve; commissioners collectively review all the data available and make recommendations to institutions that represent, in their shared/collective experience, the best steps for a struggling institution to get ahead of its challenges and recover the vitality it enjoyed before (hopefully) passing challenges arose.

Faculty want every student to succeed, provided every student is willing to do the work; commissioners want every institution to thrive. Faculty are saddened when a student with evident potential fails to meet the expectations expressed in the syllabi; commissioners feel the same disappointment when the integrity of the standards and the accreditation process compel them to sanction or even withdraw the accreditation of an institution. At the other end of the scale and perhaps akin to a student graduating *cum laude*, accreditors recognize consistently superior institutional outcomes. For example, WSCUC features a Thematic Pathway for Reaffirmation for those consistently financially stable, high-performing, low-risk institutions that demonstrate strong evidence of ongoing student success—itself the Alpha and the Omega of accreditation.

What Commissioners Want You to Know: What, When, and How to Align Efforts

What Commissioners want you to know is summarized in Exhibit 15.2 and described in greater detail in the sections that follow.

Exhibit 15.2: What, When, and How to Align Efforts

Proactive Alignment of Strategic Plan Development as Part of Comprehensive Review Preparation

The 2023 WSCUC *Handbook* includes 4 standards of accreditation and 41 specific criteria for review. Among other things, the

Handbook lays out the review process for reaffirmation of accredited institutions and serves as a guide to commission decisions. As with all accreditors, institutions are expected to adhere to all WSCUC Commission policies and applicable federal regulations; indeed, as part of becoming accredited in the first place, institutions commit to staying in compliance with the accreditation standards they have voluntarily accepted. The *Handbook* provides a Compliance with WSCUC Standards and Federal Requirements Worksheet similar to templates provided by other accreditors. Not only is that worksheet a required element of the self-study itself, but it provides institutions an opportunity to include multiple constituencies in an institution-wide reflection on the school's current status relative to the accreditation standards and criteria.

Until its most recent standards revision, the ACCJC had 4 standards and 128 criteria that had to be fully met within 2 years or else the clock would start ticking towards show cause review. Relative to WSCUC, ACCJC standards prescribed *much* more precisely how schools would demonstrate their quality. To the great relief of all parties working on accreditation, the number of standards that must be addressed in a written narrative has been reduced by 75 percent, which should have the effect of focusing all parties—institutional leaders and the institutional community at large—on the central policies and practices that establish and maintain the quality of the institution. Still, many standards remain, and *any* number of standards begs the question: Why would institutions faced with preparing for a comprehensive accreditation review not want to achieve economies of effort and effectiveness by checking two boxes (planning and accreditation) rather than one in their institutional efforts?

In our first example of what and when to align efforts (and much to the delight of one of the authors), a recently reviewed institution had been highly proactive in aligning its strategic planning process with an accreditation review. It had used the WSCUC Standards

Worksheet to obtain input from across all sectors of the institution and had developed a SWOT (Strengths, Weaknesses, Opportunities, and Threats) analysis review as a core input to the strategic planning process that was begun simultaneously with preparations for the upcoming comprehensive accreditation review. In that case, alignment with the WSCUC Standards and Criteria was built into the strategic plan from the outset, saving the university thousands of person hours and expediting commission approval of the comprehensive review.

Alignment in Responding to Recommendations: Find Common Ground to Economize Efforts

This second approach involves aligning accreditation recommendations received from the accreditor with extant institutional strategic goals. One of the authors has long made it a practice of developing matrix representations of the relationships between accreditation recommendations received and goals/objectives of the current institutional strategic plan to determine how efforts to meet each accreditation recommendation will contribute clear evidence of progress on the strategic plan. Here, there is a strong need to practice good writing as a reflection of good thinking beforehand! First, formulate clear conceptual connections and relationships between the plan and the accreditation recommendations. Then get it written up, socialize it with campus decision-makers and constituencies, and begin to create a compelling cascade of evidence to demonstrate both alignment and accomplishment.

Align Goals of Major Institutional Changes With Accreditor Standards and Requirements

A third approach is to use major institutional modifications such as mission revision, mergers, and changes of control as an opportunity to align strategic goals with accreditor standards and requirements.

Institutional mergers only show signs of steady further growth as demographic shifts take place and birth rates continue to decline. Achieving financial sustainability is frequently the overarching merger goal. But what does that mean for the students? How will student outcomes be enhanced through the merger? Institutions that put in the time planning both for student outcomes and for financial impacts in a merger will have greater credibility with commissioners, who *want* to see the merged institution and its students succeed. These institutions may also encounter fewer delays/requests for rework. As a case in point, one of the authors is familiar with an acquisition and merger that ended up taking over a year from initial proposal submission to final commission approval in part due to a lack of sufficient focus on the students and preparation for impacts to student outcomes.

How to Align?

Know the visible and invisible parts of the iceberg: Understanding how to align involves timing, a nuanced sense of the institution's culture, and a grasp of what motivates institutional actors. At the end of the day, even hardened cynics within the institution should shake their heads and acknowledge that alignment, when deployed correctly, just makes good sense.

For accreditors as well as institutional faculty, staff, and administrators, it's about student success: Frame accreditation as something institutions would already want to do to help their students succeed. People don't like projects for projects' sake but rather for the value they bring to institutions and to students. Accreditation keeps us from missing good opportunities.

Call it one degree of separation: frame what we are being asked to do so that it is fairly close to what we are already doing, so that we won't be wasting our time, and so that faculty will be excited about participating since doing so will help their students learn.

Aligning Accreditation and Institutional Processes: Advice from Other Accreditors

The experience-based perspective presented by the authors is by no means limited to a West Coast approach, but rather one that finds resonance in the accreditation and self-study preparation documentation of multiple comprehensive accreditors across the continent. The Middle States Commission on Higher Education (MSCHE) has developed a Self-Study Institute and accompanying self-study guides for institutions preparing for and proceeding through a self-study process. The expectations for alignment of institutional planning or other processes with the self-study process are clearly presented. For example, the Self-Study Institute Module 3, *Developing an Effective Self-Study Design*, includes specific directions to pinpoint several priorities of the institution to focus on within the self-study, and to provide information about:

- How institutional stakeholders were consulted in identifying the priorities.

- Alignment of the selected institutional priorities with the institution's mission and goals (and strategic plan, as appropriate).

- Alignment of the selected institutional priorities to the Standards for Accreditation and Requirements of Affiliation (Fourteenth Edition). (2023, pp. 4-5)

An example of accreditor advice to combine accreditation self-study with planning and with other institutional processes, as the authors have recommended in this chapter, is provided in the New England Commission on Higher Education's (NECHE) *Self-Study Guide:*

Because it helps various constituencies come together with a common purpose—candid self-evaluation and direction-setting—self-study is well suited to the development of a comprehensive strategic planning process or the audit of quality assurance systems. The process can also be especially valuable during institutional transitions, expansions, and system changes, as it helps institutions define challenges and create plans for addressing them. (2021, p. 9)

In the most compelling (and required) case of accreditor guidance to align accreditation standards with institutional processes, the Southern Association of Colleges and Schools, Commission on Colleges (SACS-COC) has long considered the alignment of accreditation requirements, planning, and institutional actions to further student success to be of such importance that a major component of the reaffirmation process is devoted to it. The Quality Enhancement Plan (QEP) is described in the SACS-COC *Handbook for Institutions Seeking Reaffirmation:*

The QEP describes a carefully designed course of action that addresses a well-defined and focused topic or issue related to enhancing student learning and/or student success. The QEP's topic should be identified through or in concert with the institution's ongoing integrated institution-wide planning and evaluation process. Hence, the QEP standard (7.2) is closely related to Core Requirement 7.1 (*Institutional planning*) (2020, p. 33).

To one of the authors, having served as a QEP evaluator, there is no secret to why the QEP is such a successful part of the SACS-COC reaffirmation process: It enables institutions to unite accreditation requirements with exactly what they exist to promote—student success—and to demonstrate evidence of that success to the community while simultaneously meeting accreditation requirements. In this case, it's not just making all efforts count double, but rather triple!

Concluding Thoughts

This chapter began by describing the makeup and roles played by volunteer accreditation commissions (in some cases boards of trustees) among comprehensive institutional accreditors in the United States. Based on their experience as commissioners, the authors argue from several different vantage points for institutions to adopt a fully integrated approach to accreditation, one that unites planning, budgeting, and other institutional processes with the expectations of accreditors, as stated in standards and criteria for accreditation. As explained in this chapter, the rationale for aligning accreditation standards and institutional processes is inherently practical: Accreditation preparation is difficult, time-consuming work, but when paired and aligned with structural processes of the institution, not only can the normal work of the institution proceed, but planning, communicating, and preparing for periodic accreditation reviews is accomplished with much less disruption. When such alignment is made evident to accreditation commissions, the task of those commissioners reviewing an institutional case is greatly facilitated, and generally better outcomes of a commission review result. This experiential perspective also finds validation in the self-study and reaffirmation guides of multiple comprehensive accreditors.

Discussion Questions

1. Is your institution's mission clearly stated and widely known throughout campus?

2. Does your institution evaluate and revise established policies and practices in light of their alignment with mission and their effectiveness in producing their intended outcomes?

3. Are the courses and programs offered at your institution meeting the needs of the students served? What qualitative

and quantitative data make you confident of the answer?

4. Are the student service programs offered by your institution utilized by the students who need them most? Could you demonstrate to your students that those dollars invested are making a significant difference in their lives and academic outcomes?

5. Are your institution's budgets and plans related to staffing, facilities, and technology clearly based on meeting the needs of the academic programs you have or might begin to develop?

6. Are the planning processes at your institution aligned with your accreditation timetables?

7. What steps would you take to begin aligning accreditation standards with institutional processes at your institution? What would be the most logical place to start? With whom, what body, or what group?

8. Is the work of accreditation at your institution respected as an element in maintaining and enhancing institutional quality?

9. Would you want to serve as a commissioner at some point? If so, how would you begin preparing yourself? What steps would you take? What steps have you already taken?

References

Accrediting Commission for Community and Junior Colleges. (2023). *Accreditation handbook.* https://accjc.org/wp-content/uploads/Accreditation-Handbook.pdf.

Accrediting Commission for Community and Junior Colleges. (2023). *Accreditation standards with review criteria and suggestions for evidence.* https://accjc.org/wp-content/uploads/ACCJC-2024-Accreditation-Standards-with-Review-Criteria-Evidence.pdf.

Higher Learning Commission. (2023). Decision-making bodies and related processes. https://www.hlcommission.org/Accreditation/decision-making.html.

Middle States Commission on Higher Education. (2023). *Self-study institute (SSI) Module 3: Developing an effective self-study design (pp.4-5).* https://www.msche.org/self-study-guide-for-institutions-in-ssi-2023/.

New England Commission on Higher Education. (2021). *Self-study guide (p.9).* https://www.neche.org/wp-content/uploads/2018/12/Self-Study-Guide-2021.pdf.

Southern Association of Colleges and Schools, Commission on Colleges. (2020). *Handbook for institutions seeking reaffirmation (p. 33).* https://sacscoc.org/app/uploads/2020/03/Handbook-for-Institutions-Seeking-Reaffirmation.pdf.

Southern Association of Colleges and Schools, Commission on Colleges. (2022). *Standing Rules: SACSCOC Board of Trustees, Executive Council, and the College Delegate Assembly.* https://

sacscoc.org/app/uploads/2020/12/standingrules.pdf.

Western Association of Schools and Colleges, Senior College and University Commission. (2023). *2023 handbook*. https://www.wscuc.org/handbook2023/.

Chapter 16

Insights from an Accreditation Staff Liaison

Denise York Young

In this chapter, readers gain unique insights from an accreditation staff liaison, who shares their extensive knowledge and experience working with accrediting bodies. Through their perspective, readers learn about the accreditation process, key considerations for successful accreditation, and practical tips for navigating the complexities of the accreditation journey.

This chapter is written from the viewpoint of an experienced accreditation staff liaison for the Southern Association of College and Schools Commission on Colleges (SACSCOC). SACSCOC is one of the seven institutional accreditors formerly known as regional accreditors. The U.S. Department of Education changed the nomenclature from "regional" to "institutional" accreditors in 2019. These seven accreditors, along with their founding dates and website addresses, are listed in Exhibit 16.1. The oldest three (NECHE, HLC, and SACSCOC) were founded between 1885 and 1895.

Exhibit 16.1: Former Regional Accreditors Now Known as Institutional Accreditors

Accrediting Body (Acronym) Website	Founding Date Listed on Website	Institutions[7]	Students[a] (certificate and degree-seeking)
Accrediting Commission for Community and Junior Colleges (ACCJC) https://accjc.org/	2012-13 with predecessor organizations dating back to 1924	133	1,070,072
Higher Learning Commission (HLC) https://www.hlcommission.org/	1895	925	4,682,373

---

7   Source data for institutions and students is the National Advisory Committee on Institutional Quality and Integrity (NACIQI; 2023, July) https://sites.ed.gov/naciqi/files/2023/07/InstitutionalAccredData.xlsx. These data represent Title IV participating institutions listed with the primary accreditor for Title IV gatekeeping purposes. For example, SACSCOC has approximately 20 non-Title IV participating institutions (primarily seminaries and foreign institutions) not included in the numbers in Table 16.1.

Accrediting Body (Acronym) Website	Founding Date Listed on Website	Institutions[7]	Students[a] (certificate and degree-seeking)
Middle States Commission on Higher Education (MSCHE) https://www. msche.org/	1919	480	2,614,375
New England Commission of Higher Education (NECHE) https://www. neche.org/	1885	205	992,313
Northwest Commission on Colleges and Universities (NWCCU) https://nwccu. org/	1917	156	1,041,305

Accrediting Body (Acronym) Website	Founding Date Listed on Website	Institutions[7]	Students[a] (certificate and degree-seeking)
Southern Association of Colleges and Schools Commission on Colleges (SACSCOC) https://www.sacscoc.org/	1895	757	4,915,324
WASC Senior College and University Commission (WSCUC) https://www.wscuc.org/	2012-13 with predecessor organizations dating back to 1924	170	1,230,251

Together, these seven accreditors form the Council of Regional Accrediting Commissions (C-RAC; https://www.c-rac.org/) and include approximately 56% of Title IV participating institutions and 96% of certificate- and degree-seeking students at Title IV participating institutions. These organizations have a relatively small number of staff members. SACSCOC, with the second largest number of institutions and highest number of students enrolled in its institutions, has 50 staff, of which 12 have responsibilities as accreditation staff liaisons. Much of the work of accrediting bodies is accomplished through volunteers serving as peer reviewers.

Purpose and Role of Accreditation Staff Liaisons

According to their websites, all seven institutional accreditors have accreditation staff liaisons. While their specific titles vary, all accreditation staff liaisons are at the level of vice president. Statements from accreditor websites regarding the purpose and role of accreditation staff liaisons are excerpted below.

- "HLC assigns each member college or university a staff liaison, who serves as the institution's primary contact. Staff liaisons advise institutions about HLC's policies and procedures and help coordinate the peer review and decision-making process." (Higher Learning Commission, n.d.).

- "NWCCU assigns a staff liaison to each affiliated institution. This staff liaison serves as the primary resource person to that institution. The staff liaison explains NWCCU policies and procedures and draws on the skills of other staff members to provide effective assistance and service to colleges and universities." (Northwest Commission on College and Universities, n.d.).

- "Each college has an assigned vice president who serves as the college's staff liaison and primary point of contact for accreditation activities." (Accrediting Commission for Community and Junior Colleges, n.d.).

In a 2022 recruitment posting, SACSCOC stated that a "Vice President has administrative and management responsibilities and authority as delegated by the President of SACSCOC. Vice Presidents may represent the President and shall share joint responsibility for the quality and integrity of SACSCOC policies, processes, and procedures for an assigned portfolio of institutions, and/or for a program or project."

Based on these statements from the various institutional accreditors, it is clear that the accreditation staff liaison is the primary contact for member institutions. The accreditation staff liaison provides advice on policies and procedures and guidance for the peer review process. Depending on the accrediting body, the position may have additional duties as well.

Understanding the Accreditation Staff Liaison View

At SACSCOC, accreditation staff liaisons are vice presidents and have a portfolio of approximately 75 institutions. A vice president's portfolio consists of a wide range of institutions in terms of location, size, governance structure, and mission. Exhibit 16.2 presents some characteristics of the portfolio of institutions assigned to the author.

Exhibit 16.2: Characteristics of Typical Institutional Portfolio Assigned to SACSCOC Vice President

Characteristic	Number
State	
Alabama	4
Florida	9
Georgia	2
Kentucky	4
Louisiana	3
Mississippi	1
North Carolina	12
South Carolina	4
Tennessee	5
Texas	18
Virginia	13

Characteristic	Number
Total	75
Highest Degree Offered	
Associate	24
Baccalaureate	9
Master	20
Education Specialist	1
Doctoral	21
Total	75
Control	
Public	44
Private, Not-for-Profit	31
Total	75

The institutions in this portfolio range in size from 100 to 45,000 students and encompass community colleges, liberal arts colleges and universities, regional universities, research universities, seminaries, and health science institutions.

To be an effective accreditation staff liaison, the vice president needs to understand the context of each of the institutions in their portfolio. At SACSCOC, institutions are assigned to a new vice president about 2.5 to 3 years prior to the decennial reaffirmation committee visit. A leadership orientation for those institutions is held in conjunction with the SACSCOC Annual Meeting approximately 2 to 2.5 years prior to the decennial committee visit. For example, institutions in the SACSCOC reaffirmation class of 2026 (decennial committee visits in fall 2025 and spring 2026) were assigned to a new vice president in February 2023 and had their leadership orientation at the December 2023 Annual Meeting. The leadership orientation is considered the "kickoff" for the reaffirmation of accreditation process and is an important milestone in the accreditation staff liaison's relationship with the institution.

Prior to the leadership orientation, institutions complete an "Institutional Summary Form" that provides a brief narrative history and information about the institution's governance structure, academic programs, locations, distance education, and accreditors. This information is key to providing the accreditation staff liaison with a contextual understanding of the institution. Opportunities for institutions to meet their accreditation staff liaison are typically provided at conferences sponsored by the accreditor once or twice each year. In addition, SACSCOC offers institutions the opportunity to place an observer on a decennial reaffirmation committee visit committee within two years of their own reaffirmation visit. Not only does this allow the observer to see how review committees function, but it also gives them a chance to network with the accreditation staff liaison, who in turn can learn more about the institution they will be visiting in the future.

The advisory visit is another opportunity for the accreditation staff liaison to understand the context of institutions assigned to them. Vice presidents at SACSCOC typically conduct an advisory visit to an institution within 3 to 10 months of the decennial reaffirmation committee visit. This is an opportunity for the accreditation staff liaison to meet institutional leadership, provide feedback to the institution on compliance concerns, and discuss logistics of the upcoming visit, including trips to off-campus instructional sites.

In addition to accreditors assigning a vice president to each member institution, many accreditors require that each institution designate an institutional accreditation liaison (IAL), as its primary point of contact for the accreditation staff liaison. Examples of the expectations of the IAL can be found in *The accreditation liaison officer (ALO): Role and responsibilities* (Middle States Commission on Higher Education, 2017); *The accreditation liaison* (Southern Association of Colleges and Schools Commission on Colleges, 2020); *Accreditation liaison officer* (New England Commission of Higher Education,

2021); and *Accreditation liaison officer policy* (WASC Senior College and University Commission, 2023).

The peer review process is the cornerstone of accreditation (Council of Regional Accrediting Commissions, n.d.). Bischoff (2018) states that peer review is one of the most important features of the accreditation process. A committee of peers selected by the accrediting body reviews the institution and makes preliminary determinations as to compliance with accrediting standards. Final determination is made by the accrediting body's board based on the written report produced by the peer reviewers. Not only do peer reviewers bring their knowledge of generally accepted practices, but they benefit by taking what they learn on a review committee back to apply at their own institutions.

A large part of the accreditation staff liaison's time is spent facilitating the work of peer review committees. This includes selecting committee chairs and members, making writing assignments, and working with the chair and the institution to ensure appropriate logistical arrangements. At SACSOC, the vice president assigned to an institution accompanies peer review committees on their visits to serve as a resource and ensure consistency of the accreditation process. Arranging the committee visit is a three-way partnership between the accreditation staff liaison, the Institutional Accreditation Liaison, and the visit committee chair.

Accreditation staff liaisons have a busy schedule. Exhibit 16.3 lists the typical travel events (25 to 30 per year) for a SACSCOC vice president.

Reaffirmation of accreditation by SACSOC is a multi-step process. Institutions have three opportunities (Compliance Certification, Focused Report, and Response Report) to demonstrate compliance with standards before the board of trustees makes a decision on their accreditation status. Thus, this process is a model of continuous improvement, as shown in Exhibit 16.4. Accreditation staff liaisons are in a unique position to observe how institutions

Exhibit 16.3: List of Typical Travel Events for a SACSCOC Vice President Each Year

Event	Number per Year	Duration of Each
Decennial Reaffirmation Committee Visits[1]	8	4 days
Substantive Change Committee Visits[2]	3	3 days
Fifth-Year Committee Visits to New Off-Campus Instructional Sites[3]	2	3 days
Institutional Advisory Visits	8	2 days
SACSCOC Board of Trustee Meetings	2	4 days
SACSCOC Summer Institute	1	4 days
SACSCOC Annual Meeting	1	3 days
Invited Conference Speaker	1	2 days

---

1   Some committee visits may require separate trips to off-campus instructional sites located in other states or countries.
2   Ibid.
3   Ibid.

leverage accreditation as a catalyst for institutional improvement. The following three examples related to the SACSCOC Quality Enhancement Plan (QEP), number of full-time faculty, and library staffing are illustrative of how institutions can use the accreditation process as more than a compliance exercise.

Exhibit 16.4 SACSCOC Reaffirmation Process

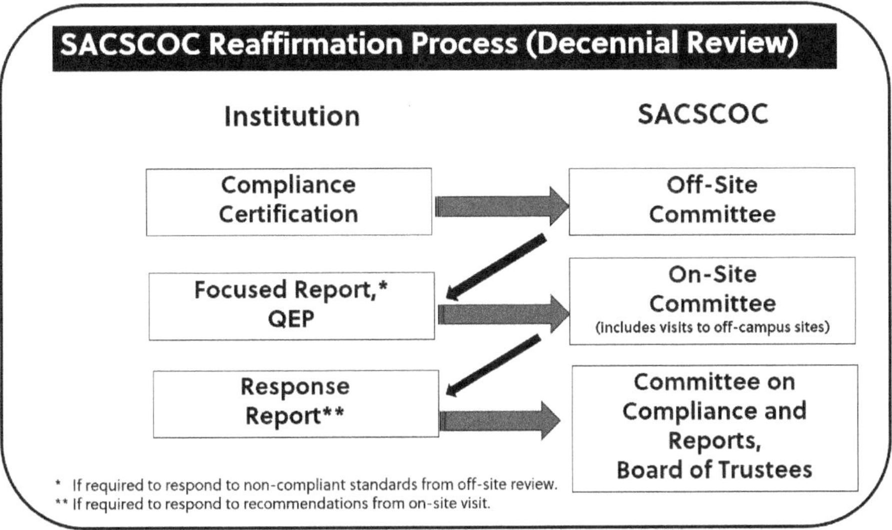

As part of their decennial reaffirmation of accreditation process, SACSCOC-accredited institutions must develop a QEP. As noted in *The Quality Enhancement Plan:*

The Quality Enhancement Plan is… derived from an institution's ongoing comprehensive planning and evaluation processes. It reflects and affirms a commitment to enhance overall institutional quality and effectiveness by focusing on an issue that the institution considers important to improving student learning outcomes and/or student success (Southern Association of Colleges and Schools Commission on Colleges, 2022, p. 1).

A one-page summary of each institution's QEP since 2007 is available on the SACSCOC website (https://sacscoc.org/quality-enhancement-plans/). The QEP can be an impetus for an institution to make improvements that might not otherwise be possible. For example, one institution's QEP involved moving to a blended model of advising, using faculty mentors and professional advisors to enhance student engagement in setting and achieving academic goals. This advising model required the hiring of at least 30 full-time professional advisors over a 3-year period, which would not have been approved through the typical institutional budgeting process. However, as part of the QEP, the hiring of professional advisors was deemed an institutional priority and was fully funded.

In completing its self-study for an accreditation review (referred to as "Compliance Certification" by SACSCOC), an institution may uncover areas for enhancement. For example, it may have plenty of faculty overall but may not realize that certain programs don't have enough full-time faculty until responding to an accreditation standard relating to the sufficiency of full-time faculty at the program level (Southern Association of Colleges and Schools Commission on Colleges, 2019). Self-discovery, as opposed to discovery by a peer review committee, allows the institution time to adjust faculty hiring prior to submitting materials to the accreditor.

Being found non-compliant on an accreditation standard by a peer review committee can be used strategically to improve institutional processes. For example, a peer review committee found a university out of compliance on an accreditation standard relating to the adequacy of library staff because the institution relied heavily on faculty external to the library, graduate assistants, and student workers to perform functions that are typically the responsibility of library faculty and staff. The library had been subjected to budget cuts in recent years, and requests for restored funding had not been approved. The finding of non-compliance made the hiring of additional library staff an institutional priority. Rather than quickly adding a librarian, the university took time to engage in process improvement techniques to identify ways to optimize people, resources, and efforts. Among other things, that analysis revealed a previously unrecognized need for a digitization librarian.

Effective Preparation and Communication With Your Accreditation Staff Liaison

It is helpful to review the accreditor's website for pertinent policies and procedures before contacting the accreditation staff liaison. Given the travel schedule of most accreditation staff liaisons, email is the preferred communication method. A telephone call or videoconference may be needed, but it is best to begin the communication process with an email that provides context for the current concerns or questions. Remember that the accreditation staff liaison has a portfolio of diverse institutions across several states, so it is important to provide adequate background on your situation. Do not presume that the accreditation staff liaison knows the inner workings of your institution, system, or state.

Communicate and consult with the accreditation staff liaison prior to major institutional changes such as offering a new level of degree; merging or acquiring other institutions, programs, or locations; or initiating innovative collaborations or partnerships. These are complex processes with multiple steps that often have to be coordinated with another institutional accreditor, a disciplinary accreditor, or the U.S. Department of Education. Timing is critical so that students are not negatively affected relative to financial aid status. The three examples below (institutional merger, cooperative academic arrangement, and library staffing) illustrate the importance of holding institutional discussions with the accreditation staff liaison prior to pursuing strategic moves that may impact accreditation:

A SACSCOC-accredited institution is exploring the possibility of acquiring or forming some type of partnership with a small private college that is experiencing financial distress and is accredited by another institutional accreditor. The location in another state is attractive to the SACSCOC-accredited institution. Furthermore, some of the programs and the student population at the beleaguered institution are a good fit for the SACSCOC institution. The institution contacts its accreditation staff liaison to discuss options ranging from simply establishing an off-campus instructional site on the campus of the other institution to completely merging the two institutions. Each potential partnership opportunity, while falling under the SACSCOC Substantive Change policy (Southern Association of Colleges and Schools Commission on Colleges, 2023), has different accreditation implications. The merger is the most complex because of the involvement of two different institutional accreditors.

Another SACSCOC-accredited institution would like to establish a partnership with a non-profit non–Title IV entity that would provide a semester-long residential experience for undergraduate students focused on a specialized area within the humanities. The institution contacts its accreditation staff liaison to understand the implications of such an arrangement on accreditation. One approach would be for the courses offered by the non–Title IV entity to be transcripted by the member institution, as allowed by SACSCOC Standard 10.9 (*Collaborative academic arrangements*, Southern Association of Colleges and Schools Commission on Colleges, 2017). To do this, the institution would need to submit a substantive change prospectus to obtain approval for a cooperative academic arrangement with a non–Title IV entity, which will offer 25% to 50% of multiple academic programs for the member institution.

Another approach could be for the institution to establish an off-campus instructional site on the premises of the non–Title IV entity and offer the courses itself using employees of the non–Title IV entity as faculty. Even though this approach would not require a substantive change prospectus, it might be more cumbersome because of the need to get courses approved through the member's governance structure so they are in the catalog. Furthermore, joint faculty appointments would need to be established. Regardless of the approach, the student experience would likely be the same; however, the administrative impact for the institution could be very different.

SACSCOC has three standards that relate to the adequacy of library and learning/information resources, staff, and access (Core Requirement 11.1, Standard 11.2, Standard 11.3; Southern Association of Colleges and Schools Commission on Colleges,

2017). The librarian at a small rural college is nearing retirement. Recognizing changes that have occurred in the past 20 years, the college administration is discussing the role of a librarian. Students at this institution rely almost exclusively on technology to locate research and use inter-library loans for materials in print. The college is exploring the possibility of hiring someone with expertise in instructional technology in place of a librarian.

The institution contacts its accreditation staff liaison to determine if this would have a negative impact on accreditation. Discussion ensues as to how an instructional technology person might contribute to the adequacy and access of library and learning/information resources as required by the accreditation standards. Though it is peer reviewers and ultimately the SACSCOC Board of Trustees who make compliance determinations, the experience of the accreditation staff liaison suggests that this type of personnel change would likely result in findings of non-compliance later. However, a case for compliance could be made if someone with expertise in instructional technology were hired in combination with sharing a librarian at another college.

As the three preceding examples illustrate, the accreditation staff liaison can help the institution think through accreditation concerns related to proposed institutional changes. The accreditation staff liaison may be able to provide options for approaching the change, but ultimately it is the institution's decision as to how to proceed. Often there is no bright line for determining compliance. Peer reviewers are expected to exercise professional judgment and rely on good educational practice when making compliance determinations.

Career Path and Skillset of an Accreditation Staff Liaison

A review of the biographical sketches of the accreditation staff liaisons available on the websites of the seven institutional accreditors reveals that the people in these positions had significant higher education administrative experience prior to their employment with an accrediting body. Most have held institutional positions in academic affairs or institutional effectiveness/research; others have experience in student affairs, and a few have been a college or university president. Many have served as an IAL and/or on peer review committees. Except for a few who have interim titles, all have doctoral degrees.

A 2022 position announcement for a SACSCOC vice president listed the following as required knowledge, skills, and abilities:

- Knowledge of and commitment to the philosophy and goals of regional accreditation and SACSCOC

- Knowledge of current educational issues, principles, practices, and organizations, and of pertinent literature in the field of quality improvement and assurance in higher education

- Ability to create and maintain cooperative working relationships with others

- Ability to anticipate, analyze, and prepare needed plans and programs

- Ability to present oral and written comments, opinions, and program interpretations clearly and concisely, including public presentations

In addition, the education and experience requirements were listed as an earned doctorate, five years fulltime experience in higher education administration, and familiarity with the accreditation process.

A review of the backgrounds of recent SACSCOC vice presidents reveals two pathways from which they typically emerge. One pathway has been that of a career capstone, with the accreditation staff liaison position being sought approximately five to seven years prior to retirement. In some instances, people have already retired from a senior institutional position. The second pathway is where the accreditation staff liaison position is sought mid-career but after holding key administrative positions at an institution. There is value to an accrediting body in having accreditation staff liaisons from both pathways because of the different perspectives they bring to the organization.

Concluding Thoughts

In summary, experience in higher education administration and knowledge of accreditation provide the foundation on which other skills are developed for a career as an accreditation staff liaison. Oral and written communication skills, attention to detail, and an ability to see the big picture while working at a detailed level all contribute to the success of an accreditation staff liaison. The use of technology in accreditation processes has increased greatly in recent years, and one must be willing to learn new technologies as they evolve. Examples include accrediting agency online databases, cloud-based storage for peer review committee materials, specialized software for institutional preparation of accreditation materials, and videoconferencing capabilities on laptops and cell phones. Furthermore, the ability to develop and maintain cooperative working relationships is vital for accreditation staff liaisons as they interact with institutional accreditation liaisons, chief executive officers at colleges and universities, and chairs and members of peer review committees.

Discussion Questions

1. What are some ways to cultivate a relationship with the accreditation staff liaison assigned to your institution?

2. How can an accreditation staff liaison understand the context and become familiar with key personnel at the institutions in their portfolio?

3. What are some responsibilities of an accreditation staff liaison?

4. What is an example of a course of action your institution is considering for which it would be prudent to discuss with your accreditation staff liaison to understand accreditation implications before pursuing?

5. How can you prepare for a position as an accreditation staff liaison?

Discover and Propel

It is important for accreditation staff liaisons to maintain currency on major issues and trends in higher education. This can be accomplished in several ways. Reading daily higher education news sources such as *The Chronicle of Higher Education*, *Inside Higher Education*, and *Diverse Issues in Higher Education* allows one to stay up to the minute on happenings in the field. Holding individual memberships in, reading publications from, and attending conferences of professional organizations such as the Association for Institutional Research (AIR), Society of College and University Planning (SCUP), Association for the Study of Higher Education (ASHE), and American Educational Research Association (AERA) can provide a scholarly base for understanding higher education issues and trends.

Organizations geared more toward institutions (rather than individuals), such as the American Association of Colleges and Universities (AAC&U) and Council for Higher Education Accreditation (CHEA) offer a wealth of practical learning opportunities through publications and conferences. United States Department of Education regulations related to accreditation are fundamental and authoritative for accrediting bodies, as are materials from the National

Advisory Committee on Institutional Quality and Integrity (NACIQI). Accreditation staff liaisons are often invited as guest speakers to discuss accreditation issues at state-level higher education conferences.

References

Accrediting Commission for Community and Junior Colleges (n.d.). *Commission staff.* Retrieved December 17, 2023, from https://accjc.org/find-your-institutions-staff-liaison/

Bischoff, T.J. (2018). Accreditation under fire: How striking a balance between accreditor accountability and autonomy can strengthen educational quality. *Roger Williams University Law Review, 23*, 203 -228).

Council of Regional Accrediting Commissions (n.d.) *For policymakers.* Retrieved January 5, 2024, from https://www.c-rac.org/for-policymakers

Higher Learning Commission (n.d.). *Staff liaisons.* Retrieved December 17, 2023, from https://www.hlcommission.org/About-HLC/staff-liaisons.html

Middle States Commission on Higher Education (2017, August 16). *The Accreditation liaison officer (ALO): Role and responsibilities.* https://msche.box.com/shared/static/6qpzp8e52w9bt2ko0x95pkzl1ubn2z21.pdf

National Advisory Committee on Institutional Quality and Integrity (NACIQI) (2023, July). *Recognized institutional accreditors: Federal postsecondary education and student aid data.* https://sites.ed.gov/naciqi/files/2023/07/InstitutionalAccredData.xlsx

New England Commission of Higher Education (2021, August).

Accreditation liaison officer. https://www.neche.org/wp-content/uploads/2018/12/Pp01_Accreditation_Liaison_Officer.pdf

Northwest Commission on College and Universities (n.d.). *Institutional staff liaisons.* Retrieved December 17, 2023, from https://nwccu.org/tools-resources/institutions/institutional-staff-liaisons/

Southern Association of Colleges and Schools Commission on Colleges (2017, December). *The principles of accreditation: Foundation of quality enhancement.* https://sacscoc.org/app/uploads/2019/08/2018PrinciplesOfAcreditation.pdf

Southern Association of Colleges and Schools Commission on Colleges (2019, June). *Full-time faculty (Core Requirement 6.1 and Standard 6.2.b).* https://sacscoc.org/app/uploads/2019/08/Full-time-Faculty_Guideline.pdf

Southern Association of Colleges and Schools Commission on Colleges (2020, September). *The accreditation liaison.* https://sacscoc.org/app/uploads/2019/08/accreditation-liaison.pdf

Southern Association of Colleges and Schools Commission on Colleges (2022, August). *The Quality Enhancement Plan.* https://sacscoc.org/app/uploads/2020/01/Quality-Enhancement-Plan-1.pdf

Southern Association of Colleges and Schools Commission on Colleges (2023, March). *Substantive change policy and procedures.* https://sacscoc.org/app/uploads/2019/08/SubstantiveChange.pdf

WASC Senior College and University Commission (2023, July).

Accreditation liaison officer policy. https://wascsenior.app.box.com/s/wzdca1fvd8244ykh56vi

Chapter 17

Innovating with Accreditation as a New Senior Leader

Jeremy Moreland

In higher education, the average tenure of a president is approximately five years; vice president roles have much more variability. Thus, each year, there are thousands of new presidents and vice presidents. A new president or vice president has to dive into accreditation matters quickly. This chapter focuses on practical strategies for incoming senior leaders to make the most of being new by fostering innovation and growth. From encouraging big ideas and creative thinking to establishing learning excursions, these leaders can promote a culture of innovation to drive success in higher education institutions. By empowering employees, engaging stakeholders, and leveraging diverse perspectives, they can align institutional goals with impactful strategies to thrive in a competitive higher education landscape.

In the dynamic landscape of higher education, new presidents and vice presidents step into leadership roles each year, bringing fresh perspectives and a drive for innovation. As a new president or vice president, diving quickly into accreditation matters is vital for ensuring institutional success and growth. This chapter focuses on what senior leaders can do to make the most of their new roles by trailblazing and innovating, with accreditation as a crucial tool for doing so.

The chapter explores leadership strategies and tactics that accelerate institutional improvement. Effective leadership is essential for driving change and promoting a culture of continuous improvement. From building strong relationships with stakeholders to creating a shared vision and fostering collaboration, senior leaders can lay the foundation for successful accreditation efforts and drive positive change within their institutions.

This chapter serves as a guide for new presidents and vice presidents, presenting 5 leadership strategies (see Exhibit 17.1) and 36 tactics to drive institutional impact, thus positively influencing the accreditation landscape and maximizing its potential in thoughtful ways that advance the institution. Utilizing accreditation as a tool for innovation and improvement, senior leaders can play a significant role in shaping the future of their institutions and enhancing their contributions to higher education.

Exhibit 17.1: Leadership Strategies

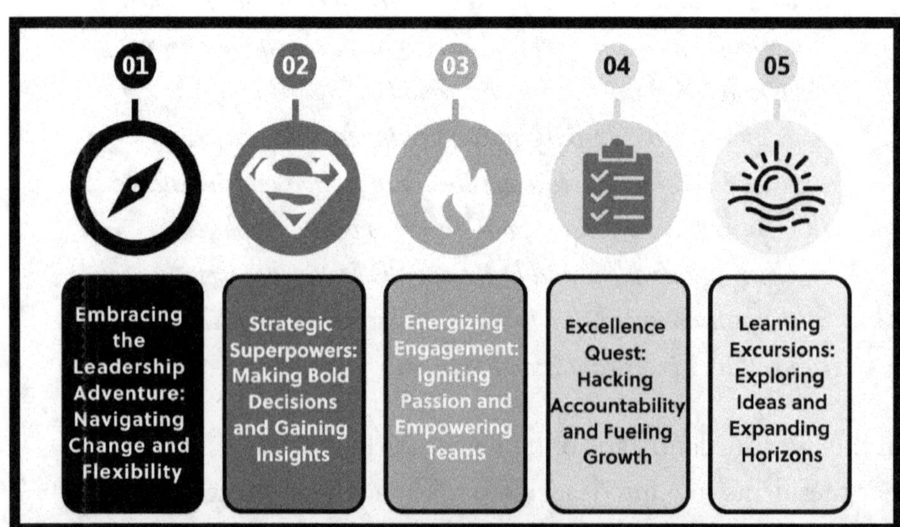

Leadership Strategies That Accelerate Institutional Improvement

The first of the five leadership strategies is to have a clear vision and inspire teams to align with it. By setting strategic goals and communicating a compelling vision, leaders can motivate their teams to achieve remarkable results and drive institutional improvement.

Prioritizing effective communication is the second leadership strategy. Through open and transparent communication channels, leaders can build trust, encourage collaboration, and ensure alignment across all levels of the institution. This facilitates faster and more effective improvement, as everyone is on the same page.

Fostering a culture of innovation is the third leadership strategy. Leaders play a crucial role in creating an environment that encourages creativity, risk-taking, and continuous learning. By promoting an atmosphere of experimentation and providing resources for innovation, leaders can spark and sustain a culture of improvement, enabling institutional growth.

The fourth leadership strategy is to embrace data-driven decision-making. Leaders need to harness the power of data to inform their decisions and drive improvement. By collecting and analyzing relevant data, leaders can gain valuable insights, identify areas for improvement, and make informed decisions that lead to positive change and better institutional outcomes.

The fifth and final leadership strategy is to develop other leaders and create a succession plan.. Effective leaders understand the importance of investing in the development of their team members and cultivating future leaders. By providing mentoring, training, and growth opportunities, leaders ensure a pipeline of capable individuals who can continue to and even accelerate institutional improvement in the long term.

Embracing the Leadership Adventure: Navigating Change and Flexibility

This section delves into the mindset and strategies that effective higher education leaders can adopt to thrive in an ever-changing and dynamic environment. In today's fast-paced world, leaders must possess the ability to navigate through uncertainty, embrace new challenges, and drive impactful change. This section explores key qualities that leaders can cultivate, including pragmatism, flexibility, an entrepreneurial spirit, and the ability to challenge assumptions. By embracing the qualities and strategies shown in Exhibit 17.2, leaders can lead with confidence, inspire their teams, and successfully guide their college or university through the unpredictable terrain of modern-day higher education.

1. Be a Genuine You: Being a genuine you is far superior to being a bubbly fake one. However, it's equally important for leaders to be aware of their own motivations, hot buttons, and triggers. By understanding themselves better, leaders can regulate their own emotions and behaviors, maintaining a positive and supportive presence even in challenging situations. This "game face" of affirmation helps leaders inspire and motivate their teams, fostering a culture of innovation and continuous improvement. Being true to oneself creates an environment where trust and transparency flourish, leading to open and honest communication.

2. Embrace Pragmatism: Embracing pragmatism means focusing on practicality and realistic solutions. Leaders should analyze the available resources, constraints, and potential outcomes to make informed decisions. They should prioritize those actions most likely to drive results and positively impact the college or university. By adopting a pragmatic mindset, leaders can navigate change and flexibility with a practical lens, ensuring a balanced and efficient approach to problem-solving.

Exhibit 17.2: Embracing the Leadership Adventure Navigating Change and Flexibility

3. Be Flexible: Being flexible as a leader means being open to change, adaptable, and willing to adjust plans based on unexpected circumstances. Flexibility enables leaders to welcome new opportunities, respond to shifting priorities, and accommodate different perspectives. It involves being able to pivot when needed, deviating from established norms or processes to explore innovative approaches. A flexible leader encourages creativity and empowers their team to think outside the box, fostering a culture of agility and adaptability within the college or university.

4. Be Entrepreneurial: Adopting an entrepreneurial mindset means taking a proactive and innovative approach to leadership. Entrepreneurs are driven by seeking out opportunities, embracing calculated risks, and capitalizing on potential rewards. Leaders with an entrepreneurial spirit encourage experimentation, creativity, and a willingness to challenge the status quo. Such leaders inspire their teams to think like entrepreneurs, empowering them to take ownership of their work, explore novel solutions, and drive higher education growth through calculated risks and bold initiatives.

5. Challenge assumptions: Challenging assumptions is about questioning established beliefs, norms, and processes. It involves encouraging a culture of curiosity, where leaders and team members continuously question why things are done a certain way and seek new approaches. By challenging assumptions, leaders can identify gaps, unearth innovative ideas, and uncover hidden opportunities. This strategy encourages critical thinking, fosters a growth mindset, and inspires individuals to break free from limitations, enabling rapid adaptation in an ever-evolving landscape.

6. Use discussion to get through impasses: When faced with an impasse or disagreement, leaders can bridge gaps and find common ground by using good discussion techniques, such as encouraging active listening, constructive feedback, and open-mindedness. This creates an environment of trust and respect, where all viewpoints are heard and valued. By fostering healthy debates and facilitating effective communication, leaders can navigate conflicts, explore diverse perspectives, and find collaborative solutions to move forward collectively.

7. Declutter: Some things don' t fit, so it's not necessary to see everything through to the end: Recognizing that not everything aligns with the institution' s goals or values is essential for effective leadership. Leaders should be able to prioritize and make decisions, ensuring that valuable time, resources, and energy are allocated to the most impactful initiatives. Understanding the importance of letting go of endeavors that are no longer aligned or fruitful allows leaders to embrace change and remain focused on what truly matters. This strategy promotes efficiency, agility, and the ability to adapt quickly to emerging circumstances.

8. Keep egos in check: To foster innovation, senior leaders must be sure to keep their egos in check. They should recognize that their authority comes from their role, not their personal identity. When faced with resistance, leaders should refrain from taking it personally and instead approach it with an open mind. By maintaining humility and creating a safe space for dialogue, leaders can learn from opposition and foster a culture of innovation.

By cultivating qualities such as pragmatism, flexibility, and an entrepreneurial spirit, leaders can successfully navigate uncertainty and drive impactful change. Challenging assumptions and using effective discussion techniques are also crucial to fostering innovation and resolving conflicts. Furthermore, recognizing when to let go of initiatives that don' t align allows leaders to focus on what truly matters. By embracing these strategies, leaders can inspire their teams, adapt to the evolving landscape, and achieve meaningful outcomes.

Strategic Superpowers: Making Bold Decisions and Gaining Insights

In a rapidly changing and complex higher education landscape, leaders must possess the strategic superpowers necessary to navigate uncertainty, drive growth, and make informed decisions. These encompass various facets, including fostering innovative thinking, embracing collaboration, leveraging metrics and processes, and cultivating a culture of continuous improvement. By adopting these strategies in Exhibit 17.3, leaders can unleash their full potential, empower their teams, and position their college or university for long-term success.

1. Assemble the senior team twice a week for strategic conversations: Regular team meetings provide a dedicated space for strategic conversations. By meeting frequently, leaders can ensure alignment, discuss progress, and make timely decisions. These meetings enable effective collaboration, facilitate information sharing, and foster a collective understanding of the college's or university's strategic direction.

2. Align the processes to the metrics: To drive success, leaders should align their processes with measurable metrics and key performance indicators (KPIs). By clearly defining objectives, leaders can design processes that are focused on achieving desired outcomes. Aligning processes to metrics enables leaders to assess progress, identify areas for improvement,

Strategic Superpowers: Making Bold Decisions and Gaining Insights

9. Assemble the senior team twice a week for strategic conversations
10. Align the processes to the metrics
11. Accelerate the process
12. Innovate, emulate, evaluate
13. Allow innovation
14. Listen to understand rather than to respond
15. Use a collaborative hiring process
16. Really get to know each person
17. Practice unconditional positive regard and assess situations rather than dispositions
18. Give specific feedback
19. Highlight what's working well and identify action plans for what's not

and take data-driven action to enhance effectiveness and efficiency. For example, if the admissions team recruits during the academic year (July to June), then align their performance evaluation to a similar timeframe. This information can then serve to support accreditation by demonstrating data use, data-driven decision-making, and continuous improvement.

3. Accelerate the process: In a fast-paced environment, leaders need to create a culture of speed and agility. Accelerating the process involves identifying bottlenecks, streamlining workflows, and reducing unnecessary bureaucracy. Leaders should empower their teams to make quick decisions, embrace experimentation, and identify opportunities to expedite initiatives without compromising quality; it can be frustrating to work within the arbitrary confines of "one week." This strategy allows colleges and universities to navigate change swiftly and stay ahead in competitive markets. Although the speed of the process will vary depending on the size and type of institution, creating a culture of speed and agility within the sector and size constraints is key.

4. Innovate, emulate, evaluate: Leaders should encourage a culture of innovation by fostering an environment where new ideas are welcomed and nurtured. They can promote innovation by emulating successful practices from other industries or colleges or universities while continuously evaluating their own processes for improvement. This strategy promotes a growth mindset, inspires creativity, and enables leaders and teams to anticipate and adapt to evolving market trends and student needs.

5. Allow innovation: Leaders should provide a supportive environment where team members feel empowered and

encouraged to innovate. By giving permission to innovate, leaders remove barriers, instill confidence, and create a sense of psychological safety. This strategy fosters a culture of experimentation and learning from failures, allowing individuals to take calculated risks, explore creative solutions, and drive continuous improvement.

6. Listen to understand rather than to respond: Effective leaders prioritize active listening, seeking to understand the perspectives and insights of their team members and stakeholders. They create a safe space for open and honest communication, where everyone' s opinions are valued. By listening to understand, leaders can gain valuable insights, foster collaboration, and make informed decisions that consider diverse viewpoints and potential implications.

7. Use a collaborative hiring process: By involving representatives from different departments or silos in the hiring process, leaders promote cross-functional collaboration and a more holistic evaluation of candidates. This strategy ensures diverse perspectives in evaluating candidates' fit for the college or university and encourages collaboration from the early stages.

8. Really get to know each person: Leaders should invest time in building relationships with team members to develop a deep understanding of their interests, roles, and aspirations. By getting to know each person individually, leaders can better support their growth, align their strengths with college or university objectives, and foster a positive and engaged work environment.

9. Practice unconditional positive regard and assess situations rather than dispositions: Assume that people come to work wanting to do good every day. They overwhelmingly do.

Assume that folks are acting in good faith and have a rationale behind their decisions. Finding out their rationale will provide background on issues and may reveal new solutions.

10. Give specific feedback: Effective feedback includes specific examples and highlights the contributions that have led to progress or success. By offering precise feedback, leaders help individuals understand their impact and provide guidance for further improvement. This strategy enhances performance and promotes a culture of continuous learning and development. An example of specific feedback is, "This project is really moving along because you did X, Y, Z. Thank you for your attentiveness on this important project."

11. Highlight what's working well and identify action plans for what's not: Leaders should acknowledge and celebrate the parts of a project or initiative that are working well to motivate and inspire their teams. Simultaneously, they should identify areas that are lagging and collaboratively develop action plans to rectify the issues. This strategy promotes accountability and continuous improvement while ensuring that projects stay on track towards desired outcomes.

12. By adopting these strategies, leaders can unlock their full potential, empower their teams, and position their college or universities for long-term success in a constantly changing higher education landscape.

13. *Energizing Engagement: Igniting Passion and Empowering Teams*

14. Leaders can employ the strategies in this section to foster a culture of engagement, passion, and empowerment within their teams. Engaged teams are more likely to be productive, innovative, and committed to the college's or university's goals. By implementing the strategies in Exhibit 17.4, leaders

Exhibit 17.4: Energizing Engagement Igniting Passion and Empowering Teams

can unleash the full potential of their teams, cultivate a positive work environment, and drive exceptional results.

15. Forge relationships: Building strong relationships is a fundamental aspect of effective leadership. By investing time and effort in getting to know team members on a personal level, leaders can create a sense of trust and belonging. These relationships provide a foundation for open communication, collaboration, and mutual support, fostering a positive and engaged team culture.

16. Get comfortable with uncomfortable conversations: Effective leaders do not shy away from difficult or uncomfortable conversations. Instead, they embrace them as opportunities for growth and understanding. By using phrases such as "Help me understand" or "I don't understand," leaders encourage open dialogue, promote transparency, and address issues proactively, ensuring that concerns or misalignments are addressed promptly rather than ignored.

17. Drop by team members' offices to say thank you: Showing genuine appreciation for team members' efforts and contributions is essential for boosting engagement and morale. Leaders can make a positive impact by taking the time to personally acknowledge and thank individuals for their work. By dropping by employees' offices or reaching out in an individualized manner, leaders convey their gratitude and reinforce the value they place on their team members' efforts.

18. Know individual personalities: Understanding the personality traits and preferences of team members can enable leaders to tailor their approach and communication style to best support each individual. For example, some team members may need

time to process information, so providing them with materials or information in advance allows them to fully engage and align with others during discussions. This personalized approach demonstrates that leaders value and respect the unique qualities of each team member, enhancing overall engagement and productivity.

19. Be an energetic catalyst: Leaders have the power to infuse energy and enthusiasm into their teams. By leading with passion, enthusiasm, and a positive attitude, leaders can inspire and motivate their team members. Being an energetic catalyst involves setting an example through one' s own behavior, fostering a dynamic and vibrant work environment, and encouraging team members to approach their jobs with passion and positivity.

20. Keep your spirits high: Energy flows from the top down in colleges and universities. By maintaining high energy levels and consistently modeling excitement and dedication, leaders create an uplifting and motivating atmosphere for their teams. This positive energy becomes contagious, fueling increased engagement, creativity, and commitment among team members.

21. Hold end-of -semester assemblies for the entire faculty and staff: Bi-annual get-togethers, including the "party" after, are excellent for team morale and also accomplish many things, including highlighting successes, saying a big thank you to the entire team, and just keeping everyone engaged and enthusiastic about working for the college or university.

In summary, by implementing these strategies, leaders can cultivate a culture of engagement, passion, and empowerment, igniting the full potential of their teams and driving extraordinary results.

Exhibit 17.5: Excellence Quest Hacking Accountability and Fueling Growth

Excellence Quest: Hacking Accountability and Fueling Growth

Leaders can leverage the strategies in this section to cultivate a culture of accountability, growth, and innovation. In today's fast-paced and dynamic higher education environment, colleges and universities need to be agile, responsive, and adaptable to succeed. The strategies in Exhibit 17.5 enable leaders to drive growth, encourage accountability, and promote a vibrant culture of excellence.

1. Don't suck red ink: Financial responsibility is essential for the long-term sustainability and growth of colleges and universities. Leaders should carefully evaluate each program and initiative to ensure that it aligns with institutional goals and is financially feasible. By taking a responsible and strategic approach to resource allocation, colleges and universities can achieve greater success and profitability.

2. Welcome accountability: Accountability is essential to promoting a culture of excellence. Leaders must hold themselves and their team members accountable for meeting performance goals, achieving desired outcomes, and adhering to college or university values. By clearly defining expectations and providing regular feedback, leaders can ensure that team members stay on track and produce high-quality work.

3. Encourage big ideas, and follow up feasibility studies and proformas: Ideas come from faculty, staff, and students alike. Encouraging big ideas and creative thinking is vital for fostering innovation and growth. Leaders should provide employees with the opportunity to share their ideas and provide feedback. A feasibility study and three-year proformas will ensure that the idea is realistic, financially feasible, and aligned with college or university goals.

4. Identify first followers for new ideas: When implementing new ideas, it' s essential to identify first followers who will champion the initiative and help spread the word. These individuals can offer valuable feedback, provide support, and help generate momentum towards achieving the objectives of an initiative.

5. Make decisions to get started faster: In a rapidly changing environment, colleges and universities must be agile and make decisions quickly. By empowering decision-making at all levels, leaders can create a sense of energy and urgency, inspiring teams to work collaboratively and delivering results.

6. Don' t get bogged down by governance: A short pilot could yield all the results you need to know to advance a project or sunset the efforts and move on to another option. Leaders must balance governance with flexibility, recognizing that excessive bureaucracy can hinder innovation and progress. By trialing projects with a short pilot, colleges and universities can assess viability and make informed decisions about continued investment or discontinuation.

In summary, by implementing these strategies, leaders can foster a culture of accountability, growth, and innovation, creating a strong foundation for college or university success.

Learning Excursions: Exploring Ideas and Expanding Horizons

The strategies in this section focus on expanding knowledge and gaining new perspectives by leveraging the experiences and insights of peers and institutions. By actively seeking out counterparts from other institutions, following similar institutions on social media, organizing book clubs, and hosting lunch- and- learn sessions, colleges and universities can foster a culture of continuous learning and knowledge sharing. The activities in Exhibit 17.6 serve as opportunities for employees to explore ideas, expand their horizons, and discover innovative approaches that can be applied within their own institution.

Exhibit 17.6: Learning Excursions Exploring Ideas and Expanding Horizons

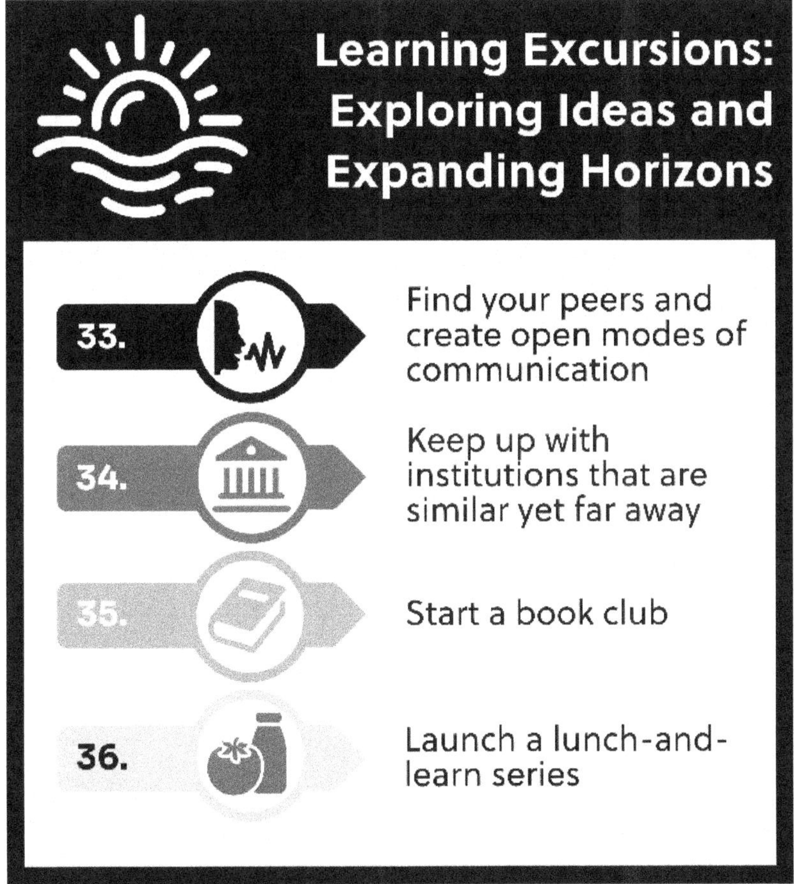

1. Find your peers and create open modes of communication: Identifying 5 to 10 professional counterparts from institutions that are not direct competitors allows for confidential questions to be exchanged within a trusted group. Creating an email list will allow members of this group to collaborate with

and seek assistance from each other with a quick turnaround time. This open mode of communication fosters a sense of camaraderie and enables knowledge sharing.

2. Keep up with institutions that are similar yet far away: Becoming familiar with institutions that are similar in key areas, such as size, sector, and program offerings, but geographically distant helps prevent any overlap of ideas. Following these institutions on social media platforms allows for regular observation and learning from their practices. If the chosen institutions do not post frequently (i.e., at least twice a week), it may be beneficial to find other model institutions that share relevant and useful information. Tracking their social media presence can provide valuable insights into how they present information and what types of content they share, helping to inform and inspire ideas within your own college or university.

3. Start a book club: Establishing a higher education book club within the institution encourages continuous learning and the exploration of new ideas. Employees who wish to participate can select a book relevant to their field or area of interest. The book can be purchased by the vice president or another designated host. Regular book club meetings provide an opportunity not only to discuss a book's content but also to explore how ideas presented in the book can be applied within the institution. The purpose is not simply to discuss the book but also for the group to ask "How can we apply that idea here at our institution?" To follow up, invite relevant stakeholders to discuss the group's ideas. For example, if the group has an idea about recruiting, invite the head of admissions to discuss its feasibility, any past experiences, etc.

4. Launch a lunch- and- learn series: A lunch- and- learn series

allows faculty to choose topics they want more information about or find intriguing. Subjects might include AI in the classroom or the relationship between athletics and academics. By inviting speakers from relevant stakeholder groups, such as experts in the field or administrators, faculty can engage in open and honest conversations. This safe space provides an opportunity for faculty to ask questions, have myths debunked, and gain valuable insights that can fuel innovation and improvement within the institution.

The learning excursion strategies provide valuable platforms for exploring new ideas, expanding horizons, and promoting a culture of continuous learning within a college or university. By leveraging the knowledge and experiences of peers, other institutions, and experts, employees can tap into a wealth of insights that can inform and inspire innovative approaches to challenges and opportunities.

Discussion Questions

1. How can you encourage authenticity and self-awareness among your team members at your institution, and what impact might that have on your institution as a whole?

2. How can you collaborate with institutions that are not direct competitors with your institution, and what benefits might that bring?

3. What are some of the key takeaways from the "learning excursion strategies," and how can you implement them at your institution to leverage the power of accreditation?

4. How can you integrate the concept of "unconditional positive regard" into your day-to-day operations at your institution, and what impact might that have on your accreditation process?

5. What are some challenges your institution faces when it comes to keeping egos in check, and how can you mitigate them?

6. How can you develop a lunch- and - learn series that is meaningful and relevant to your campus community, and what steps do you need to take to make it successful?

7. What are some specific challenges your institution faces that you might learn how to mitigate from other institutions facing similar challenges?

8. In what ways can you incorporate the concept of financial responsibility to ensure the long-term sustainability and growth of your institution?

9. How can you nurture strong relationships with team members at your institution to better support their growth, align their strengths with institutional objectives, and foster a positive and engaged work environment?

10. Using the strategies from this chapter, how can you promote a culture of accountability, growth, and innovation at your institution, in line with the strategies discussed in the section "Excellence Quest: Hacking Accountability and Fueling Growth"?

Biographies

Book Editor and Chapter Author

Kristina 'KP' Powers, PhD is Vice President for Finance and Administration at Menlo College (Silicon Valley). She is also the Founder and President of the Institute for Effectiveness in Higher Education, an organization that elevates forward thinking to accelerate colleges and universities. She has headed institutional research, institutional effectiveness, and assessment offices as well as served as an accreditation liaison at multiple public, private not-for-profit and private for-profit institutions. Other higher education roles have included, serving as an IPEDS Trainer (15 years), the President of the California Association of Institutional Research (CAIR), the NC-SARA Data Advisory Council, teaching and developing institutional research and higher education administration courses at four institutions (12 years), conducting policy education research at the Florida Legislature, and an admissions advisor at the State University of New York, College at Brockport.

Kristina earned her PhD from Florida State University in Educational Leadership and Policy Studies with a concentration in Higher Education Policy and a Master's in Higher Education Administration from Florida State University, and a Bachelor of Science from the State University of New York, College at Brockport. She publishes and presents in the areas of higher education administration and organization, institutional research, as well as student success with a focus on retention and graduation rates using national databases and institutional data. Her books, *The Power of Strategic Accreditation: Driving Institutional Impact* (2024), *Second-in-Command, First in Excellence: An Organization's Secret to Achieving Phenomenal Success* (2023), *Organization and Administration in Higher Education* (2012, 2017, 2022), *Data Strategy in Colleges and Universities: From Strategy to Implementation* (2019), and *Cultivating a Data Culture in Higher Education* (2018). She has served as issue co-editor and author for *New Directions of Institutional Research*.

Chapter Authors

Biographies of Contributing Chapter Authors

Melanie Booth, EdD has been an independent consultant to multiple colleges, universities, and higher education organizations in areas of innovation and change, quality assurance, work/learn partnerships, Credit for Prior Learning, accreditation, learning assessment, program review, faculty development, and student success initiatives. She currently serves as the Executive Director of the HLC Credential Lab with the Higher Learning Commission. Over her career, she has held executive leadership positions with the National Council for State Authorization Reciprocity Agreements, The Quality Assurance Commons for Higher and Postsecondary Education, and WASC Senior College and University Commission. She has also served as a dean, academic and student services department director, and faculty member at a variety of postsecondary institutions in California, Oregon, and Washington. Melanie holds an Ed.D. in Higher Educational Leadership and Change from Fielding Graduate University, a master's degree from San Diego State University, and a bachelor's degree from Humboldt State University.

Mary Ann Coughlin, DPE is the Provost and Vice President for Academic Affairs at Springfield College in Springfield, Massachusetts.

Across her tenure at Springfield College, Mary Ann has served in a variety of positions; as a faculty member, President of the Faculty Senate, Senior Associate Vice President for Academic Affairs and her current role as Provost. Across these positions, she has supervised academic support services and provided leadership for outcomes assessment initiatives, academic progress reviews, and institutional research. Currently, she works with the School Deans and Academic Leadership with a focus on delivering quality academic programs and supporting student success. Mary Ann has also presented numerous times at the NECHE accreditation conference as well as served as a NECHE evaluator for nearly a decade. Mary Ann is a Past President of AIR and was awarded the 2012 AIR Outstanding Service and the 2018 AIR Distinguished Member Awards. In addition to being well known within AIR for her training and workshops in the area of statistics and as a content developer and faculty member for the AIR Holistic Approach to Institutional Research course, she also contributes significantly to the development of training materials and resources on the use of data tools for IPEDS.

Nancy D. Floyd, PhD is Senior System Director for Research at the Minnesota State Colleges and Universities; in that role she oversees production of system submissions to the state Office of Higher Education, reports to the State Legislature on behalf of the system, and IPEDS submissions for seven universities and twenty-six colleges, as well as a number of systemwide data applications and long-range reporting projects. In this role she also serves on the Minnesota P-20 Education Partnership and specifically on the Learner Lifespan workgroup, as well as the National Postsecondary Education Cooperative (NPEC). Her research interests include the use of risk assessment in higher education leadership, and shared data governance.

Angela E Henderson, PhD serves as Chief Data Architect at TriviumBI, where she is responsible for development and dissemination of institutional data reports and analytics for multiple colleges and universities. Henderson's areas of expertise and interest include data-informed analyses, data visualization, and integration of data to guide institutional decision-making and accreditation processes. Throughout her 16 years of higher education experience, she has presented and published on these topics, most recently serving as co-editor of *Cultivating a Data Culture in Higher Education* (2018).

Resche D. Hines, PhD is Chief Executive Officer at TriviumBI. Previously, he served as the Assistant Vice President for Institutional Research and Effectiveness at Stetson University. Prior to joining Stetson, Dr. Hines served as the Assistant Vice President for Enrollment Management and Director of Institutional Research at Chicago State University. Dr. Hines is a results-driven, focused, and effectual leader with the proven ability to provide enhanced organizational leadership through data-informed decision-making in academic affairs, strategic planning, enrollment measurement, and institutional change management in higher education and not-for-profit sectors.

Jillian Huot, MBA, CAPM is the Director of Accreditation and Program Review at Macomb Community College and serves as the College's Accreditation Liaison Officer to the Higher Learning Commission (HLC). Jillian is an educator, business professional, and a passionate advocate for student success and continuous improvement in higher education. She has worked in higher education since 2010 and has served in many roles including an admissions advisor, an academic and financial aid advisor, and a learning outcomes assessment specialist. She is also an instructor of project management and serves as one of the project managers for the College's strategic plan. She earned a Bachelor of Science in Psychology from Central Michigan University, a Master in Business Administration, a Master in Project Management, and graduate certificates in both project management and business administration from DeVry University's Keller Graduate School of Management. She is a Certified Associate in Project Management (CAPM), as recognized by the Project Management Institute, has presented at the HLC conference (2023), and contributed to the creation of the National Survey of Accreditation Liaisons through the Institute for Effectiveness in Higher Education (2022).

J. Joseph Hoey, EdD serves as Assistant Chief of Staff, Vice President for Assessment and Accreditation at National University, and as the NU Accreditation Liaison Officer to WSCUC. Dr. Hoey brings to the position over 30 years of experience in accreditation, institutional effectiveness, planning, board governance, and assessment. He also serves as a WSCUC Commissioner and as a consultant to the Ministry of Education and Higher Education in Qatar. Joseph holds an Ed.D. from North Carolina State University, a Master of Music from Florida State University, and a BA in Music from UC San Diego.

Rebecca Hong, PhD serves as the Vice Provost of Student Success, Inclusive Excellence, and Curricular Innovation at the University of San Francisco. In her 20+ years as a higher education leader-practitioner, Rebecca has held leadership roles advancing assessment, accreditation, institutional research, curricular innovation, and institutional change efforts to forge equitable learning environments. She has published articles, book chapters, and presented at national conferences on assessment, educational effectiveness, and creating human-centered organizations. Hong earned her Doctorate in Education from the University of Southern California, her master's degree in education from Biola University, and her bachelor's degree in economics from the University of California, San Diego. She is also a graduate of the Institute of Management and Leadership in Education from the Harvard

Graduate School of Education. Hong regularly serves the higher education community as a consultant and on accreditation review teams and her local community as a board member and basketball coach.

Richard Mahon, PhD, was Vice President for Instruction (retired) at Mt. San Antonio College. He holds a Ph.D. in history of consciousness from UC Santa Cruz with specializations in history of ideas and political theory. After completing his doctorate, he taught at Deep Springs College, Diablo Valley College, West Valley College, Cabrillo College, and UC Santa Cruz before becoming a Professor of Humanities at Riverside City College in 1998. At RCC he also taught courses in history, philosophy, and political science, and served as Curriculum Committee chair and Academic Senate President. During his tenure at RCC, Dr. Mahon served on the Executive Committee of the Academic Senate for California Community College (ASCCC) and on the Board of Governors for the Faculty Association for California Community Colleges (FACCC). He served on the Accrediting Commission for Community and Junior Colleges from 2012 to 2018. He was awarded the Hayward Award by the Board of Governors of the California Community Colleges for service as an outstanding faculty member in 2013. Dr. Mahon moved to Allan Hancock College in 2016, where he served as Dean of Academic Affairs and adjunct faculty member in history and philosophy. He served as Vice President of Instruction at Mt. San Antonio College from 2019 until his retirement in 2021.

Lashonda Kennedy, MAEd, is the Director of Student Engagement and Belonging at Menlo College. In her role as Director of Student Engagement and Belonging, LaShonda oversees a comprehensive suite of programs and services designed to support the holistic development of students. Her broad background includes expertise in areas such as new student orientation, student organization advising, leadership development, and career exploration. Whether planning engaging cultural and social activities, advising the student government, or facilitating career readiness workshops, LaShonda's ultimate goal is to help today's students connect to tomorrow's careers. In addition to her administrative responsibilities, LaShonda also serves as an Adjunct Faculty member, teaching courses that support first-year student transition and the integration of classroom learning with real-world experience. Outside of her professional responsibilities, LaShonda enjoys staying active through her passion for community engagement by serving on multiple boards and non-profit committees locally, nationally and internationally.

Sundra D Kincey, PhD, is Associate Provost of Program Quality and SACSCOC Institutional Liaison at Florida Agricultural and Mechanical University (FAMU). In her role as Associate Provost, Kincey brings a wealth of experience and expertise that encompasses myriad aspects of academic administration and leadership in ensuring the university's programs meet the highest quality and accreditation standards. She also champions and advocates for student access by improving textbook affordability. Externally, Kincey serves as a commissioner and trustee on boards that provide oversight of institutional and discipline-specific accreditation. In addition to her administrative responsibilities, Kincey is actively engaged in research that seeks to explore and identify effective strategies to inspire and empower women and future leaders in academia, student achievement, retention, and persistence.

Valerie Martin Conley, PhD is the incoming vice president and chief academic officer at St. Norbert College in De Pere, Wisconsin. Known for being a mission-driven data-informed leader and scholar in higher education, Dr. Conley is the former provost and Vice President for academic affairs at Idaho State University, and dean of the College of Education at the University of Colorado Colorado Springs. Dr. Conley was a member of the faculty at Ohio University for thirteen years, where she also served as director of the Center for Higher Education and chair of the department of Counseling and Higher Education. Prior to serving in academic leadership roles, Dr. Conley worked in private industry as a consultant to the National Center for Education Statistics and in institutional research. Dr. Conley received her B.A. and M.A. degrees in Sociology from the University of Virginia and her Ph.D. in Educational Leadership and Policy Studies from Virginia Tech.

Bethany L. Miller, PhD is Associate Provost & Chief Data Officer at Macalester College. With a focus on equity and inclusion as well as assessment, Bethany has published, presented and consulted, building on her work experiences at Cornell College and Mary Baldwin University. Bethany is an expert faculty member with the Institute on General Education and Assessment Institute and have served on multiple AAC&U research initiatives, from contributing to the creation of the most recent VALUE ADD (Assignment Design and Diagnostic) tool to the development of its forthcoming campus guide for implementing open educational resources as tools for promoting diversity, equity, and student success. She was recently named a Senior Fellow for AAC&U in the Office of Curricular and Pedagogical Innovation. Supported by an undergraduate degree in English, and a Ph.D. in Education with an emphasis in Research, Evaluation, Statistics, & Assessment, her work lays a foundation for collaboration to build shared understanding and using data to support student and institutional success. Bethany is currently co-authoring a book on equity-centered collaboration in the use of data to inform student and institutional success.

Jeremy Moreland, PhD is President of William Woods University. A dynamic academic leader in professions-based, student-centered higher education, Dr. Jeremy L. Moreland has served in a variety of roles in his nearly quarter-century higher education career including provost/chief academic officer, dean, faculty member and research associate, Dr. Moreland joined WWU after serving as Provost and Chief Academic Officer for St. Thomas University. He was responsible for oversight of academic programs, instruction, classroom and online delivery, curriculum, assessment and quality assurance among other areas, St. Thomas enjoyed remarkable enrollment growth during his tenure, including consecutive record-breaking incoming traditional age freshman classes. He was also instrumental in helping achieve operating surpluses in the university's budget after years of deficits, innovative new academic programs and the implementation of a multi-point, hybrid advising model. He also led successful responses to fully resolve existing accreditor concerns regarding earlier years' financial and assessment matters, thus ending his tenure at St. Thomas with zero accreditor concerns for the institution. Dr. Moreland earned both his Doctor of Philosophy (1998) and Masters of Science (1996) in General Experimental Psychology from TCU, with a research focus on applied cognition and innovative learning media. He is also a 1993 graduate of Stephen F. Austin University in Nacogdoches, Texas, where he received a Bachelor's Degree in Psychology with a minor in Hearing Impaired Studies/Sign Language. He is a member of the International Leadership Association, American Educational Research Association, and the Association of Psychological Science.

Alana Olschwang, PhD is Associate Vice President for University Effectiveness, Planning, & Analytics (UEPA) at California State University at Dominguez Hills. As the leader of UEPA, Dr. Olschwang organizes, evaluates, assesses, and supports improvement to operations, initiatives, and efforts so that the university can determine how well it is fulfilling its mission and achieving its goals. Her focus for over twenty years has been combining principles and theories from organizational behavior, evaluation, education, and other fields to support institutional planning, decision-making, and effectiveness. She has done this work in both public and private institutions, serving undergraduate and graduate degree programs. While not currently in the role that is directly responsible for accreditation (ALO), she works very closely with the person in that role and has held the role in the two previous positions. Additionally, she has served on a WASC steering committee and as a review team member across visit types and to institutions ranging from San Diego and Hawaii to Peru. Additionally, she has been an organizer and key support role for specialty accreditation ranging from CCTC to CEPH and AACSB. In her current role, she has developed an Office of Workforce Integration, which has grown out of the use of economic modeling data to inform curriculum and program planning, prepare students for their careers, and demonstrate the return on the investment of a college degree. Additionally, she has enhanced the program review process significantly through greater access to meaningful data, with an emphasis on examining equity. Adopting a critical quantitative lens, she has worked with partners across the CSU to develop Faculty Student Success Dashboards that have enabled faculty to evaluate the impact of their interventions and course corrections. The work with equity and economic modeling has been presented at multiple conferences and resulted in several grant projects, most recently including a $5.3 million dollar multi-year project to close the digital divide for minority communities.

Terra Schehr, MA, Principal, SchehrStrategies, LLC has over 20 years of experience in institutional research, effectiveness, capacity building, and strategic planning in higher education. Terra has led the development and implementation of student learning assessment practices at multiple institutions and regularly presents at professional conferences. She has been involved in institutional engagements with the NCAA and two of the nation's regional accreditors, has served as her institution's accreditation liaison officer, has participated on multiple peer review teams, and has experience with several discipline-specific accreditation organizations.

Angela Schmiede, PhD, is Vice President for Student Success & Strategic Planning at Menlo College. She has over 25 years of experience supporting college student success in the areas of student affairs, experiential learning, career services, academic advising, academic support services, international student services, and institutional effectiveness at institutions as diverse as Menlo College, Stanford University, and Vanderbilt University. She is currently Menlo College's WSCUC Accreditation Liaison Officer (ALO), serving since 2015. Angela is a graduate of the WSCUC Assessment Leadership Academy and was appointed to serve as a member of the WSCUC Substantive Change Committee in 2019. She earned an M.Ed. in Human Resource Development from Vanderbilt University, and an M.A. in Sociology and a Ph.D. in Higher Education from Stanford University.

Jessica M. Shedd, MA, is Assistant Provost for Assessment & Institutional Research at Tulane University, leading efforts to leverage data for decision-making. In this role, she serves as Tulane's Institutional Accreditation Liaison to the Southern Association of Colleges and Schools Commission on Colleges (SASCOC), leading the university through its decennial reaffirmation in 2022. Prior, Jessica led the research and reporting team at The University of Texas System's Office of Strategic Initiatives after having served as IPEDS Team Leader and acting Program Director at the U.S. Department of Education's National Center for Education Statistics. She has also served as Director of Research & Policy Analysis at the National Association of College and University Business Officers (NACUBO), and held analyst positions in the institutional research office at the University of Maryland and the Institute for Higher Education Policy

(IHEP). Jessica is a past member of the AIR Board of Directors and has been an active member of NEAIR, MdAIR, TAIR, CSRDE, and AAUDE serving these organizations in various leadership roles. She received her B.A. in psychology and women's studies from the College of the Holy Cross and her M.A. in education from Stanford University.

Janet Simon Schreck, PhD, is Senior Associate Vice Provost for Academic Affairs & Accreditation Liaison Officer, and Associate Professor, School of Education at Johns Hopkins University. In this role, Schreck collaborates with the Vice Provost of Graduate and Professional Education and a broad cross-section of the campus community to identify cross-cutting goals and initiatives that improve undergraduate and graduate education. In addition, she directs academic compliance, institutional and learning assessment, and accreditation. Schreck serves as the Accreditation Liaison Officer to the Middle States Commission on Higher Education (MSCHE) and the Institutional Academic Grievance Officer. She is a faculty member in the School of Education where she teaches and advises doctoral students in the Ed.D. program. Schreck earned her B.A. and M.S. in Speech-Language Pathology from Loyola University Maryland and Ph.D. in Gerontology from the University of Maryland, Baltimore.

Marjorie A Trueblood, EdD, is Dean of the Student Center for Inclusion and Belonging, Rollins College. In this role, she creates initiatives to further underrepresented student success, increase the cultural humility of multiple stakeholders, and assists with the implementation of Rollin's Diversity, Equity, Inclusion, and Belonging strategic plan. Throughout her career she has served in multiple capacities within higher education, including Residence Life, Title IX, Student Support and Intervention, Admissions, and Diversity and Inclusion. Outside of work, she is active in nonprofits and provides DEIB training and consultation to various entities.

Marjorie enjoys supporting multiple stakeholders to be their best selves works to infuse social justice principles in building inclusive communities.

Jennifer E. Walsh PhD, is senior vice president of Strategic Initiatives and Chief Strategy Officer at Hawai'i Pacific University, which is a comprehensive non-profit private institution with more than 5,000 students. She is also the author of *Three Strikes Laws* (Greenwood Press, 2007) and has published peer-reviewed articles and book chapters on topics related to criminal justice policy and other political topics. Dr. Walsh is frequently consulted by print and broadcast media on a range of issues related to local, state, and national politics and speaks regularly on crime and justice, constitutional freedoms, women in leadership, and higher education policy.

Lori Williams, PhD is Executive Vice President and Chief of Staff at Excelsior University and has over 25 years experience in higher education. Prior to this role, she served as president of the National Council for State Authorization Reciprocity Agreements (NC-SARA), vice president at the Western Association of Schools and Colleges Senior College and University Commission (WSCUC), and provost, vice provost of curriculum development and innovation, vice president of product strategy and development, executive director for student success, and other administrative roles. Lori speaks at conferences about adult and online learning, and has served as professor, thesis advisor, and mentor.

Denise York Young, PhD joined the Southern Association of Colleges and Universities Commission on Colleges (SACSCOC) as Vice President in 2017. Immediately prior, she was Associate Provost at the University of North Georgia with responsibility for SACSCOC accreditation, assessment, institutional research, and planning processes. She has 30+ years of experience in teaching and administration at a wide range of institutions — community college, small faith-related universities, and public universities. She completed the SCUP *Planning Institute,* CCCU *Leadership Development Institute*, and Harvard *Institute for Management and Leadership in Higher Education.* Her PhD (higher education/educational research) is from the University of North Texas with other degrees from North Carolina State University and the University of Nevada, Reno.